PROFESSIONALIZING THE POLICE

CLARENDON STUDIES IN CRIMINOLOGY

Published under the auspices of the Institute of Criminology, University of Cambridge; the Mannheim Centre, London School of Economics; and the Centre for Criminology, University of Oxford.

RECENT TITLES IN THIS SERIES:

Getting Out: Early Release in England and Wales, 1960–1995
Guiney

Sentencing Policy and Social Justice
Henham

Cold Case Reviews: DNA, Detective Work, and Unsolved Major Crimes
Allsop

Justice, Mercy, and Caprice: Clemency and the Death Penalty in Ireland
O'Donnell

Young Criminal Lives: Life Courses and Life Chances from 1850
Godfrey, Cox, Shore, and Alker

The Chinese Mafia: Organized Crime, Corruption, and Extra-Legal Protection
Wang

Professionalizing the Police

The Unfulfilled Promise of Police Training

NIGEL G. FIELDING

OXFORD
UNIVERSITY PRESS

OXFORD
UNIVERSITY PRESS

Great Clarendon Street, Oxford, OX2 6DP,
United Kingdom

Oxford University Press is a department of the University of Oxford.
It furthers the University's objective of excellence in research, scholarship,
and education by publishing worldwide. Oxford is a registered trade mark of
Oxford University Press in the UK and in certain other countries

First Edition published in 2018

Published in the United States of America by Oxford University Press
198 Madison Avenue, New York, NY 10016, United States of America

British Library Cataloguing in Publication Data
Data available

Library of Congress Control Number: 2018942485

ISBN 978–0–19–881747–5

Acknowledgements

We are grateful to the following for permission to quote copyrighted material: Council of Europe for permission to reproduce Table 7.2 Council of Europe Code of Ethics: Training of Police Personnel; Elsevier for permission to reproduce Table 1.1 from Susan Lentz and Robert Chaires (2007) 'The invention of Peel's principles', *Journal of Criminal Justice*; Marian FitzGerald for permission to reproduce Figure 2.3 Influences on Stop Patterns; Metropolitan Police Service for permission to reproduce Table 3.1 Responses to Question 'Neighbourhood Policing is not "real policing" ', Table 6.2 Metropolitan Police Diversity, and Table 6.3 Police Officers by Rank and Gender; RAND Corporation for permission to reproduce Table 1.2 Vollmer's Police Professionalism and Table 1.3 Huntington's Tenets of Professionalism from Russell Glenn, Barbara Panitch, Dionne Barnes-Proby, Elizabeth Williams, John Christian, Matthew Lewis, Scott Lerwehr, and David Brannen (2003), *Training the 21st century police officer*; Taylor and Francis, Harper Collins, and Joan Drucker Winstein for permission to reproduce Table 6.4 The Three E's from Peter Drucker (1993) *The Effective Executive.*

The following Tables and Figures contain public sector information licensed under the Open Government License v3.0: Table 1.4 Officer Time Use; Table 1.5 Trend in Police Establishment; Table 2.2 Proportions of Recorded Crimes Solved; Table 3.2 How often people saw a police foot patrol; Table 4.1 Learning Requirement; Table 4.2 Initial Police Learning; Table 6.1 Deaths In or Following Police Custody; Figure 2.1 Crime Incidents; Figure 2.2 The police are dealing with antisocial behaviour in the area.

The following Table contains information available under the Parliament Open License: Table 2.1 Cost of the Police Force.

The following Tables contain information licensed under the Non-Commercial College of Policing Licence: Table 7.1 Professionalism in Practice; Table 7.3 Code of Ethics for Policing; Table 7.4 Ten Standards of Professional Behaviour.

Contents

General Editors' Introduction

The Clarendon Studies in Criminology series aims to provide a forum for outstanding theoretical and empirical work in all aspects of criminology and criminal justice, broadly understood. The Editors welcome submissions from established scholars, as well as excellent PhD work. The Series was inaugurated in 1994, with Roger Hood as its first General Editor, following discussions between Oxford University Press and three criminology centres. It is edited under the auspices of these three centres: the Institute of Criminology at the University of Cambridge, the Mannheim Centre for Criminology at the London School of Economics, and the Centre for Criminology at the University of Oxford. Each supplies members of the Editorial Board and, in turn, the Series Editor or Editors.

In *Professionalizing the Police*, Fielding tackles a subject that is at the forefront of contemporary policing, detailing the historical context and the challenges police professionalization has faced and continues to face. This unique, book-length treatment of the topic provides a one-stop resource for those interested in how policing works (and, in some instances, where it doesn't) which will appeal to academics of policing as well as police professionals seeking to better understand their craft, how it has evolved, and the directions in which it is currently advancing. This balance of academic and practical discussion allows the book to bridge the gap between previous academic work on the topic, and available vocational guidance.

One of the real strengths of this book is its in-depth discussions of the function of policing, how this has evolved, and the implications for the role of the police and their interactions and relationships with the public. For example, it considers how the advent of new technologies affects the day-to-day activities of police personnel, and similarly how service-oriented policing changes the expectations of police responsibilities. It also considers how challenges like austerity, changing funding models, and moves towards privatization affect police efficacy, and challenges contemporary practices that have led to the increasing influence of politics on policing, for example in the role of elected Police and Crime Commissioners.

Throughout the book there is an emphasis on the importance and current limitations of police training. The author calls for the curriculum, packaging and delivery of police training to take into account both policing needs as well as the wealth of knowledge from educational fields and sciences like criminology which are compiling large bodies of research on good practice. He also highlight the importance of both classroom and experiential learning, and the challenges this raises for police professionalization.

In the final chapters, the book tackles several of these challenges head-on, including issues of diversity in recruitment and promotion, policing culture and misconduct, and police competence and legitimacy.

As a one-stop-shop following policing practices in the UK from their inception to the present day, and detailing the challenges policing faces in contemporary Britain, this book will appeal to both police professionals and academics who desire a grounding in where UK policing has been, where it currently stands, and where it is headed. As Editors, we commend Nigel Fielding's book for making significant contributions to the field of policing through this sweeping and scholarly treatment of police professionalization, and warmly welcome *Professionalizing the Police: The Unfulfilled Promise of Police Training* to the *Clarendon Studies in Criminology* series.

Kyle Treiber and Loraine Gelsthorpe
Institute of Criminology, University of Cambridge
May 2018

Introduction

In 2009 Michael Banton, whose seminal book *The policeman in the community* was published around the time Westley, Reiss, Bayley, and Black were founding police studies in the US, spoke at the University of Surrey. Banton made a sharp distinction between policy-oriented and scholarly research. Many see the distinction as less clear, amongst them the late John Alderson, former chief constable of Devon and Cornwall. On retirement Alderson held fellowships at Cambridge, then Oxford. His objective was to stimulate more academics to research policing. As consultant to the European Human Rights Commission, Alderson feared the demise of policing by consent in favour of a paramilitary style. At Lord Scarman's inquiry into the 1981 Brixton riots he said 'if we are to save ourselves from incessant conflict we must start talking hearts and minds, not CS gas and plastic bullets'. Without labouring the point, there are fundamental issues both of policy and of intellectual discipline here. To confirm their intersection, we might note Alderson's declaration that: 'if the police, either universally or locally, come to feel alienated it is likely the fundamental nature of their functioning will change from an essentially proactive to a reactive force ... The Rubicon will have been crossed'. He did not write that in an academic publication but in his last annual report as chief constable. In his perception, social science needed to engage with policing in an effort of 'balancing social control and freedom'.

Banton's and Alderson's views relate importantly to the vexed question of police professionalism. At the time Alderson championed police research, law, education, and medicine all attracted extensive scholarship. Not so the British police. It seemed that there had to be some failure of policing so colossal as to warrant a Royal Commission or judge-led inquiry before there was any research effort. The sole centre for police studies was

Professionalizing the Police: The Unfulfilled Promise of Police Training. Nigel G. Fielding © Nigel G. Fielding 2018. Published 2018 by Oxford University Press

at Strathclyde, directed by Roy Wilkie. In the US, police science thrived at Berkeley, Michigan State, and Maryland, and in France at the Lyons Ecole de Supérieure. Alderson was able to cite only five scholarly books on the British police (an under-report, but not by much), of which one was a history and another was written in 1943.

Police research is transformed since Alderson's time, and police studies, already growing in the 1990s, has been further propelled by recent reforms of recruit training. There is independent academic research, official research, and research by officers completing academic or vocational qualifications. This led Brown (1996) to develop her typology of research stances ('insider insiders', 'outsider insiders', 'insider outsiders', 'outsider outsiders'), pithily capturing the constraints on each type of research relationship; Weatheritt's (1986) critique of 'doomed to succeed' in-house evaluations of policing innovations was also a landmark contribution.

To those who doubt the relevance to professional policing of the large questions that lie behind policy decisions, a final point regarding Alderson pertains. During his tenure as Chief he was taken to court by the Central Electricity Generating Board (CEGB) for refusing to evict protestors from a field where the CEGB wanted to drill foundations for a nuclear power plant. Alderson refused to use force absent a breach of the peace, seeing 'great constitutional principles' at stake. The case ended in a fudge (Lord Denning ruled that the police did have powers to evict the protestors, but also refused to grant the CEGB's writ of *mandamus* against Alderson), but after the ruling, Alderson simply went to the field, spoke to the protestors, and asked them to leave. They did so. Their point had been made and had been understood at the highest level of their local force. If professionalism, and training as a means to instil it, is more than just a policy matter, then Alderson's action exemplifies the way that policing policy often revolves around large intellectual questions, in this case, lawful dissent, and thus, ultimately, public consent.

The interaction between police socialization and police competence is a driver of role conflict (Fielding 1988b). Such conceptual matters inevitably require consideration of policy, practice and evaluation. For instance, role conflict leads us to conceptualizations like Festinger's 'cognitive dissonance' but also to empirical indicators like patterned rates of resignation. A prominent policy-relevant finding is the rapidly declining salience of formal versus informal agencies of occupational socialization. Classroom training has high salience while it remains the sole or principal mode in the training sequence, then falls steadily in salience as exposure to field experience grows, with a sharp drop following first patrol. That tells us something about the effectiveness of formal training but also that enculturation is not just something 'done to you' but a co-produced resource. Agencies of informal socialization greatly exceed agencies of formal socialization in impact on job-relevant attitudes and enduring attitude change, and affiliation to occupational culture actively devalues knowledge rendered via formal socialisation.

This effect can be observed in other occupations. It is hardly a surprise that on-the-job experiences progressively modify the importance placed on early learning; lawyers, medics, academics and many other trades leave training and/or higher education into the embrace of seasoned members of their occupation whose stance is generally 'now you will find out how things really work around here'. What may be different in policing is the active negation of classroom-based learning, the premise that formal socialization was not just a partial story but a lie. All of us are used to modifying our knowledge base by experience but it is a different thing to discard altogether what we first thought we knew. The process one encounters in occupations like law is that formal knowledge and on-the-job experience proceed in dialogue; new entrants may well challenge what they find not just on the basis that it is not what they expected but that it does not measure up to the standards they first learned. That seems less apt to happen in the police service.

In pursuing why this may be so, socialization theory, micro-sociologies of workplace interaction, and the interplay between theories of the self and occupational culture are drawn into encounter with the increasing professionalizing project of the police. The balance of the academic and the vocational in police training has been central in contemporary debates over professionalism. In the UK it has marked the character of the Initial Police Learning and Development Programme (the unmemorable abbreviation 'IPLDP' can more readily be recalled by pronouncing it 'ippledip', as do police), and its incorporation into a system involving colleges, universities, and education businesses alongside force training. But this book aspires to do more than evaluate training. To understand training against the yardstick of professionalism we must understand the nature of what the police do. This requires an attempt to capture the nature of contemporary society and sociality, for that is what police professionals must themselves attempt.

1

Professionalism and Police Training

Sir Robert Peel's nine principles for policing take a particular construction of police professionalism (Table 1.1). Peel does not have sole credit. The first Metropolitan Police commissioners, Charles Rowan and Richard Mayne, had a large part in their development (Lentz and Chaires 2007), with Mayne declaring 'the primary object of an efficient police is the prevention of crime: the next that of detection and punishment of offenders if crime is committed. To these ends all the efforts of police must be directed. The protection of life and property, the preservation of public tranquillity, and the absence of crime, will alone prove whether those efforts have been successful'. In fact, Peel never formulated the principles as such. They were constructed in the form we know them by Charles Reith in the 1940s, as a guide to Peel's conception of policing (Lentz and Chaires 2007). Shared credit apart, the essential thing is that the principles have a relentless emphasis on the relationship to society in a way not found in the established professions.

The police service's uncertain debate about the claim to professional status notably lacks grounding in any detached appraisal of what a profession is and how professions like law or medicine function. In economics, law enforcement is a 'defective market' because uncontrolled market competition for profit cannot deliver a universal good. This is why professional codes are important in law and medicine (Wolf 2017). The distribution of policing services to those who cannot pay but are subject of police attention makes it right to pursue police professionalism. Meanwhile sociological understandings of professions as mechanisms for social closure around guarded knowledge enabling self-regulation for monopoly profit leave one wondering whether a profession is the right model for any worthy kind of occupational practice. Functionalist sociology's inclination to regard professions like

Professionalizing the Police: The Unfulfilled Promise of Police Training. Nigel G. Fielding © Nigel G. Fielding 2018. Published 2018 by Oxford University Press

Table 1.1 Sir Robert Peel's Principles

1. To prevent crime and disorder, as an alternative to their repression by military force and severity of legal punishment.

2. To recognize always that the power of the police to fulfil their functions and duties is dependent on public approval of their existence, actions and behaviour and on their ability to secure and maintain public respect.

3. To recognize always that to secure and maintain the respect and approval of the public means also the securing of the willing cooperation of the public in the task of securing observance of laws.

4. To recognize always that the extent to which the cooperation of the public can be secured diminishes proportionately the necessity of the use of physical force and compulsion for achieving police objectives.

5. To seek and preserve public favour, not by pandering to public opinion but by constantly demonstrating absolutely impartial service to law, in complete independence of policy, and without regard to the justice or injustice of the substance of individual laws, by ready offering of individual service and friendship to all members of the public without regard to their wealth or social standing, by ready exercise of courtesy and friendly good humour, and by ready offering of individual sacrifice in protecting and preserving life.

6. To use physical force only when the exercise of persuasion, advice and warning is found to be insufficient to obtain public cooperation to an extent necessary to secure observance of law or to restore order, and to use only the minimum degree of physical force which is necessary on any particular occasions for achieving a police objective.

7. To maintain at all times a relationship with the public that gives reality to the historic tradition that the police are the public and that the public are the police, the police being only members of the public who are paid to give full-time attention to duties which are incumbent on every citizen in the interests of community welfare and existence.

8. To recognize always the need for strict adherence to police-executive functions, and to refrain from even seeming to usurp the powers of the judiciary of avenging individuals or the State, and of authoritatively judging guilt and punishing the guilty.

9. To recognize always that the test of police efficiency is the absence of crime and disorder, and not the visible evidence of police action in dealing with them.

Source: S. Lentz and R. Chaires (2007), 'The invention of Peel's principles', *Journal of Criminal Justice*, 35 (1), 69–79.

medicine and law as distinctive and 'noble'—which led to an uncritical search for distinctive 'traits' of the professional—long ago gave way to interactionist sociology's view that professions are essentially similar to occupations (Atkinson 1983: 226–7), 'profession' being no more than a title claimed by occupations under certain circumstances and masking their mundane reality and self-serving practices. The apparatus of professionalism includes licensing, accreditation, an ethical code, and laying down and promulgating the body of knowledge required for professional practice (Lee 2010: 131). Professional bodies produce exclusion and elitism. In jealously guarding admission, membership, expulsion, practice, and practitioner discipline, this take on professions is preoccupied with opacity and lack of accountability. It highlights professional status as a means of vesting in the hands of the professional the control of price and the quality and extent of services provided. While acknowledging the theoretical value of a profession's authorship, control and licensing of professional practice standards, the social sciences tend to approach the professions as symptomatic of what is offensive to a free society and obstructive to democracy.

This is not to say that these sceptical, even jaundiced, perspectives are necessarily right, although they have proven convincing empirically and useful in addressing policy issues like social constraints on entry to the judiciary. Certainly, the term 'profession' is more loosely used now than formerly (Wilensky 1964); a Victorian would be bewildered to hear of a 'nursing profession' and even now some blanch at there being a 'hairdressing profession'. Central to the marks of a profession is the control of entry via a prescribed path of accredited education. It is now possible to register for a foundation degree in hairdressing, but it is not a graduate-only occupation. Core characteristics that in most people's eyes make some work a profession rather than an occupation are now less firm, but the distinction endures. Yet in the 90 years between the Desborough Committee Report (1920) and the Neyroud Report (2010) there has been little elaboration of what might make policing a profession. Nevertheless, researchers such as Chan (Chan 2001; Chan et al 2003), Hayes (2002) and Otwin (2004) all address how training can promote ethical, democratic policing. Rather than address ourselves to the sociology of professions the necessary focus is a sociology of professional education, including the latent functions of the curriculum in reproducing knowledge and of training in differentially distributing cultural capital such as to form the *habitus* of police work (Bourdieu 1992).

During the formative period of Peel's 'New Police', recruitment, not training, was seen as the path to sound policing standards. There was much attention to the necessary qualities of constables and how to recruit and select to secure such qualities. Despite Peel having declared that officers should be men of above average intelligence, good character, and sound physical fitness, the latter two qualities were prime during the nineteenth century. There was more faith in the recruitment of upright, tractable, and able-bodied men than interest in imparting the finer points of the constable's role (Steedman 1984). Training was perfunctory, largely based on the military model, with a great deal of drill, some rote learning of the legal basics, and recruits pressed into service hastily. Such preparation as there was came from accompanying an experienced officer on one or two tours of duty and from conversation in station house interludes. Nineteenth century policing was marked by high staff turnover, suggesting that selecting for qualities was ineffectual in securing satisfactory officers and/or that the job's obnoxious qualities were too much for many recruits.

A plausible anchor point for the contemporary period of police training is the 1919 Desborough Committee, convened by Parliament after the 1918 police strikes over pay and conditions. Amongst its fifty-one recommendations was 'the system of training and education be improved and assimilated throughout the Police Service'. The Committee notably emphasized an idea that until then had been subordinate in public discourse about policing, that policing was a 'profession'. Desborough highlighted the exceptional demands that policing made and the special characteristics needed to meet them. This underpinned its policy on pay and conditions. Pay rose substantially, pensions were enviable, but the police were forbidden a union or right to strike. The 'exceptional demands' and 'special characteristics' line buttressed for generations the idea that the police should themselves lead the 'design and delivery of police training and policy development' (Neyroud 2010: 30). In the 1964 Royal Commission on Policing, good pay and training were a defence against corruption and guarantor of respectability. It is generally held that the Sheehy Report of 1993 was so widely reviled in the police service because of its view that policing was much less unique an occupation than police imagined. Whatever Peel's view of the level of intelligence needed (backed by *The Times*, which declared that 'a much more enlarged degree of attainment and intelligence' was needed for 'this more complicated service'; editorial, 25 September 1829), police were largely trained in the style of an artisan trade for much of the modern period. Yet Desborough declared 'the duties the police have to perform are varied and exacting; they are increasing, and will probably still increase in variety and complexity, and a man cannot make a good policeman unless his general intelligence, memory and powers of observation are distinctly above average' (Desborough Committee 1920: para. 29). Nevertheless, this is less an agenda for professionalism than a narrow (and Holmesian) statement of qualities that assist the competent investigation of a crime.

In the US the so-called 'professional era' of policing emerged in response to the corruption associated with the political control of police departments in the early twentieth century. The US reforms included distinctive uniforms, centrally despatched vehicle patrol, and codes of conduct. The latter stood in tension with the adoption of paramilitary command and control. The approach called 'scientific police management' was associated with August Vollmer, and was underpinned by his conceptualization of professionalism (Table 1.2). These principles were applied during Vollmer's tenure as police chief in the university town of Berkeley, California, and expounded during his time in the 1920s as President of the International Association of Chiefs of Police. Vollmer persuaded the University of California to teach criminal justice and became first chair of the programme. He promoted recruitment of women and African-Americans, and was the first chief to introduce motorized patrol, police car radios, and the lie detector. Such things were the basis of his reputation as a leading advocate of scientific police management. From early in the modern era of policing, technology has been a prime icon of

Table 1.2 August Vollmer's police professionalism

* serving a higher purpose
* rigorous officer education
* broad police discretion
* collegial control

Source: Glenn et al (2003).

modernity and a sign that policing was keeping abreast of changing times. These were accessible symbols readily understood by the public and the mass media, rather more so than people-based initiatives like 'intelligence-led policing' or 'community policing' that raise questions like 'who exactly is the community?', matters harder to grasp than a new kind of gun.

Vollmer was briefly Chief of the Los Angeles Police Department (LAPD), which later came to be seen as a leading adopter of Vollmer's approach. However, the LAPD experience demonstrated that the scientific management approach created professionally remote, internally-oriented, legalistic, formalized, and rigid police departments. A large factor was the emphasis on a particular construction of police ethics, an example of a bad policy inspired by noble motives. Corruption was rampant in urban American forces for generations before Vollmer. Chiefs were elected officials, and votes were orchestrated by 'machine politics' based on ethnicity. All ranks were subject to corruption by gangsters and organized crime, aggravated by America's futile experiment with temperance. Reacting against this, Vollmer sought a system that insulated police from the community. If the problem was that the police had got too close to the public, close enough to take backhanders and parley with machine politicians, the solution was to keep a long arm's length away from the people. However, it is doubtful such an approach was ever suited to the cities of California. These were relatively less marked by the corruption found in the old cities of the East Coast. The issue in big West Coast cities was rapid population growth caused by economic boom, circumstances not designed to engender sociality and a sense of community, a situation aggravated by the sprawling nature of cities dependent on automobiles (the cover of the 'Portrait of LA' book my family received on moving there in 1957 is a photo of an elevated highway intersection). Such places were not so much cities as agglomerations of separate residential areas, some being communities in the accepted sense, some being amorphous collections of apartments with a ceaseless population turnover, and some being ethnic minority ghettos including unregistered, disenfranchised migrants.

Vollmer's principles were incapable in such places of handling the civil unrest around race, opposition to the Vietnam War, and the counter-culture that featured in the 1960s. Ironically, the International Association of Chiefs of Police (IACP) Code of

Police Ethics, seen as Vollmer's crowning achievement, was complicit in causing decades of troubled police/public relations. The LAPD's separation from the community left it with no understanding of the new cultural currents and particularly, the tensions around ethnicity. This led to complete unpreparedness for events like the 1965 Watts race riots, which left thirty-four dead and caused $40 million of property damage. Confronted by a population it did not understand, the LAPD sought refuge in technology, brutalizing relations with the community by the liberal use of weaponry and reluctance to get out of squad cars and talk to people. The disaster-waiting-to-happen culminated in the 1991 Rodney King beating, in which technology turned on the LAPD. Images from a bystander's video-recording of the virtually unprovoked, near-fatal beating of King by a dozen police officers were seen worldwide as epitomizing the reality behind America's promise of liberty and justice for all. The officers' acquittals sparked the 1992 Los Angeles riots, in which fifty-three died, ending only when the military was deployed. The so-called 'professional model' was seen as having failed. Reform efforts shifted to Community Policing.

In 2003 researchers at RAND led by Russell Glenn published their analysis of what was required to bring police training into the twenty-first century. It was commissioned by the LAPD but has been widely influential. It works from Samuel Huntington's (1957) concept of professionalism. Huntington, a controversial neo-conservative political scientist, argued that tenets of 'corporateness', responsibility and expertise should guide the development and practice of military training and Glenn et al extrapolated this to the police (Table 1.3).

Huntington advocated the carpet bombing of Vietnam, advised dictatorships, and was twice denied membership of the US National Academy of Sciences. Perhaps his neo-conservative pedigree helped police organizations to embrace the relatively humane principles of his approach to professionalism, and Glenn et al's socially liberal rendering of them. Huntington's thinking has, however, found little resonance amongst scholars. Few have sought to connect his rendering of corporateness with the empirical knowledge we now have about the way frontline officers monitor each other's conduct, such as their intolerance of shirkers or those who are untrustworthy, issues that have come to the fore in contemporary attempts to understand the dimension of police

Table 1.3 Huntington's tenets of professionalism as applied by Glenn et al to policing

Corporateness: Instilling an understanding of professional duty and building a minimum level of expertise before admission to the job. Collectively maintaining professional standards; using lessons learned for sustaining expertise; creating quality instruction; developing structures and procedures to maximise potential from training.
Responsibility: Duty extends beyond serving officers' own interests. This sense of service requires a Community Policing approach that recognises social diversity. Diversity awareness must underlie every aspect of training.
Expertise: Formal training remains the responsibility of trainers but every supervisor and officer must commit to constantly improving skills and knowledge. Training should not only help recruits qualify but extend to every echelon beyond graduation.

Source: Glenn et al (2003).

legitimacy relating to how officers regard their own authority. Although we know that officers are powerful influences on each others' style of policing, the organization has not exploited what is known about informal social control by peers in furtherance of standards of professional behaviour.

The RAND researchers were tasked by California's State government to apply Huntington's principles to five core skill areas seen as fundamental to future police training: the use of force; search and seizure; arrest procedures; community policing; and diversity awareness. Glenn et al conceptualized the skills as interconnected in frontline policing, so their principal recommendation was that the training curriculum must be integrated in ways that allow officers to realistically practice combining relevant skills and knowledge. They judged that training conveyed technical skills like weapons and vehicle handling but struggled with interpersonal and verbal communication skills. Most officers needed more training in these, especially interpersonal skills relevant to de-escalating conflict and getting people to do what they do not want to do. Police needed to think in terms of a 'communications continuum' that even extended to handling the media who may pass judgment on their actions.

Training for Community Policing (CP) was isolated in many training systems and Glenn et al found that many officers struggled to define what CP is. It needed to be integrated throughout training. Use of force, search-and-seizure, and arrest policies, all needed to be understood in the context of Community Policing and diversity awareness. It is hard to disagree, despite officer resistance. Nevertheless, as the 'Review of Police Core and Ancillary Tasks' (Home Office 1995) insisted, police still have backstage service functions that help give police a human face and balance their law enforcement role. Schools liaison, community and safety education, and even handling lost property, broaden the police role in the community while also exposing police to the community's concerns. Perhaps the most significant backstage function is crime prevention advice. Engaging with prevention at local level extends basic investigation/detection skills to the frontline. Yet while officers spend 80% of their time dealing with crime in some respect, only a small fraction involves crime prevention (HMIC 2012c). These backstage activities help keep the police a service organization but feature little in recruit training.

We speak of policing as though everyone knows what it is. Yet many debates hinge on whether something is within or outside the frame of what we understand as policing. Does the function that 'bouncers' perform at nightclubs constitute policing? That private security firms perform in shopping centres or, increasingly, public order situations? They can *in extremis* use physical contact to move people on from the property whose owner is paying them, but having only a citizen power of arrest they often prefer to call the police. Private sector policing does not occur solely in private space, nor does public sector policing occur exclusively in public space (Jones and Newburn 1998). Public police agencies sell services as if they were businesses, while the private sector, through the questionable agency of blundering giants like G4S and Serco, deliver services to the public sector, including leaving a terminally-ill prisoner handcuffed and waiting in the street for forty minutes while guards went to lunch and applying an illegal restraint that killed a fourteen-year old boy (*Howard League News*, 2014, Autumn edition).

In his early work Robert Reiner treated policing as something that only a publicly-constituted and publicly-accountable organization could perform. His view changed, although he remained opposed to privatization of policing. The Crawford et al (2005: 4) definition is helpful in such debates: 'policing is intentional action involving conscious exercise of authority that is directed to law enforcement, order or an assurance of safety'. Neither the State nor criminal justice appears in the definition. Yet it readily covers what the public police do, while helping us to see what we should look for in private police to identify what of their work involves something we should call 'policing'.

However, order of any kind produced by social control is a *particular* order, with a particular balance of interests. The point raises a constitutional paradox. The police institution exists to impose and safeguard the 'specific order' of the State, but itself poses a threat to the preservation both of that specific order and the underlying constitutional order (Walker 2000: 6). Britain's unwritten constitution poses a unique problem in controlling and making accountable the police, because it rules out a definitive statement protecting our fundamental rights. Unlike states where the executive and legislative branches of government are kept distinct to avoid concentration of powers, in Britain whoever controls Parliament controls the executive, leaving control of the police vulnerable to political expediency. Since parliamentary sovereignty is an 'indivisible property', it is not possible through a federal arrangement to lodge residual police powers at regional level, as in US states.

Bar the European Arrest Warrant, policing arrangements did not fall under European Community law either. Brussels could not challenge Britain's domestic constitutional arrangements for policing, but even the Warrant was threatened by politicians running scared from euro-scepticism prior to 'Brexit'. The core doctrine of constabulary independence (under which police are responsible for their actions to the law and only to the law) itself relies on constitutional convention, and while such conventions represent 'rules of political behaviour' they are not enforceable by the courts (Walker 2000: 16). The doctrine is silent in respect of who controls the policies under which forces operate. Neither chief officers nor the public can look to it to resolve awkward matters such as the precise boundary between policy and operational practices.

That boundary has been to the fore in quarrels that go beyond teething troubles in the imposed relationship between chief officers and Police and Crime Commissioners. But it also registers daily, as forces juggle priorities between calls for service. A chief can set a policy to favour one or another type of call, but the exact balance between policy and operational imperatives falls, at best, to intermediate supervisors and more often to call-handlers and the frontline. Moreover, the history of the independence doctrine's application since the inter-war years of the twentieth century is 'a history of failure to come to terms with the requirements of legitimate governance of the police' (Walker 2000: 46).

Authorities like Reiner (2011) have bemoaned the contemporary eclipse of a social democratic politics of social control, a victim alongside other communitarian values of increasing 'competitive egoism'. For many, this bespeaks the enduring grip of neo-liberalism, a 'zombie category' that neither the banking crisis, recession, nor Brexit have loosened from its hold over government. Loader and Sparks have argued for a more nuanced approach. Thus 'there is a good case to be made in the UK, but not just there, that we have witnessed greatly reduced tolerance towards discrimination, and the use of undue force, by police ... and significantly enhanced means of investigating these' (Loader and Sparks 2011: 19). There is evidence that police do not resent the Human Rights Act 1998 and indeed feel it aids their daily work (Bullock and Johnson 2012), albeit the story is one of clearer bureaucratic processes rather than a prompt to actively embrace human rights.

The definitional debate engendered by private policing tells us that public policing has the elements of a public good. Loader and Sparks' 'principles of just ordering' encourage us to consider how we might build on them. As well as defending and extending the application of human rights law, we should promote a critical understanding of government's urge to use police for projects of social engineering, and exploit the surviving remnants of the social democratic project. Technology can help; video functionality in citizens' smartphones has prompted greater caution over deploying force (Brown 2016).

However, the Loader and Sparks argument with most traction concerns governance, 'thinking more imaginatively about how to extend the democratic credibility and responsiveness of crime control institutions and ... foster[ing] experimentation with deliberative institutions and mechanisms that help make good the claim that [police] decisions are legitimate' (Loader and Sparks 2011: 32).

The concept of 'procedural justice' derived from political science theories of institutional legitimacy has much resonance in policing. The idea that the public are highly responsive to the perceived fairness of police actions, and that the way that police conduct themselves in such dealings heavily influences such perceptions, has a lineage running from the Black and Reiss studies of police legitimacy in the wake of the 1960s US race riots through UK research in the 1980s and 1990s showing the importance of police demeanour in interaction with citizens (Fielding et al 1992) and on to survey measures of public confidence (Hough et al 2013).

Peel, Rowan and Mayne's fifth principle of policing was that the police should 'seek and preserve public favour ... by ready offering of individual service and friendship to all members of the public without regard to their wealth or social standing; by ready exercise of courtesy and good humour; and by ready offering of individual sacrifice in protecting and preserving life'. This conception may be rather idealized but is a useful motivational fiction. It has fed a strong belief in the generic or 'omni-competent' constable, which is a useful way of approaching the evaluation of training and the wider issue of police professionalism. There is an ongoing debate about whether the constable role can remain generalist or specialists should be trained as such from the outset. Since it is generally desirable for organization members to understand the role of those elsewhere in the organization it makes sense to preserve the notion of the generic nature of the office of constable during initial training and early service. Future policing will require officers with even more 'multiple skills', but street sense will still count. There may be a drive for greater consistency across forces but equality before the law does not mean identical treatment everywhere, it means delivering treatments that are appropriate to circumstances.

Despite growth in specialist squads, around 55% of officers are still assigned to 'general patrol'. Combined with attending incidents, it accounts for about 40% of an officer's time. Classic research (Singer 2001; see Table 1.4) provided a detailed picture based on activity logs differing little from more recent studies discussed later. Officers spent nearly as much time in the station (43%) as in dealing with incidents and making enquiries. Each arrest took an average three and a half hours in station, with officers queuing for their prisoner's turn at the breathalyzer, photo ID, fingerprint, and criminal record check. Singer estimated that to get one more officer permanently out on patrol five further officers would be needed.

Table 1.4 Officer time use

% of respondent time by activity	
Working inside the police station	
Relief management	7.0%
Prisoner processing	5.7%
Prosecution, file and enquiries	6.2%
Cover duties	3.5%
Dealing with public	1.2%
Individual administration	0.5%
Station based training	0.7%
Break	5.1%
Other	13.1%
Working within the community	
Community support	1.7%
Patrol (including uncommitted patrol and travelling between pre-planned tasks)	17.0%
Attending incidents	23.3%
Crime related	9.0%
Other duties	3.3%
Policing events	0.5%
Break taken outside station	0.3%
Other work in the community	1.0%
Working with the criminal justice system	
Within the police force (other than own police station)	0.2%
At court	0.6%

Source: Singer (2001) *Diary of a Police Officer*, London: Home Office.

Singer's is an old, if revealing, study. Some of its recommendations have been implemented—more civilianization and more IT to deal with paperwork, delegating certain duties to other agencies, laptops in vehicles, and hand-held devices for connectivity on foot patrol. However, these things have been overtaken by 'policing under austerity', with civilian staff made redundant to 'protect the frontline', and diminished resource for IT. So the importance of training for patrol should not be underestimated.

Investigators depend heavily on intelligence collected by patrols. Interventions conducted spontaneously on patrol help build interpersonal skills, and reduce the use of force.

Recruitment and training cannot be isolated from broader currents. Today's recruitment and training environment has political roots in the 1982 White Paper 'Efficiency and Effectiveness in the Civil Service', the iconic statement imposing market discipline on the public sector. It was followed by Home Office Circular 114/1983 on 'Manpower, Effectiveness and Efficiency in the Police Service', which curbed police pay and staffing and required cases for new posts to be based on new beat and shift patterns and evidence that civilians could not do the work. By the end of the 1990s the combination of performance measurement and understaffing created rising fear of crime and demands for a more visible police presence. Government responded in 2000 with the Crime Fighting Fund. Trends in officer numbers are shown in Table 1.5. The Fund provided £726 million toward recruiting 9,000 additional officers. In 2002, when Her Majesty's Inspectorate of Constabulary (HMIC) published a highly critical review of recruit training, the training programme cost over £200 million a year (including salaries).

Training is often a source of savings when times are hard. For instance, when South Wales resisted civilianization the funding to continue using uniformed staff was taken from training. Force inspections regularly reported a 'training deficit' throughout the 1990s (Fielding and Fowles 2000a). When the Home Office published its consultation 'Police Training' in 2000 it floated greater commitment to CPD, reorganization of the Police Training Council, an 'employer-led National Training Organisation', a core curriculum, a qualifications framework, a central police college to train leaders, a dedicated training inspectorate, more IT-based provision, new powers for the home secretary to intervene if training was failing, joint training with other criminal justice agencies, and community input (Fielding and Fowles 2000b). This foreshadowed much of the agenda that was to come, but that does not mean these priorities were achieved.

Although the police reform agenda features numerous reviews and reports, the Neyroud Review (2010) has been the most substantial of recent years in impact on training and the professionalism debate. Neyroud identified the period 1990–2010 as critical for the professional knowledge base for policing. Yet

Table 1.5 Trend in police establishment 1939–2016

Year	Police Officers	% increase or decrease over time period	Time period (years)	% Change/ year
1939	60,262			
1963	76,195	20.91	24	0.87
1974	102,901	25.95	11	2.36
1978	109,075	5.66	4	1.42
1982	120,951	9.82	4	2.45
1986	122,993	1.66	4	0.42
1990	126,193	2.54	4	0.63
2000	124,614	−1.27	10	−0.13
2001	125,519	0.72	1	0.72
2003	133,366	5.88	2	2.94
2004	140,563	5.12	1	5.12
2005	142,795	1.56	1	1.56
2008	141,859	−0.66	3	−0.22
2009	143,769	1.33	1	1.33
2010	143,734	−0.02	1	−0.02
2011	139,110	−3.32	1	−3.32
2012	134,101	−3.74	1	−3.74
2013	129,584	−3.49	1	−3.49
2014	127,909	−1.31	1	−1.31
2015	126,818	−0.86	1	−0.86
2016	124,066	−2.22	1	−2.22
2017	123,142	−0.75	1	−0.75

Sources: A. Dixon (1963) 'Home Office and Police', unpublished MS, National Police Library; Home Office Police Workforce England and Wales series.

work he cites as adding to 'the knowledge and the level of professional skill across policing in the UK' was almost entirely motivated by response to episodes of disastrous service delivery. We are told, for example, that the period saw the 'professionalization of the investigator' as a result of the Byford Report on the bungled Yorkshire Ripper case, the 1993 Royal Commission on Criminal

Justice (prompted by widespread concern about stop-and-search of minorities), and 'the combined work on patrol in the 1990s', a reference to research demonstrating the ineffectiveness of cherished frontline practices. More recent work on Neighbourhood Policing ('NP') is cited as giving 'a significantly enhanced knowledge and skills base for patrol officers'—which is true, but the story is also one of surreptitious removal of NP resources from the outset.

Even more surprisingly, this rendering of the professionalism evidence base turned the idea of evidence upside down by arguing that, actually, we know too much. Although 'systematic documentation of … the skills and competence required to perform each role in the organisation … shows that the service has already begun to professionalise itself', unfortunately 'this quantity of guidance, advice, standards and competency frameworks is overwhelming' and needed drastic pruning. It is not just commentators who see in this curious position a reflection of the jockeying for advantage between the Association of Chief Police Officers (ACPO), HMIC, and Home Office. Neyroud himself commended a single professional body 'making the priority decisions about what really matters' (Neyroud 2010: 46). The take-home message from Glenn et al (2003) and Neyroud (2010) is that the character of training, and prevailing constructions of professionalism, reflect response to crisis and political imperatives at least as much as any considered rendering of what professional policing is and how training can bring it about.

2

Mission and Challenges

It is an easy headline when politicians declare that 'fighting crime' is what the police are for. However, when we delve beyond headlines the crime-busting myth disintegrates. It is not simply that the founders of the modern police knew that public order is the precedent condition of crime control because one cannot control crime without public cooperation. Nor is it the radical thesis that the police are so ineffective that it is absurd to say they are for crime control. Bittner's (1970) argument that the police are the default service to whom people turn when they feel 'something needs to be done about this, and it needs to be done now' comes closer. Waddington (1999: 20) makes the important point that 'what the police *do*, as opposed to have the potential to do, is exercise authority'. In their own way, dealing with lost children and burst water mains, delivering death notices, and advising schoolchildren on road safety all draw on such authority. None concern 'cutting crime'.

Some calls suggest considerable public confusion over the police role, including one from a woman worried about missing 'East Enders' on her broken TV, another asking officers to deliver a crate of beer, and a woman requesting removal of a bathroom spider (*The Guardian* 27 July 2013). Despite the national non-emergency number, citizens still use 999 for calls such as asking the best time to drive to Newcastle. Police are an 'agency of first resort'. Over a third of calls to Greater Manchester Police in 2010 were for social work-type issues. The bind is that while only a minority of contacts relate directly to crime, over half *might* involve or lead to a crime. Public-facing work accounts for 44% of officers' time, 27% is administration (mostly post-incident reports), another 27% is in the custody suite, at court, in training, briefings, or meetings (McLean and Hillier 2011).

The order maintenance element of policing's 'dual function' of law enforcement and order maintenance (Banton 1964) particularly calls for the exercise of discretion, interpreting whether action is warranted and if so, what. The dilemmas of police discretion are illustrated by the case of taxi driver Chris Halliwell and the detective superintendent who investigated him, Steve Fulcher. Halliwell was arrested as prime suspect in the kidnapping of Sian O'Callaghan, missing for five days. Halliwell refused to talk. Fulcher used his discretion to instruct that Halliwell be driven to an isolated hilltop rather than the police station. Without reading Halliwell his rights or arranging for a solicitor, Fulcher persuaded Halliwell to take him to O'Callaghan's body. Halliwell cooperated. Fulcher was preparing for him to be taken into custody when Halliwell asked 'do you want another one?'. At this point Fulcher should by law have cautioned Halliwell. Instead, he let Halliwell take him to the burial site of Becky Godden-Edwards, whom Halliwell had killed nine years earlier.

Fulcher's exercise of discretion in breach of the law meant none of Halliwell's evidence in respect of the Godden-Edwards murder could be used and, as it was then the sole evidence available, no prosecution was possible. In the O'Callaghan case, other evidence was available. Halliwell pleaded guilty and received a life sentence (a prosecution for Godden-Edwards' murder succeeded in 2016, Halliwell receiving a full-life sentence). Fulcher's reasoning brings alive the dilemma between the course of action he took and the requirements of the law. Fulcher said in pre-trial argument 'my duty was clear—to find and protect Sian if I could. It's what any parent would have wanted a police officer to do'. Fulcher instructed colleagues to interview Halliwell, then issued a statement that he was 'very close to identifying Sian's whereabouts'. Halliwell was then spotted dumping a car seat cover and headrest, and buying pills sufficient to overdose. Fulcher immediately ordered his arrest. Colleagues conducted an 'urgent interview' without a solicitor, permissible when delay could lead to a death. Halliwell did not cooperate and demanded a lawyer. It was at this point that Fulcher had Halliwell taken to the hillside site and persuaded Halliwell to take him to O'Callaghan. In the pre-trial hearing Fulcher acknowledged that, with full cognisance of legal requirements, he had ignored Police and Criminal Evidence Act (PACE) procedures. 'On the one hand, I was cognisant of Mr Halliwell's rights. But my primary duty was to save Sian's life ... There was an equation to balance between Mr Halliwell's right to silence and Sian O'Callaghan's right to life. My view was that Sian's right to life took a prior claim' (*The Guardian* 20 October 2012).

Asked why he did not caution Halliwell when the latter offered to take him to another burial, Fulcher said they had achieved rapport and that reading him his rights could have made him clam up. Once granted a lawyer Halliwell did exactly that. The defence depicted Fulcher's choice as a reversion to a 1970s style of policing and denial of Halliwell's fundamental rights under PACE. The judge agreed the hilltop questioning had pressurized Halliwell and that, post-arrest, there were deliberate 'wholesale and irrefutable breaches of PACE'. Halliwell's barrister argued Fulcher prevented a fair trial because he had revealed on live TV that Halliwell had taken him to the bodies, which no juror could ignore. However, because the seat covers had traces of O'Callaghan's blood, and there was CCTV linking her to Halliwell, the evidence was sufficient to successfully prosecute for O'Callaghan's murder.

In a final, vital coda, both victims' families expressed support for Fulcher's approach, as did his chief constable. The O'Callaghans were thankful for Fulcher doing all he could to save her in case she was alive, and the Godden-Edwards were thankful to know the truth of their daughter's disappearance. The Chief said 'there may be occasions where police officers have to make a decision in terms of saving life to step outside rules ... I would like to think I would make a similar decision in his circumstances', views echoed by other senior police, lawyers, and court reporters. While such dilemmas can only be resolved by values, and the balance one sets between law and commonsense is personal rather than analytical, the case illustrates the dilemmas of discretion that professionalism must address.

Governments' enthusiasm for putting new offences on the statute books runs alongside increasing limits on police discretion. The conceptual space the law enforcement/order maintenance distinction inhabits will always remain relevant. However, the resources available have changed considerably. Policy imperatives are manifest in the technological and legal tools made available, which determine the particular balance between law enforcement and order maintenance. Although there is value in the greater transparency associated with PACE Codes of Practice we increasingly regulate interventions that were formerly left to officers' judgement. Out-of-court disposals are a means to resolve minor matters informally using police discretion, but are subject to policy. Such disposals declined between 2007 and 2012 because targets prioritized serious crimes. The 232,200 police cautions in 2011 were a 36% decrease on 2007 (Ministry of Justice 2012, Statistical Bulletin). Similarly, the 127,500 Penalty Notices for Disorder issued in 2011 were 38.6% down on 2007. Police discretion thus varies with administrative targets.

Training must accommodate how these trends impact on recruits' understandings of the police mission and its performance. New officers must reach a contemporary accommodation to the order maintenance conundrum. For a behaviour to disrupt public order to the point requiring intervention police have to determine whether it breaches the norms the public applies to the place and time in question. Establishing prevailing norms in contemporary urban communities will remain contentious, making order maintenance decisions more open to challenge. Today's recruits are likely to spend most of their frontline time on the high-volume relatively minor offences which present most problems in exercising discretion. Understanding how training affects the standards recruits bear on joining is important in preparing them for the situations they will commonly encounter.

Where law allows scope for interpretation, guidance from supervisors is sparse, and the community provides little clear lead—some wanting more enforcement and others more tolerance—where do novices look for guidance on how to exercise their discretion? Research suggests it is to other police, so the practical definition of discretion lies largely with tutor constables and other seasoned officers. Personnel are policing's major resource—and cost—86% of the police budget in 2013 (HMIC 2014a). To such matters we now turn.

Defining and Measuring Police Work

London and other cities were largely self-policed up to the eighteenth century under the medieval ward and precinct-based system involving householders (or their placemen) exerting community social control. When Henry Fielding established a police office at Bow Street in the 1750s he had six 'thief takers'; by the end of the century there were 70 Bow Street Runners, with seven other police offices across London by 1792 (Ackroyd 2001). The City of London formed its Day Police in 1784 performing regular patrols, 1798 saw foundation of the Thames Police Office dealing with quays, docks, and warehouses, and 1805 saw a horse patrol to deter highwaymen. When the office of Peel's 'New Police' was established in a Whitehall courtyard called Great Scotland Yard it oversaw three thousand men organized into seventeen divisions (ibid). Within four years less than a sixth remained, the rest having found other work or been dismissed for drunkenness or immorality.

Politicians are guaranteed a positive reception when they increase police numbers to 'fight crime'. Changes in police strength have an uncertain effect on crime rates (Bradford 2011) but complete absence of police increases crime (Sherman and Eck 2002). High or low budgets do not translate directly into high or low detection rates. One study found that a 10% increase in Sweden's officer numbers produced a 2% decrease in burglary (Lindstrom 2013) but detection rates can be poor despite generous funding or high despite severe cuts. Notwithstanding 22% cuts, recent detection rates by police in England and Wales stand at their highest since the present statistical definitions were enacted in 2002. By 2014 police strength fell for the fifth year running, to a twelve-year low, at 127,909 officers (from a peak 143,734 in 2010). In the same period recorded crime fell 14% (ONS 2014a).

Her Majesty's Inspectorate of Constabulary's (HMIC) 'Valuing the Police' (2010d) maintained that police visibility is key to public confidence, and that confidence is highest when police numbers are highest. On average, 12% of officers and Police Community Support Officers (PCSOs) are visible and available at 0900 Monday; 1900 Wednesday; 0030 Saturday morning, where 'visible' means staff who wear uniform and mainly work in public and 'available' means being ready for duty rather than attending court or receiving training. More solo patrol, and shift patterns correlated with demand, can improve visibility, but large cuts inevitably mean fewer officers and less visibility. Since visibility is a function of numbers, numbers have an additional indirect effect on public confidence (Sindall and Sturgis 2013). The ONS 2012/2013 survey found 34% of adults reported sighting an officer on foot patrol compared with 38% in 2011/12, the first decline in seven years. Those never seeing officers on foot patrol rose to 27%. The link between visibility and public confidence was indicated by falls in the proportion of people rating police as doing an 'excellent' job, to 9.6% (51.8% said their performance was 'good'). Combining 'excellent' and 'good', in 2011/12, 62.3% rated police positively but in 2012/13 it was 61.4%. Those feeling the police did a 'very poor' job rose from 1.8% to 2.2%.

HMIC (2010d) was important not just as a historical reminder of the agonies with which governments' traditional favour towards the police budget finally died. HMIC was prescient in arguing that central targets were becoming counter-productive, that the performance regime had become clogged by an excess of indicators, and that forces would adopt uncoordinated and counter-productive innovations to address cuts. It was a perceptive forecast of the police vista for the austerity years ahead.

The 2010 comprehensive spending review cut Home Office budget from £9.3 billion in 2010/11 to £7 billion in 2014/15 while imposing Police and Crime Commissioners (PCCs), new procurement and back office functions, new terms and conditions of employment, and the diversion of £1.8 billion to border control and counter-terrorism. Government expected improved productivity—'modernizing' pay and conditions would help police 'do more with less'. These euphemisms amounted to cutting officer numbers. Stories appeared of cases like that of a couple who found a two-metre California King Snake in their kitchen cupboard; police told Mr Gamble he must chase it away himself (*Evening Standard*, 29 July 2014).

These portents of drastic action on pay and conditions were confirmed in a radical review by former Rail Regulator Tom Winsor, advised by a labour market economist. Forces were to use pay and conditions to maximize frontline visibility, make remuneration 'fair to the taxpayer', and enable 'modern' management practices (Winsor 2011). Pay was 10% to 15% higher than comparable public sector workers, sometimes 60% above median local earnings. It included an element for anti-social hours, but fewer officers now worked them. A £2,000 boost for working unsocial shifts and a £3,000 cut for those in middle and back office roles would encourage experienced officers back to the frontline; 43% of Police Federation ranks worked nine-to-five in offices. Winsor cut starting salaries from £23,000 to £19,000 but chiefs could offer up to £22,000 for desired skills and qualifications. Officers were concerned about pension changes and retirement age, but less about fitness testing and role/skill-based pay (Hoggett et al 2013). Winsor duly became HM Chief Inspector.

HMIC (2012b) reported the frontline was being 'protected but not preserved'. As well as officers, forces planned to cut IT, facilities, equipment, and training by £474 million. A common contingency is shedding civilian staff, an example being sharing fingerprint experts with adjacent forces—delaying trials. Others include selling stations, not replacing police cars, and reducing training (with one PCC commenting 'we've cut training so officers are all less well-trained at all ranks, from constables to senior officers'; *Surrey Advertiser* 30 May 2014). There would still be a shortfall of £302 million against the required £2.4 billion saving by 2015, requiring a cut of 8,100 frontline posts and a 33% cut in non-frontline posts. Prime for back office cuts was training.

Cuts in strength affect response times. Fourteen out of twenty-one forces responding to a Freedom of Information (FoI) request reported rising 999 call response times from 2011 to 2013; Devon and Cornwall reported a 50% increase (*Daily Telegraph* 19 May 2014). Workload pressure, reduced supervision, and weak/absent training due to understaffing also cause under-recording of crime. In a sample of 3,102 incidents reported to police, 20% were no-crimed, including rapes and serious violence (HMIC 2014b).

Accompanying the bare numbers is the crumbling distinction between local response, investigative, and community teams. Increased staffing of investigative teams and public protection roles like sex offender management rob Neighbourhood Policing (NP). Solo patrol increases. But while officers work hard—starting early on e-mail and working through meal breaks—researchers saw opportunities for greater efficiency in 56% of shifts observed (McLean and Hillier 2011). Inefficiencies obstructed 9% of tasks, most often custody work, with officers having to wait in a third of cases for a sergeant to initiate booking. NP and response work increasingly overlaps. Community work takes 32% of NP officer time but also 13% of response officer time, and incidents take 23% of response officer time but also 10% of NP officer time, revealing the sticking plaster approach forced on supervisors. While efficiency experts call for 'a cultural shift' one suspects the real culprit is the intransigent realities of police work, like chasing after 'victim engagement' when victims do not want contact (Millie 2014) or multiple units attending incidents, earlier noted by Singer (2001).

Repeated reference in official austerity pronouncements to prioritizing 'frontline policing' led the Home Affairs Committee (2011b) to demand that the Home Office systematically define 'frontline', 'middle office', and 'back office'. HMIC (2011a) surveyed public and police. Most agreed that officers responding to 999 calls or performing NP duties, and detectives, were frontline. Such roles accounted for 61% of the workforce. Training and finance were back office. 'Middle office', where operational and support functions overlap, such as processing intelligence, holding prisoners, or answering calls from the public, was less certain. A clear majority of the public saw call-handlers as frontline, and a small majority custody officers, but only a minority saw processing intelligence as such. Adding call-handlers and custody officers increased the frontline by 7%. HMIC ventured this definition: 'The police frontline comprises those who are in everyday contact with the public and who directly intervene to keep people safe and enforce the law.'

The Police Allocation Formula (PAF) captures relative force workload using indicators including population inflow (affects violence and sex offences); being 'hard pressed' (incidence of high cost crimes, vehicle crime, exceptional need for reassurance); proportion on income support/benefits and in overcrowded households; bars per 100 hectares (affects personal violence, sexual offences, vehicle crime, burglary, need for reassurance); population density (affects robbery, traffic, high cost crime); residents in 'routine/semi-routine occupations' or who have never worked or are unemployed; amount of terraced accommodation, single parent households, student housing; proportion of 'wealthy achievers'. However, while PAF provides the gearing for force budgets, funding is received as a lump sum that PCCs and forces distribute according to local priorities (Table 2.1).

Home Secretary Theresa May's 'Business Partnering for Police programme' (BPP) sought extensive privatization, including crime investigation, NP, and managing high-risk individuals. Despite G4S and Serco being convicted for claiming non-existent 'services' on electronic tagging contracts, ministers allowed these multinationals to bid, but forces backed out and BPP folded. A private sector partner called police the 'customers from hell' (Perpetuity Research 2011). The service demanded low profit margins, and negotiating contracts with the private sector was often the first time police had to specify job components and

Table 2.1 Cost of the police force

£ million	Current prices		2008 Prices		
	2000–2001	2009–2010	2000–2001	2009–2010	Change
Home Office Core Settlement	3,412	4,683	4,210	4,602	9%
Home Office Specific Grants	72	1,233	88	1,212	1273%
Rate Support Grant and National Non-Domestic Rates	2,661	3,627	3,282	3,565	9%
Central Government Sub-Total	**6,144**	**9,543**	**7,581**	**9,379**	24%
Precept (from Council Tax)	1,242	3,106	1,532	3,052	99%
Total	**7,386**	**12,649**	**9,113**	**12,431**	36%

Source: N. Johnston and B. Politowski (2016) *Police Funding*, London: Commons Library.

required standards (Police Foundation 2011). Policing cannot be characterized in profit-making terms, so perhaps the lack of understanding is mutual.

For many years the only information about what police do was crime statistics. Social histories document their manipulation in the 1900s, with 'no-criming' and 'classificatory differences between crimes and offences … used to redefine them in a manner suitable to practitioners' (Weinberger 1995: 85). Detectives locked up crime books to stop uniformed officers recording certain types of crime. Recording was based on levels of crime perceived as creditable or compelling, low when seeking to show effectiveness, high when seeking resources.

A revealing case is homophobic violence (Moran 2007). Police data suggested most was of the 'stranger-danger' kind; 65% of police reports indicated no relationship between perpetrator and victim. When Moran scrutinized the reports he identified two new perpetrator categories—neighbours, and locals. The former accounted for 21% of reports, the latter for 28%. 'No relationship' thus fell under 15%. But LBGT groups rejected Moran's re-analysis, disliking its implication that many perpetrators knew their victim. So did police, arguing that 'community' data was fuller and more valid while police data was partial and mediated by 'policy concerns'. Police rubbished their own data because their strategy was committed to the 'stranger-danger' model, hence mobilized against random violence outside gay bars.

The British Crime Survey (BCS) (since 2012 the 'Crime Survey for England and Wales' (CSEW)) is regarded as more reliable than police-generated statistics. Victim surveys are less susceptible to gaming. In 2012 responsibility for crime statistics transferred from the Home Office to the Office for National Statistics (ONS). In 2010/11, when the police recorded 4.2 million offences, the BCS recorded 9.6 million. The 1.15 million offences detected (cleared up) by the police were 28% of police-recorded crimes but only 12% of those reported to the BCS (Table 2.2). Average detections per officer vary little, about ten per officer per year.

Long-term trend shows crime rising steadily from 1981, peaking in 1995 and falling since 2000 (Figure 2.1). Rather than better policing this is largely due to better household and vehicle security, changes in drug markets, and more effective community penalties.

Crime reported to the CSEW fell 14% in 2014. Violence fell 20%, criminal damage 17% and theft 10%. Violent crime fell from 3.8 million incidents in 1995 to 1.3 million in the 2016 CSEW, but improved recording practices following concern over

Table 2.2 Proportions of recorded crimes solved

Year to March, per cent	2009	2011
All Crimes	28.3	27.7
Fraud and Forgery	25.5	22.0
Violent Crimes	39.7	38.7
Sexual Offences	29.8	28.7
Involving Stealing	18.3	17.4
Of which, Domestic Burglary	*16.3*	*17.0*
Criminal Damage and Arson	13.9	13.5
Public Disorder	71.4	65.9
Drug Offences	94.8	93.5

Source: Crimes solved and detection type breakdown, Her Majesty's Inspectorate of Constabulary, http://www.hmic.gov.uk/data/crime-and-policing-comparator-data/

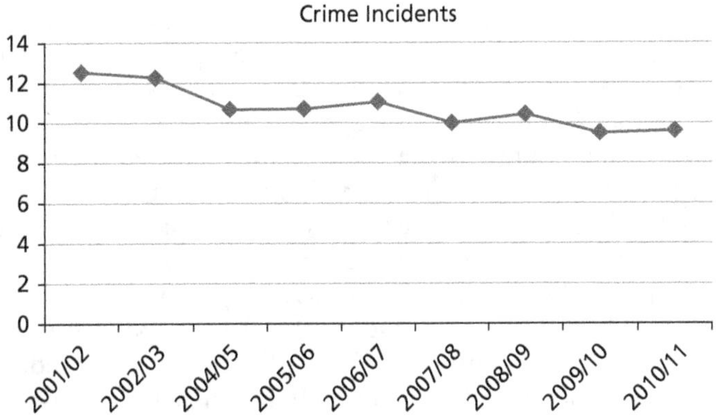

Figure 2.1 Crime incidents

Source: Crime Survey for England and Wales 2013.

gang-related violence (Home Affairs Committee 2009a) saw *police-recorded* violent crime rise 27% in 2015. In 2012/13 sharp instruments accounted for the largest share of homicides; knife and gun crime rose 14% in 2016. England and Wales have low homicide rates, in most years comparable to those of large US cities like New York. In 2010, there were 619 homicides (and 536 in New York), giving a risk of eleven offences per million but thirty-three per million for children (infants under one have highest risk). In 2013 there were 551 homicides in England and Wales—143 being domestic (ONS 2014a).

Public beliefs about crime are inaccurate. In 2011, 60% believed crime rates had risen nationally, yet declining crime rates were well-established (*Society Now*, Autumn 2011: 19). The risk of criminal victimization was 40% in 1995, 27% in 2003 and 21.5% in 2010. A possible cause of public misunderstanding is media sensationalism—42% of tabloid (populist) newspaper readers thought crime had risen, but only 26% of broadsheet ('quality') newspaper readers. Knife and gun crime show particularly large gaps between perception of national crime rates (81% thought it was up in 2010) and local (13%). Serious gun crime has actually fallen—thirty-nine died from gunshots in 2011 against ninety-six in 2001 (*The Economist* 28 July 2012: 23–4)—but overall gun crime rose 1.2% in 2015/16 due to increased non-injury gun discharges.

Both a reduction in crime and a rise in crime can prompt police self-congratulation. According to police, crime fell in London in 2014 by 6.2%, with robberies falling 24% after a force campaign (BBC News 22 April 2014). Rape and domestic violence rose (rape by 32%), but the Met claimed victims were more confident about reporting. In 2013 a whistleblower said forces routinely manipulated statistics to meet targets, and the Commissioner agreed there was 'some truth' in the claim (*Police Foundation News*, April 2014). The UK Statistics Authority withdrew the national statistics 'kitemark' (endorsement) from police-recorded crime data in 2014, citing HMIC's (2014b) concerns and parliamentary concerns (Public Administration Select Committee 2014). The Office for National Statistics (2014c) found 'gradual erosion of compliance' with the national counting rules and evidence of massaging figures to hit targets by classifying offences as 'no crime' or 'crime-related incidents', neither of which count in national figures. Targets distort policing in other ways; in 2012 five Kent officers were arrested for inducing confessions to meet detection rate targets and a 14% drop in serious sexual violence reported to the Met reflected declining victim confidence after officers faked evidence to halt a rape inquiry (Brunger 2013). Home secretaries May and then Rudd were so enraged at the Met losing a human rights case brought by two rape survivors that they repeatedly appealed, dragging the women through the courts again and again, and, as prime minister, May set out to repeal the Human Rights Act. Statistics are politics writ small.

Policing Strategies

Conventional policing strategies favour crime control by random patrol, emergency response, stop-and-search, investigation and detection, and intensive enforcement 'crackdowns' (Karn 2013). These are relatively ineffectual. Identifying and managing risk is more promising; it shifts resources towards specific individuals (e.g. prolific offenders, repeat victims) and locations (crime hotspots) and rather than relying on arrest, conviction, and punishment it deters by certainty of detection. The deterrent effect of certainty is far stronger than punishment severity (Durlauf and Nagin 2011). Officer visibility raises perceived risk of apprehension; when the Wehrmacht arrested all Danish police, crime immediately rose. Combining increased police presence and preventive strategies with measures to prevent repeat victimization and actively involve the community secures best deterrent effect (Karn 2013: 3). Tactics include *intelligence-led policing* (ILP), *problem-oriented policing* (POP), and *Neighbourhood Policing* (NP). ILP delivers responses to crime other than formal criminal justice interventions, but its effectiveness is uncertain. POP effectively reduces crime but is hard to implement. NP, like Community Policing (CP) more generally, is diffuse, and where it impacts on crime, it does so by reinforcing community resilience (Fielding 2002).

Policymakers seeking an evidence-based approach to policing would find little to recommend in traditional approaches. Yet the evidence-oriented policymaker must also negotiate public opinion, which rates these ineffective strategies highly, as do many police. The public puts first priority on responding to emergency calls, second on detecting and arresting offenders, and third on foot patrol (ONS 2013). To the public, *foot patrols* are the essence of crime prevention and community safety (Wakefield 2006); internationally, forces devote from 40% to 65% of their personnel to it (Waddington 1999). *Random patrol* is ineffective in crime control terms (Skogan and Frydl 2004), the classic calculation being that an officer could expect to be within a hundred yards of a burglary in progress once every eight years (Clarke and Hough 1984). It has long been known that neither car nor foot patrol reduce crime, only fear of crime (Kelling 1981; Pate 1986). Random patrol is for reassurance.

Where patrol is focused rather than random, the evidence is more positive. *Directed patrols* reduce the carrying of illegal weapons (Koper and Mayo-Wilson 2006) and personal robberies (Jones and Tilley 2004). They are effective in hotspots policing and problem-oriented policing (Ratcliffe et al 2011). But achieving these effects is resource-intensive, requiring extra officers to achieve higher 'dosage'. They also elevate use of stop-and-search, which, even as a disruption tactic only reduces 'disruptable' crime by 0.2% (Miller et al 2000).

Nevertheless, the evidence is that preventing crime, and disruption tactics, are more effective than pursuing formal criminal justice disposals. Intensive enforcement is then reserved for *zero tolerance policing* or *broken windows policing*. Despite tough labels, these involve responding rapidly to minor signs of deteriorating social order, such as vandalism, abandoned vehicles, public drunkenness, and street prostitution, to tip the balance toward the law-abiding, encouraging them to exert informal social control. These approaches have an indirect effect on crime but can make those subjected to them less cooperative with police (Howell 2009). Zero tolerance increases misconduct complaints and reduces public trust. Crime rate reductions touted by New York police and politicians as due to zero tolerance were seen elsewhere (including Britain) where it was not used.

Thus, evidence-based assessments commend three alternatives that concentrate efforts on specific crimes, offenders, victims, and locations: hotspots policing, targeting repeat victimization, and focused deterrence (Karn 2013). *Hotspots policing* targets micro-locations. Half of US crime occurs at 5% or fewer of all addresses (Weisburd et al 2004). Hotspots policing needs more than just patrol and arrests (Taylor et al 2011) and effects can be short-lived. Most promise is where efforts include situational crime prevention; some include community-building and employability coaching (Weisburd 2012). Offenders are alert to where residents watch out for each other and avoid such pockets in disorganized, mistrustful settings (Bottoms 2012). One worry is displacement but hotspots policing seldom causes this (Bowers et al 2011) because crime hotspots are also places where offenders live and they are reluctant to commit offences in unfamiliar areas (Weisburd et al 2006). Nor does it raise crime fear (Weisburd et al 2011). There are still blunders. It need not have taken a Random Control Trial to discover that a hotspot intervention against crime at bus stops would increase crime nearby. Officers arrived and departed by bus, standing at bus stops in-between, so offenders anticipated their movements and conducted their activities accordingly (Ariel and Partridge 2016).

Another way to concentrate resources for greater effect is to *focus on repeat victimization* (Pease 1998); internationally, 40% of crime against individuals and households is against targets already victimized that year (Farrell et al 2005). Repeat crime also raises risk for near neighbours (Burnasco 2008). Interventions like 'super-cocooning', which focuses crime prevention on repeat and 'near-repeat' victimization, are successful in large British cities (Grove et al 2012). A logical extension is *focused deterrence*. Referred to as 'pulling levers' in the US, the principle is to directly engage persistent offenders, emphasizing that punishment will be certain, immediate, and severe, balanced by incentives including priority access to social services, employment opportunities, and substance abuse programmes (Braga and Weisburd 2012).

Intelligence-led policing involves gathering information on a crime problem from case files, informants, wiretaps, phone intercepts, and social media (Maguire 2008), conducting a pattern analysis, planning targeted responses, and evaluating them (Ratcliffe et al 2011). ILP targets prolific offenders and/or hotspots, and employs disruption tactics, as in the British National Intelligence Model (NIM). However, in practice officers are reluctant to share information with civilian crime analysts, who in turn are reluctant to recommend courses of action (Innes et al 2004), and analyses can be unsophisticated (Deukmedjian and de Lint 2007).

A similar but more convincing pitch is made for problem-oriented policing, where, unlike NIM, frontline officers lead on problem diagnosis (Goldstein 1990). POP involves appraisal of a crime/disorder problem using empirical evidence, design of an intervention, monitoring of its effects, and organizational memory for future use (Tilley 2010). POP emerges positively from systematic reviews (Weisburd et al 2010) but confronts the police inclination to adopt the first available solution before fully diagnosing problem specifics (Myhill 2006). Transferability requires more than superficial similarity between problems (Tilley 2010).

Community Policing emerged as a labelled approach in the 1970s. CP has several meanings, although long-term beat assignment is longest-standing. CP seeks to engage citizens in crime control and improve police/public communication to inform POP-like local problem diagnosis. Its most sustained application was the Chicago Alternative Policing Strategy (CAPS), a coordinated initiative involving city administration, social agencies, and police. Officers were trained in problem-solving, partnership and communication skills, neighbourhood crime/disorder analysis, and community outreach involving novel IT applications. CAPS produced sustained improvements in public confidence, particularly amongst alienated minorities—blacks and Hispanics—and crime fear fell. But CAPS did not unambiguously deliver sustained crime rate reductions (Skogan and Frydl 2004). In Britain, similar principles of visibility, accessibility, and focus on locale, came to form the backbone of NP. In pilots there was a net gain in public confidence of 12% compared to non-pilot sites, and reductions in perceived, and in some cases actual, crime and anti-social behaviour (ASB) (Tuffin et al 2006). CP's *community engagement* efforts followed research demonstrating that even in harsh areas there were individuals who would work with police to improve resilience against crime, which then improved confidence in police (Lloyd and Foster 2009). Community engagement reduces calls about ASB and disorder by steering police interventions with sound information (Myhill 2006).

Distinct from crime control, innovations in *public order policing* have been ineffective and controversial. Legitimate public protest is increasingly shaped by Public Order Management Systems requiring advance disclosure of protestor identities and incorporating organizers into planning 'secure' protests. 'Protest permits' shrink availability of public spaces (Atak 2014; McPhail et al 1998; Mitchell and Staeheli 2005). Force-based strategies of the 1960s/70s gave way to 'Negotiated Management' in the 1980s/90s involving communication with protestors and minimum force, then to 'Strategic Incapacitation' from 2000 onwards, with its array of containment ('kettling'), electronic surveillance, pre-emptive arrests, and selective intervention (observing/seizing 'troublemakers'). There were major demonstrations in London protesting the 2009 G20 summit, the first, outside the Royal Exchange, being seriously violent, while the second, the Climate Camp, was not. Police contained the Royal Exchange demonstration by 'kettling' but then imposed the tactic on the Climate Camp, where people including mothers with babies were corralled in small spaces and denied exit for long periods, eliciting widespread public condemnation. Also controversial are 'distraction tactics', applying force against those who appear hostile, using footage from Forward Intelligence Teams. Parliament was 'deeply disturbed' that untrained officers were deployed using the new tactics (HAC 2009c).

HMIC (2009a) said police should improve dialogue with protest groups, moderate kettling, wear clear identification, and improve training. The Met upgraded public order training, reinforced officers' duties towards journalists, made officers' name badges clearer, submitted safety tactics to independent medical assessors before demonstrations, and tightened control over Forward Intelligence Teams. National 'mutual aid' arrangements were revised with refresher courses for commanders and a new public order training curriculum. The Court of Appeal ruled that 'kettling' was acceptable only in exceptional circumstances (Burns 2012) where there was a 'reasonable apprehension of an imminent breach of the peace' (Khan 2012; Scorer 2012). However, practice and training still divided on key tactics like shield formations ('running lines', which involve intermediate shields versus 'section file', combining long and round shields, with two rows). With three shield sizes, some one-handled and others two-handled, twelve variations occur across forces. Shield training proved insufficient to enable officers to use shields proportionately. At judicial review, the court heard that some officers 'appear not to have been trained for crowd control operations of this kind' (*R. v Commissioner of Police of the Metropolis [2011] EWHC 957*), declaring that both training and on-the-spot instruction were needed.

PACE and Suspect Populations

The main contemporary regulator of police powers is the Police and Criminal Evidence Act (PACE) 1984, which replaced the non-statutory 'Judges Rules'. PACE was a landmark in progress towards professional policing. Its Code of Practice governs police action prior to and during arrest, and at the station up to the point of charge. The Code goes through regular modifications but few doubt that it is an advance on what went before. To grasp why, we might cite the notorious case that followed a 1972 Fire Brigade call to the London home of Maxwell Confait. Confait, a homosexual prostitute, was found strangled in a locked bedroom. Investigators stopped the police surgeon taking Confait's rectal temperature (to establish time of death) because they thought that, as a homosexual, this part of the body might render evidence of recent sexual activity. Police initially suspected Confait's landlord, Mr Goode, who shared Confait's liking for wearing female clothing. Under interrogation, Goode mentioned that Confait wanted to move out, and admitted to being jealous (but not to a homosexual relationship). Shortly afterwards Goode was admitted to psychiatric hospital and committed suicide.

An 18-year-old, Colin Lattimore, whose mental age was eight, was taken into custody, along with Ronnie Leighton, 15, and Ahmet Salih, 14. The Judges Rules said that as far as practicable, children should only be interviewed in the presence of a parent, guardian, or someone other than a police officer and of the same sex. However, police questioned all three without any other adult present. The boys later testified that police hit them. Lattimore and Salih admitted starting the fire, with Lattimore admitting to Confait's murder and Salih to having watched.

At trial all three had alibis for the time of death estimated by the surgeon and a pathologist. Nevertheless, Lattimore was convicted of manslaughter and arson and sent indefinitely to mental hospital. Leighton received life for arson and an unrelated burglary. Salih was sentenced to four years at Approved School. An appeal failed. Lattimore's father lobbied government tirelessly. In a television documentary two pathologists insisted the time of death coincided with the boys' alibis. The case was referred back to the Court of Appeal. All three convictions were quashed and the boys immediately freed. The judge, Lord Scarman, lambasted police, saying the lack of a struggle showed Confait knew his assailant. An inquiry led by Sir Henry Fisher found blatant disregard by police for the Judge's Rules, leading directly to the Philipps Commission from which emerged the Police and Criminal Evidence Act 1984. Two prisoners sentenced for other crimes subsequently confessed to Confait's murder.

PACE regulates high volume activities—for instance, police stopped-and-searched one million people in 2012/13 (ONS 2014c). Stop-and-search is one of the most controversial police activities (27% being unlawfully conducted even made news in Turkish North Cyprus; *Cyprus Star*, 12 July 2013). Police strongly defend stop-and-search, and resent increasingly stringent recording requirements (Shiner 2010), yet only 10% result in arrest (Home Office 2014a). With 15.1% of those stopped-and-searched in 2013 being black, and 10.5% Asian, ethnic minority stops are disproportionate to population share. Minority males aged 16–29 are particularly likely to be stopped. Afro-Caribbeans are six times more likely to be stopped on suspicion of drug possession but statistically less likely to use drugs (Pears 2013). In 2014, 49% of stop/searches in London were of ethnic minorities (Home Office 2014b); across forces 13%–28% were of children (*Police Foundation Newsletter* July/August 2014). While forces must now publish outcomes after each stop-and-search and explain their use of the power (Home Office 2014a), stop/search practices continue to produce repeat encounters with 'the usual suspects'.

The prime 'stop' criterion of 'reasonable grounds for suspicion' derived from common law inherits a legacy of poor definition and loose interpretation dominated by what is *not* 'reasonable'

(Lustgarten 2002). In practice, reasonableness is contingent on exact situation and context. Some editions of PACE codes of practice intricately specify things like defining a private dwelling but offer only abbreviated guidance on reasonable suspicion (Quinton 2011). 'Tough minded suspicion' has long been treated as a defining characteristic of police officers (Skolnick 1966), and *habitus* of police work (Bourdieu 1992). Generalizations about population sub-groups are not grounds for search, but valid when stemming from suspect behaviour. Officer presumptions remain in tension with information and/or intelligence as locus of suspicion.

Despite the theoretical possibility of a 'democratic suspicion' (Young 1994) where everybody is equally suspect, police unavoidably discriminate. There is plausibility in supposing that youths nervously carrying a large bag at night are more likely miscreants than elderly women doing the same, but the basis of such generalizations lies exactly in practices that PACE seeks to control. Logically, numerous old ladies may be carrying stolen goods but remain undiscovered because police do not suspect them. Classic ethnographies document the importance of incongruity in judgements of who merits stopping (Rubinstein 1971). Incongruity relies on generalization about the typical acts, actors, and motivations for doing X in place Y. Thus, suspicion is fundamentally differentiated, and no amount of regulation can dilute its logic (Hawkins 2003). However, police also learn that behaviour meriting intervention can be excused if plausible reasons are given, as in the classic scenario of traffic police pursuing a speeding driver who, on being stopped, displays her doctor ID. Immediately switching to escorting her, they remain alert to the possibility that the emergency address is that of her beau.

Repeated stops of the same person cannot all be explained by prejudice. A meticulous longitudinal study (Farrington et al 2007) found that just 7% of 'chronic offenders' accounted for half of all officially recorded offences by the sample (similarly, Hales et al 2010). Crime runs across generations; the number of parental convictions relates positively to their children's (Besemer 2014). Police need skills to break the link when dealing with families and communities where offending is trans-generational. Currently, police contact increases the likelihood of future violent offending, with the sharpest effects on low violence offenders (Ward et al 2014). Youths subsequently stopped or arrested display higher levels of delinquency. This is aggravated by delinquent peers, deviant identity formation and decreasing bonds to non-offenders; absent these conditions, the relationship between police contact and offending weakens (Wiley et al 2013). Delinquent peers and identity-formation effects are conditions officers can influence.

The volume of young people passing through the CJS is falling. Between 2008 and 2014, 54% fewer people came into the youth justice system, with 14% fewer re-offences (Ministry of Justice 2014). Hence the concentration of offences in a sub-group of persistent offenders with whom police are repeatedly in contact. Young people do not all reach psychosocial maturity by age 25. Transition to adulthood has become more tortuous. Austerity, and housing policies, hit the young hard. They take longer to find work, are obliged to remain longer in the family, and delay child-rearing. These being major 'taking-responsibility' factors, periods of rebelliousness and boundary-testing have lengthened, such that offences committed by young adults aged 18–24 increasingly resemble those committed by under-18s (Home Office 2013c). Alcohol is a direct or contributory factor in a third of arrests (Man et al 2003). A quarter of officers feel inadequately trained to handle drunken youths. Longer periods of adolescent experimentation extend the time when youths and police regard each other through mutual stereotypes, particularly where there is experience of stop-and-search (Graham with Karn 2013). The social competence of those most often in contact with police is low; 48% of prisoners have trouble reading and 65% lack basic numeracy (Basic Skills Agency 2002). Literacy and numeracy have a statistically significant relationship to how often young adults are stopped, and arrested, even controlling for poverty, disruptive family environment, poor education, and emotional/behavioural problems.

Racism, Hate Crime, and Terrorism

A 'racist incident' is any incident, including any crime, perceived as racist by the victim or others. The law applicable to assaults, public order offences, criminal damage, and harassment requires courts to treat more seriously offences aggravated by racial or religious factors. In 2011/12 there were 47,678 racist incidents in England and Wales, the largest number (9,464) being in London, with Greater Manchester having 3,288 and West Yorkshire 2,803. While most plead guilty, conviction rates are high even in contested cases. Convictions nearly tripled between 2002 (2,300) and 2012 (6,500), and custodial sentences increased almost 80% (to 810). Police have steadily attuned to evidential standards, with prosecutors' acceptance of police assessments rising to well over 80%. Year-on-year increases in defendant numbers, high conviction rates, and increasingly close fit between police and Crown Prosecution Service (CPS) assessments all suggest that prosecutions are a small share of a widespread phenomenon. The CSEW 2011–2013 annual average was 278,000 hate crimes, the most common being race hate, at 154,000/year, followed by religion, at 70,000/year (ONS 2014b). Two-thirds were assault or vandalism.

Since 2008 police have recorded five strands of hate crime: race, faith, sexual orientation, trans-sexual (gender identity), and disability. Across England, Wales and Northern Ireland the 2010 figures were 39,311 race hate; 2,007 faith hate; 4,883 sexual orientation hate; 357 trans-sexual hate; 1,569 disability hate; and 488 anti-semitic. Of these totals, the Met accounted for a fifth. In 2012, 73.9% of defendants were White British, and 28.9% were aged 18–24 (Crown Prosecution Service 2012). Police detect 46% of racially or religiously motivated offenders. Use of the word 'hate' has been questioned, including by judges. Many incidents solely involve verbal insults. Australian law has substituted 'prejudice-motivated crime' (Wickes et al 2016). Assuming targets are 'vulnerable' also troubles victims but government rejected EHRC's (2012a) call to modify terminology to encourage reporting.

Hate crime is not simply perpetrated between the mainstream ethnicity or religion and minority individuals. In 2004 a 12-year-old Sikh boy was attacked by a 14-year-old Muslim boy who set fire to his hair and turban, and two Satanists spent three months harassing a Christian minister (CPS 2005). The charity Community Security Trust (2014) recorded 302 anti-semitic incidents in July 2014, the-then highest ever monthly total. Offenders were described in 107 incidents: 55 were of South Asian appearance, 32 white, 15 Arab or North African, and 5 black. That month Israel conducted a campaign against Hamas in which thousands of Gazan civilians were killed; previous and subsequent high tallies also coincided with such conflict. Of the July

2014 incidents, 155 directly cited Israel's action in Gaza. Hate crimes rose 40% following the EU referendum. Between 16 and 30 June 2016 there were 3,076 cases, 915 up on the same period in 2015. Unusually, most involved violence, not verbal abuse, spitting, or criminal damage. Ethnic minorities and non-British nationals were targeted, particularly Poles and takeaway staff, with 'Rights for Whites' incidents on campuses.

In 2010 the Minister for Diversity freed forces to add to the five strands. In 2013 Greater Manchester Police became the first force to separately record as hate crime any offences incurred by appearance, specifically subcultures like Goths. This followed the 2007 murder of Sophie Lancaster, beaten into a coma by her attackers while cradling her severely beaten boyfriend, who survived with life-changing injuries in an attack triggered by their Goth attire. Forces can legally do little more than record subculture hate as an element in an offence, despite widespread harassment (Leblanc 2013). All of a sample of twenty-one UK goths had experienced verbal abuse, sometimes with physical abuse like pushing or spitting (Garland and Hodkinson 2014). In 2014 the College of Policing encouraged forces to consider within a hate crime framework 'other forms of targeted hostility' like harassing prostitutes. In 2016 Nottinghamshire Police announced they would categorize misogyny as a hate crime. Only a quarter of hate crime victims report it to police, and over half tell no one, 30% thinking police would not take it seriously (Garland et al 2014).

In 2007, the remains of Fiona Pilkington and her daughter Francecca were found in a burnt-out car near their home. Francecca had a learning disability, and Fiona's son Anthony had severe dyslexia. In seven years of harassment by neighbours and local children the windows of the family's home were regularly broken, gates and fences were torched and there were taunts, insults, and verbal abuse. Children threw stones at Francecca's bedroom window and goaded her to pull up her nightie. Her gait was mocked. Anthony was beaten up, locked in a shed at knifepoint and battered with an iron bar. Fiona and concerned neighbours had contacted Leicestershire Constabulary on thirty-three separate occasions. Calls were ignored or response was delayed by days. Fiona's suicide note expressed despair at police inaction.

Hostility and violence against disabled people—who number 10.1 million adults, 21% of the population over 16—is widespread in Britain (Equality and Human Rights Commission

2009). There are no specific aggravated offences related to disability and no offence of incitement to hatred on the basis of disability (EHRC 2014). Police seldom consider disability as a factor motivating crime, consequently incidents receive low priority. Harassment of the disabled is often dealt with as anti-social behaviour but over half of force call centres cannot automatically identify repeat victims of ASB, and 23% of calls reporting ASB elicit no response. Serious attacks and murders of disabled people frequently originate in petty ASB, which, left unmanaged, worsens (EHRC 2014).

Murders of disabled people are, far more than other murders, marked by degrading treatment, torture, and extreme, sustained violence. Steven Hoskins, a 38-year-old with learning difficulties, was tortured for hours. He was tied up, dragged round on a lead, imprisoned, burnt with cigarettes, and repeatedly violently abused in his own home. He was forced to confess (falsely) to being a paedophile, coerced into swallowing a lethal dose of paracetamol, taken to a 40-metre railway viaduct, and forced over the railings where one of his five attackers jumped up and down on his fingers until he let go. This horror followed months of alerts to police as incidents became more frequent and serious. Steven contacted police on numerous occasions without any follow-up. Calls that did elicit response were treated separately and not linked. In 2010, 19% of disabled adults were victims of crime in England and Wales, and 17% in Scotland (EHRC 2014). That is 1.9 million people.

Training does not specifically encourage officers to invite people to declare disabled status. Frontline officers express nervousness about asking people if they are disabled yet readily ask people their self-identified ethnicity. Large reporting variations in disability hate crime across forces reflect the training and awareness deficit (Sin et al 2012).

Over 80% of LGBT people have suffered harassment, insults, and intimidation. Some 10% of homophobic hate crime victims have been physically assaulted, 20% threatened with violence, and 12.5% have had vehicles or property vandalized (Stonewall 2013). Some 75% do not report it to the police. Of those who do, half said it was recorded as 'no further action', and 40% said police did not record it as homophobic. Stonewall recommended training for police and call handlers in identifying such crimes, better crime pattern analysis, and for forces to be gay-friendly employers. In 2014 the Equality and Human Rights Commission (2014a) prioritized action on under-reporting of LGBT hate crime. They might start with parliamentarians. MPs who opposed extending hate speech legislation to homophobia depicted police as 'intent on suppressing the rights of people of faith' (Johnson and Vanderbeck 2011: 65). Their evidence featured fanciful anecdotes about body-armoured officers intimidating Christian pensioners circulating leaflets excoriating homosexuality.

Granting rights to same sex partners is not associated with more anti-gay hate crime but spikes in racially or religiously motivated hate crime are associated with terrorist attacks (King and Sutton 2013). Islamophobic hate crimes have risen sharply. In 2013 the Met recorded 500, against 336 the previous year, with similar surges elsewhere after Lee Rigby's murder (Corcoran and Smith 2016). Greater Manchester recorded 130, against seventy-five in 2012, Kent's figure rose from fifteen to fifty-four, and Humberside's from four to fifteen. The organization monitoring Islamophobic incidents, Tell Mama, dealt with 840 cases between April and December 2013, compared to 582 in the year to March 2013. Sixty English Defence League protests took place, the largest far-right activity in thirty years.

British forces' Muslim Contact Units rely heavily on community partnerships. In New York there are no partnerships with Muslims but instead surveillance, infiltration, and other 'hard' policing measures. Each strategy has drawbacks. In New York local police and 'high' policing agencies trip over each other while in London officers resist partnership strategies (Quinlan 2015). Despite officer scepticism, forces with well-developed relationships into potential terrorist communities are more effective against 'radicalizers' (HMIC 2009b). In UK, counter-terrorism specialists feed threat assessments to frontline officers. Depth investigation has been overtaken by breadth, extending the regular police role.

Community Policing can yield early warnings about terrorist attacks (Murray 2005: 359), but officers face a tension between acting as community stalwarts who build dialogue with local communities versus acting as field intelligence officers, discreetly gathering intelligence and developing sources (Harfield and Harfield 2005). There is evidence that all ethnic minority groups, not only Muslims, feel disproportionately targeted (Lister 2011). Communities accept intelligence-gathering but do not suspend expectations of fairness. Populations under extreme threat, as in Israel, assign understandably high importance to police effectiveness but equally to procedural justice (Tal and Weisburd 2013).

While the contemporary police mission can be characterized as the continuance of long-established practices in a new context, modern terrorism brings a pervasive sense of unease and amorphous threat. Techniques previously the preserve of armed insurgents are freely available online and we are reminded of our insecurity over the public address system every time we travel. The relevance to police training of the changes in legal powers and operational capacity that have followed terrorist outrages may seem obscure. Things like extending detention without charge may seem remote from regular policing, although others like arrest without warrant and stop/search powers not requiring suspicion in designated areas may not. Patrol constables during the Second World War had a community intelligence role. They more often detected people having affairs or selling contraband than deserters or spies, but nevertheless provided granular information to military intelligence. Such roles connect headlines about terrorism with police training and recruitment.

After the 1985 bombing of an Air India flight over Canada it emerged that the Royal Canadian Mounted Police's (RCMP) 17,000 officers included just one Punjabi speaker. Diversity was suddenly integral to crisis response. Community Policing was rediscovered as a corrective to information shortfall (Deukmedjian and de Lint 2007: 242). A typical English force invests 230 posts directly in intelligence activities. While officers receive considerable information from the public, that submitted for formal processing replicates traditional law enforcement concerns. Immediacy scores over deep background, and officers' direct observation over public engagement. Originally conceived as an alternative to rapid response policing, CP has reverted to such emphases under the intelligence agenda (Bullock 2013). Integrating CP with Intelligence-Led-Policing directs policing backwards.

ILP makes similar demands to CP: defining the community, eliciting information from it, and assessing information quality. However, CP information-gathering is more continuous, less oriented to single cases, and more readily validated than information covertly provided (Fielding 1995). ILP invites divisive suspicion and distrust, and can undermine legitimacy, a legitimacy deficit being what prompted the drive for CP in the first place.

Ruptured Communities, Polarization, and Disaffiliation

Cities like London are becoming more ethnically diverse. The minority share of London's population was larger in the 2011 than the 2001 Census for Caribbean, Chinese, Bangladeshi, Pakistani, Indian, and 'other black' ethnicities, but lower for 'other Asians' and Africans (MOPAC 2014). The white share of London's population fell from 59% to 44%. Other British cities are more diverse too, with Leicester, Luton, and Slough having no ethnic group in the majority (Simpson 2013). High diversity suppresses locally-generated hate crime because no group predominates, but can bring tensions with the wider community; hostility towards immigration drove the 2016 vote to leave the EU. Yet prejudice masks the anxieties that feed it. For instance, beyond hostility to immigrants, English Defence League supporters display anxieties about vulnerability and high fear of crime (Garland and Treadwell 2012).

Like the flow of problematic stop-and-searches that culminates in high profile disorder, low-level expressions of community divisions steadily aggravate tensions. Racist graffiti, especially near schools, exacerbate social tensions but are ignored because police see them as unremarkable in disadvantaged communities (Wilson 2014). A professional practice of policing would notify municipal services of such signs of ambient hate, but confronted by obscene drawings at a nursery school entrance, police said it was not a crime because they could be scrubbed off (*Daily Telegraph* 2 August 2014).

As Britain becomes more sharply divided, the prosperous inhabit communities of choice while the poor are trapped in communities of fate (Hirst 1994). Yet even the worst estates include individuals inclined to support police efforts (Foster 2002: 172). 'Neighbourhood sentinels' are sensitive to disturbances of local social order, maintain broad, dense social networks and spend much time in public (Innes 2014b). Volunteers, mothers with young children, cab drivers, and hairdressers are communication vectors. Their accounts of local crime/disorder often intertwine information about an incident with themes about locations and types of people to avoid (Harcourt 2005). Building an actionable picture requires patience and discrimination (Hamilton-Smith et al 2014).

Police accessibility raises minority satisfaction with police problem-solving provided officers do not simply take reports of problems but inquire how frequently they happen, encourage complainants to note details or intervene, and keep complainants informed. Only 21% of respondents in a county force's worst area said their Safer Neighbourhood Team kept them informed of action on local problems (Foster and Jones 2009). Yet more saw them as effective against crime than did not—39% against 27%. Ratings of police efforts rose strongly while the teams were operating, with 'excellent' ratings rising from 16% to 44% and 'poor' down from 27% to 12%. Harsh settings display both apathy and appreciation of NP, confidence in police but desire for more action. The austerity-driven disappearance of park keepers, concierges, train guards, bus conductors, and 'roundsmen' (Satnav-guided delivery is not the same as services visiting the same addresses daily), all of whom were 'capable guardians' in crime prevention terms, amplifies reliance on police (Crawford and Lister 2004). As society moves from relatively static, geo-local relations to more ephemeral, interest-driven relations, police have an increasingly pivotal role in sociality.

We associate social division with cities, and read the rural through pastoral lenses. However, increasing diversity of rural populations can provoke dangerous insecurities in white rural populations. Rural minority victims believe police do not take their cases seriously (Garland and Chakraborti 2007) and worry that reporting harassment could cause backlash. Stereotyped views are particularly found amongst rural officers (Cloke 2004). Reports of racist incidents are received sceptically, with officers probing whether complainants have themselves committed offences. There is more engagement with East European and Roma migrants, but as offenders, with officers warning other community members about their presence (James 2007).

Police can moderate policies that aggravate community divisions. In 2013 ultra-orthodox Haredi Jews exploited devolution of planning laws. 'Direct democracy and less bureaucracy' policies empowered a non-statutory Haredim-dominated Neighbourhood Forum that accused other Stamford residents, who objected to their plans for large house extensions to accommodate big family sizes, of anti-semitism (*The Guardian* 9 March 2013).

However, in Northampton, preparing a neighbourhood plan brought the main immigrant community, Somalis, together with local whites for the first time, with police encouraging participation. In 2014 Hull police commissioned a five-week training programme to raise understanding of East European immigrants. Across Europe, young minority men are most likely to have tense relations with police (Roux et al 2011). Yet in Germany, Turkish-origin youths trust police more than do whites, reflecting the restraint exercised by police in encounters with them. Police stops of African-origin youths in France are three times the white rate, while in Germany Turkish youths are stopped less frequently than whites (Oberwittler and Roche 2013). Minority French youths shun police, while in Germany even Turkish youths most strongly identifying with Turkey regard police positively.

Riots

Public order training is challenged by spontaneous disorder. In 2014, police in Ferguson, St Louis shot dead an unarmed black teenager suspected of stealing cigars. His 'assassination'—the term the community used—sparked days of rioting, during which police shot dead another young black man. Ferguson is largely African-American (67%), but 94% of its police are white. Rioting recurred when no officer was found responsible for Michael Brown's death, as it did a week later following the death of another black man, Eric Garner, held on the ground in a headlock by a white NYPD officer. Killing citizens is an abject failure of professionalism symbolized by the New York mayor's declaration that the whole force must be re-trained to better communicate and keep calm when making arrests.

Spontaneous unrest has a structural dimension involving perceived disadvantage, a political dimension of alienation from institutions, a cultural dimension for behaviour police regard as disorderly, a contextual dimension of poor police/public relations, a situational dimension involving struggle over contested space, and an interactional dimension—the flashpoint—where a trigger incident expresses the conflictual relationship as serious, violent disorder (D. Waddington 2007, 2013). Whatever the deeper causes, the trigger for serious disorder involving minority communities repeatedly involves two factors—frustration over iniquitous stops, and heavy-handed police conduct in performing them, both being matters for frontline officers.

When the 1981 Brixton riots were followed by further rioting in 1985 the trigger was an aggressive search for a black Briton, during which armed officers burst into his mother's home and shot her at point blank range, permanently paralysing her. Only after Mrs Groce's death did the Met apologize. It emerged that Mrs Groce, and Stephen Lawrence's family, were amongst those on whom undercover police were gathering intelligence. Those monitored included the relatives of Jean Charles de Menezes, a Brazilian shot dead by police in the aftermath of the 2005 '7/7' bombings because he stepped off one Underground carriage and into another, interpreted by officers as meaning he was 'surveillance aware' and therefore a terrorist (Waddington 2011a: 101); the wife of Harry Stanley, shot dead when police mistook a table leg he was carrying for a gun; and the family of Ricky Reel, a student whose body was found after he was attacked by whites shouting 'Pakis go home', a racial dimension police ignored. The Met's Special Demonstration Squad (SDS)—set up to infiltrate political groups in 1968—conducted covert operations on seventeen justice campaigns for murder victims or people who died following police contact. A report by Derbyshire's chief constable said Scotland Yard had disregarded 'rules and legislation that clearly set out what they should, and should not have, collected and retained' (Creedon 2014), and the SDS was 'out of control'. Evidence was collected 'just in case' and 'because we can'. Ignoring clear regulations, and covertly recording participation in legitimate exercises of freedom of expression is profoundly unprofessional, raising issues of accountability and police legitimacy (Punch 2010).

Like London 2011, the 2013 riots in Stockholm's Husby suburb were triggered by a fatal police shooting in circumstances that were immediately (and accurately) challenged by community members. The Swedish riots involved neither looting nor diffuse protest but torching cars and baiting and stoning police. Residents cited political disenchantment (Body-Gendrot 2013); structural police harassment, particularly stop/searches; neo-liberal restructuring of welfare; and a sense of entitlement betrayed, including disrespect by police (Hornqvist 2014). Response to riot police amongst the disadvantaged can function independently of positive relations with local officers. Communication between police and protestors can exert leverage over both sides and help police understand where protestors are coming from.

Well-informed policing interventions can head off riots, facilitated by technology. Since there were no organizers to engage with prior to the Million Mask March 2016, police accurately predicted protestor numbers from Facebook posts. Rioting in Lozells, Birmingham in 2005 followed tense relations between minority youths and police. Police instituted daily meetings with community representatives concerning action on grievances and employed a mediation service to improve police/gang relations. When the 2011 rioting reached Birmingham police used Twitter to disseminate information to Lozells that prevented rioting (King 2013). Similarly, before the 2011 Liberal Democrat conference, police deployed liaison and social media specialists. Two days of protest involving 5,000 protestors saw only one arrest. Based on Sweden's 'Dialogue Policing' (Holgersson and Knutsson 2011), the liaison team's pre-event interaction with organizers explained restrictions but also facilitated some protest objectives. Protestors were barred from a protest route that crossed delegates' paths but were sold on another route by officers mentioning it gave media cameras an angle maximizing protestors' apparent numbers (D. Waddington 2013: 56). During the protest liaison officers moved amongst the crowd explaining police actions (e.g. arrival of new officers being to allow others a meal break). Unexpectedly, a delegate appeared in the crowd, defending the party flouting its election pledge not to raise university tuition fees. A commander began deploying riot officers but liaison officers saw that protestors were willing to hear the delegate out and successfully urged the commander not to intervene.

Heavy-handed policing spreads disenchantment beyond those with grievances against police. In 2010 university tuition fees protestor Alfie Meadows sustained life-threatening injuries from being beaten about the head with a police truncheon. Photographs of his surgical scar elicited considerable public criticism of police. A first trial saw jurors unable to agree. A second trial collapsed. At the third the jury returned unanimous not guilty verdicts, on the basis that Meadows and a colleague were defending themselves and others from police assault. Other fee demo cases—including one where officers inadvertently recorded themselves plotting to pin charges on particular protestors (*Daily Telegraph* 14 March 2011)—indicate increasing use of section 2 of the Public Order

Act, carrying up to five years' imprisonment. It makes little distinction between the actions of a crowd and individuals within it. For example, violent disorder charges were brought against a woman who dislodged broken glass to prevent injury to protestors entering and leaving Millbank. Her employer responded exquisitely to the prosecution's question whether he was surprised at her action: 'What? This is why I am here? Because Sara kicked an already broken window! Yes, I am surprised that this is why I am here' (*Times Higher Education*, 21 March 2013). The jury took just fifteen minutes to unanimously throw out the case. Eighteen of nineteen protestors charged after the Meadows fees protests were acquitted, suggesting public antipathy to draconian public order powers. Each trial cost taxpayers £14,000 a day (*New Statesman*, 9 March 2013). With fifty-eight protestors tried over fees demonstrations, most trials lasting several days (Meadows' third lasted four weeks), and only a 48% conviction rate, enthusiasm for section 2 represents poor value for money.

Prime Minister Cameron endangered one violent disorder trial's integrity by denouncing Christopher Hilliard for supposedly dragging a constable from his horse and beating him. Video footage revealed the mounted officer pulling Hilliard by the hair so hard that Hilliard had to stand on tiptoes. The officer fell because he had forgotten to tighten the saddle girth on his horse. A protestor was charged with violent disorder for shouting at police and waving a stick, receiving ten months' imprisonment. Prior to the uptake of section 2, protestors in equivalent circumstances were cautioned or received fixed penalty notices.

Nor are harsh legal powers effective when police must respond reactively to spontaneous disorder. In the 2011 riots, London police were out-manoeuvred for the first four nights, standing in riot gear while being mocked by looters. Police stations were firebombed and shops looted. Rain calmed the rioting, not police. Participants seldom claimed structural grievances (Treadwell et al 2013). Shame was widely expressed. Sentences on rioters increased the prison population by over a thousand. The Peasants' Revolt in 1381, the eighteenth century grain riots, and the 1980s race riots in London and northern England all had an express grievance. In 2011, that was elusive.

The trigger event was plain enough: the fatal police shooting of black suspect Mark Duggan. When 300 supporters marched from the Broadwater Farm estate, a confrontation in which twenty-six officers were injured was followed by looting and torching shops, with ever-fewer references to Duggan. Media coverage helped spread rioting to backwaters like Croydon, which provided an enduring image of the riots when a furniture shop that survived Second World War bombing was razed to the ground. Three Asian men guarding a Birmingham shop were fatally rammed by a car driven by rioters. Another enduring image was the dignified appeal for calm and forgiveness by the father of one of them.

There was widespread criticism of police; 90% of YouGov poll respondents said water cannons should have been deployed, 78% endorsed tear gas, 72% Tasers, 65% plastic bullets, and fully a third wanted police to use live ammunition (*The Economist* 13 August 2011). However, water cannon were not then available and are clumsy, tear gas affects bystanders as well as rioters, and Tasers cannot be discharged into groups. Plastic bullets are much slower than regular bullets and can be dodged, striking bystanders. Public order training assumes participants want to confront police, whereas the looters sought to avoid them. Training also assumes officers should control 'the ground', but that kept shifting as rioters dispersed and re-assembled.

Mutual Aid officers were obstructed by poor communication channels to central command. This despite HMIC's 'new national formula for the provision of public order support between forces' (HMIC 2011c). Forces lacked capacity to exploit social media. Control rooms swamped with information from Twitter and Facebook were unable to distinguish fact from rumour, causing wasted deployments. Twitter was not used to convey information about targets or police movements despite Cameron's and the Met's dark claims (Procter et al 2013). Its heaviest use was to coordinate clean-up efforts.

Politicians did not seek far for explanations. Prime Minister Cameron said riots were not about race, cuts or poverty but 'criminality, pure and simple' and 'a twisted moral code', although he then managed the staccato blurt 'Children without fathers. Schools without discipline. Reward without effort' (Cameron 2011). Justice secretary Clarke snorted that rioters were from 'a feral underclass' (Clarke 2011), adding bestial overtones to Victorian 'dangerous classes' rhetoric. Statistically, 35% were on unemployment benefits (against one in eight of the working-age population), 42% were receiving free school meals (against

16% of state secondary school pupils), and two-thirds lived in the bottom quintile of deprived areas (Newburn 2012: 332).

Rioters testified to bewilderment at why they had participated, but 27% of females and 37% of males said they would riot again (Lewis et al 2011). Opportunism and being caught up in the moment featured in female rioters' accounts. Two 20-year-olds helped torch an abandoned police car because everyone was masked and there were no witnesses, describing it as 'quite satisfying'. Rioters included girls of 11. Women stole lower value items or items others dropped, including lip gloss, nappies, baby food, and rice. Asked why she was stealing, one struggling with a large box of soap power said 'because I need it'. Another felt guilty when her mother unknowingly denounced looters but remained pleased at her 'free stuff', £300 of clothes. Rioters sought a wider significance. The women who torched a police car said 'it felt like all us youths were pulling together, like just trying to make a point. There were other ways we could've gone about it, it did get a bit out of hand at the end, but still, I think we were heard'.

Poor educational attainment is a strong risk factor for crime. Two-thirds of juvenile rioters had 'special educational need' (against a fifth of all secondary schoolchildren), half had not reached the normative English and Maths Key Stage 2 level (against a quarter nationally), and at Key Stage 4 only 11% held five GCSEs, against half the general population (Newburn 2012: 332–3). Relative to others sharing disadvantage who did not riot, conflictual relations with police, especially experience of stop/search, featured in rioters' accounts (Lewis et al 2011). Some 43% of female rioters, and 78% of men, had been stopped and searched in the last year. Killing suspects, and excessive stops, are factors police can directly influence (Cabinet Office 2011).

In 1967 Detroit saw five days of riots that left forty-three dead. Three theories emerged (Meyer 1973). The 'riff-raff theory' held that rioting was a desperate act by people so deprived there was no other way to improve their lot. The 'assimilation theory' implicated problems Detroit's black population had adjusting to the industrial North, having originated in the rural South. These theories were disproved. There was no difference in education and income of rioters and non-rioters, and Northern-origin people were three times more likely to riot than Southerners. The third theory was relative deprivation. Awareness of others getting ahead made more acute the frustration of being left behind. The riff-raff theory cannot be applied to the 2011 English riots; welfare cuts had not begun. The second theory would have to be re-cast in terms of immigration rather than internal migration, and even so, rioters' families were well-established in the community or indigenous whites, not recent immigrants. There may, though, be mileage in relative deprivation given the Newburn data above.

However, public debate was framed in more elemental terms, of 'greed' or 'evil'. Lewis et al (2011) saw evidence of protest in resentment about unemployment and impending cuts, but their data conveys rioters' sense of bewilderment and chagrin mixed with lingering euphoria. Political declarations, or references to poverty, were few. Looking for these may be to go too deep. One thread is prominent throughout the testimony—profound, if nuanced, resentment of police. That is consistent with procedural justice analysis, if rendered as fairness of a kind related more to home, school, and playground than criminal justice. Home Secretary May weighed in with that rarity, a comment about methodology by a minister—the Lewis et al research lacked a control group of non-rioters. But she spoiled the point by declaring, on the basis of no evidence, that the riots were 'about instant gratification'. In the search for causes it is sensible to work from empirical evidence, and there is an abundance over a forty-year period that ethnic minorities in English cities have troublesome relationships with police, and that bad policing is often at its root. If we must involve elemental qualities of the human psyche, it is more useful to work from our fundamental sense of fairness than from the assumption that we are depraved monsters waiting for controls to be suspended so we can riot. We must also acknowledge that rioting is exciting (Katz 1990), making participants imagine that burning a cop car is an important statement, especially if everyone is masked and there are no witnesses. The police/public relationship gives us something to work on, while the 'greed' vision gives us nowhere to hide once the prisons are full. Disorder represents an acid test for police professionalism.

Police and gangs

Glasgow's Violence Reduction Unit was credited with halving youth violence and its methods were much-studied following the 2011 riots. It was modelled on the Boston Ceasefire project, which significantly reduced violent youth crime (Braga et al 2001). Glasgow's initiative involved 'call-ins' that gang members were cajoled, or obliged by probation orders, to attend. Once there, victims' families, community members, former gang members, and youth workers berated them against violence. The unresponsive were subject to harassment tactics, including daily police visits and arrests for minor offences. Manchester, Liverpool, and London emulated Glasgow.

Effective measures against gang and group violence require multi-agency coordination and engagement with gang members to elicit information and threaten crackdowns while pushing diversionary services (Bullock and Tilley 2003). But coordination is lacking between the Youth Justice Board, police and probation (HMIC 2010b). Police have a well-developed understanding of gang activity but focus on 'catch and convict'. The danger lies in labelling what may actually be loosely-affiliated individuals as gang members, elevating the perceived risk they pose (Smithson et al 2013).

Force 'Youth Intervention Teams' partner other social agencies, notably the Youth Support Service. Techniques include family group conferencing, community reparation boards and Youth Restorative Intervention, where victim and offender meet (Alarid and Montemayor 2012). These are cost-effective in reducing recidivism, and victim satisfaction is consistently higher than with normal disposals (Strang et al 2013), but frontline police are sceptical and resistant (Paterson and Clamp 2012).

Yet careful relationship-building with youths alienated from police can substantially ameliorate conflict (van de Klomp et al 2014). Following New Year's Eve riots by Dutch youths of Moluccan descent, conflict resolution techniques enabled a peaceful celebration a year later. Police analysed the history of their relations with the group to identify where other approaches would have been beneficial, highlighting opportunities in current relations. An aggressive outburst by a senior officer was contextualized by revealing that he had been seriously injured during rioting. Police dropped investigation of the throwing of Molotov cocktails. Benefits came from candour about the views of one's own side, and both sides not expecting too much too soon. Many Britons find police ineffective against ASB (HMIC 2011b; Figure 2.2). Candour about the limits on police efforts may refresh

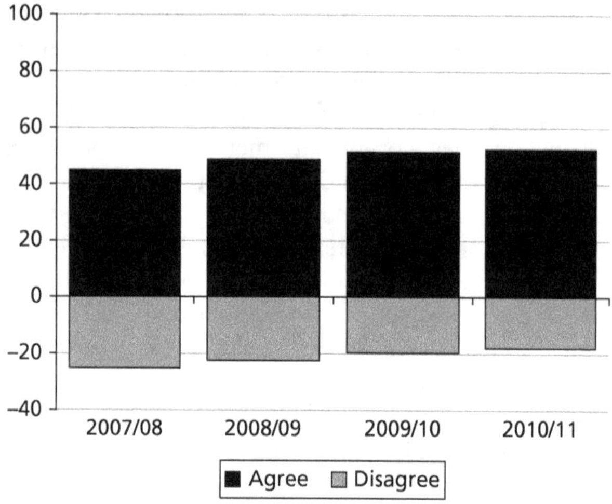

Figure 2.2 'The police are dealing with anti-social behaviour in the area'

Source: HMIC (2011) *Policing ASB*, London: HMIC.

relations with mainstream communities as well as those having a history of conflict with police.

Stop-and-search

Stop-and-search has caused friction between police and ethnic minorities for over fifty years. Despite regular legal changes and PACE guidelines, it remains divisive. Take cases like that of a black college student stopped fifty times by the Met between age 14 and 17, including two strip searches, without finding anything criminal. He was detained several times in police cells and released without charge. Charges of assault on police collapsed. Police claimed he rolled over when handcuffed, grazing their knuckles, but CCTV showed him 'lying there like a dead fish' (*The Guardian* 24 August 2012). Officers were investigating a knife threat whose suspect was white, a description they amended to 'black'. That year London's police stopped blacks eleven times more than whites.

Overall, ethnic minorities are seven times more likely to be stopped and searched than whites, only 10% result in arrest, and

27% do not contain reasonable grounds to search, making for over 250,000 illegal stops in 2013/14. Most officers do not receive in-service training in the powers; only twenty-one forces had refresher training. When the Equality and Human Rights Commission (2012b) worked with forces having the biggest racial disproportion, disparities fell without worsening detection rates. This was achieved by training, curtailing numerical performance targets, ensuring managerial commitment, and frontline officer accountability (EHRC 2013).

In research for the MacPherson Inquiry, FitzGerald (2000) established that the main influences on stop patterns were not ethnicity per se but age, and suspect descriptions in crime reports (Figure 2.3). Figure 2.3A shows black over-representation in relation to share of population. Figure 2.3B shows that this reduces considerably when age is taken into account. At the time, minorities were 45% or more of the school age population. Younger people are out in public more, thus more available to be stopped. The closest match for the ethnic composition of the search figures was with suspect descriptions (Figure 2.3C). Indeed, significantly more black people were reported as suspects than police actually stopped, implicating public suspicion of minorities. Even when controlled for socio-demographic factors, self-reported offending, area characteristics and degree of street presence, recent data show ethnic minorities are disproportionately stopped-and-searched (Ariza 2014), leaving suspect descriptions a prime influence.

Blatant racism does still occur. In 2012 a black man suffered a police torrent of abuse including 'the problem with you is you will always be a nigger, yeah?' (*The Guardian* 31 March 2012). Londoner Mauro Demetrio was arrested and held in a police van the day after the 2011 riots. One officer kneeled on his chest and set about strangling him. A second officer then uttered a succession of racist insults, concluding 'you'll always have black skin. Don't hide behind your colour'. The incident involved eight officers. Demetrio was arrested on suspicion of drug driving and for missing a court appearance. He began recording following sexually explicit innuendo about his mother. Dialogue after the strangling attempt ran: Demetrio: 'you tried to strangle me'. Officer: 'No, I did strangle you'. Demetrio: (inaudible). Officer: I strangled you 'cos you're a cunt . . . (and because) you were kicking out. Stopped you though, didn't it'.

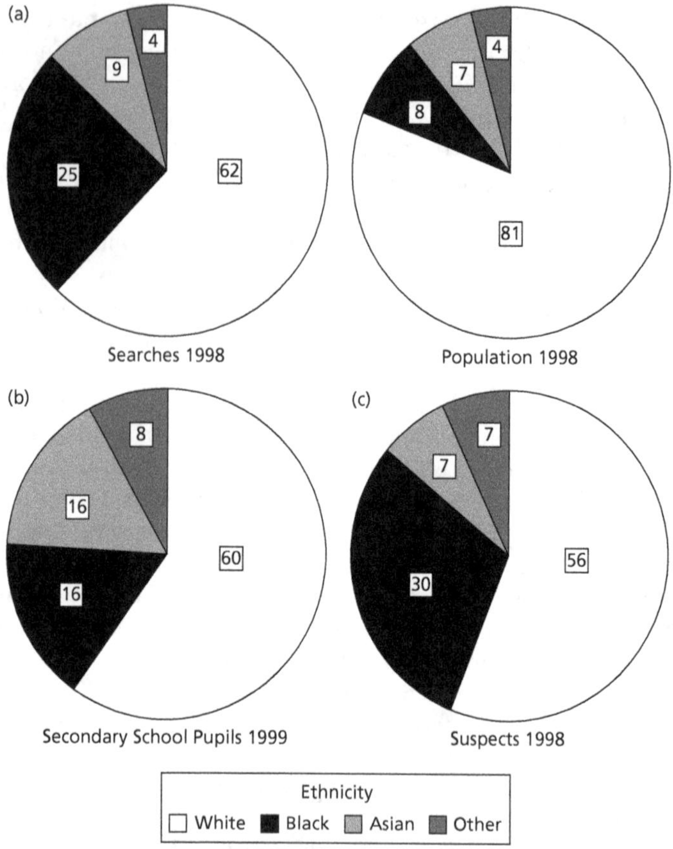

Figure 2.3 Influences on stop patterns

Searches by ethnic group compared with population (A); secondary school population (B) and suspect description (C). (% within ethnicity)

Source: M. FitzGerald (2000) Doctoral thesis, Guildford: University of Surrey.

The CPS declined to bring charges against officer MacFarlane, saying the abuse did not cause harassment, distress or alarm. A police doctor found marks on Demetrio's neck but there was no charge of assault. In two consecutive trials juries could not reach a verdict. MacFarlane's defence was that he was trying to 'defuse the situation', Demetrio having become agitated. MacFarlane said

Demetrio first used the word 'nigger' referring to himself, and that he, MacFarlane, simply repeated the word, being fatigued from policing the riots. He was attempting to help Demetrio—'I had formed the impression that he had low self-esteem. I wanted him to reconsider his lifestyle, to not view his skin colour as the reason behind the problems he had, not to blame the police, not to blame other people'. The second judge discharged MacFarlane. After disciplinary proceedings for gross misconduct MacFarlane was sacked. The Met's complaints director said MacFarlane, 'as a trained officer, was expected to behave professionally even in the face of provocation'.

An Independent Police Complaints Commission (IPCC) investigation followed an officer telling a DJ he stopped while driving a Bentley that black people in 'gangster-style clothing' would be stopped (*The Guardian* 28 January 2017). In the DJ's video of the encounter, the Met officer says 'predominantly the criminal profile of people who [commit robberies in the area] are black people. So naturally if you see a car full of black lads dressed in gangster-style clothing ... they're getting stopped'. Apparel is not grounds for suspicion. IPCC investigated after the video received over 85,000 YouTube views.

The Commission for Racial Equality (2004) found scant evidence that training gave officers an understanding of what constitutes racial discrimination, racist abuse of powers, or how to challenge workplace racism. Probationers were afraid to raise such concerns. In 2014 the Home Office announced a review of stop-and-search training and introduction of 'unconscious bias awareness training'. There would be disciplinary action for misusing the powers. Stop-and-search data became available on the national police website. The Met signed up to a best practice initiative under which participating forces must record the ostensible object of a search and its outcome, allow citizens to accompany officers on patrol, and restrict use of section 60 'no suspicion' powers to incidents where a chief officer is certain serious violence would otherwise occur. These measures remain voluntary. Perhaps Home Secretary May's comment that a black stop rate seven times the white stop rate was 'no longer sustainable' would prove sustainable after all. The success of voluntary efforts depends on sustained public and media scrutiny, but the suspect description issue suggests the importance of police discretion in moderating the most immediate form of public input.

Mythologies of New Governance: More Powers, Fewer Constraints

Between 1997 and 2012 over 3,000 new offences were created and a range of new summary measures were introduced. One tranche of new powers came from counter-terrorism legislation, another from anti-social behaviour legislation, and another from expanded summary powers. In 2006 powers of arrest were extended to every offence. Under the Conditional Caution, police can impose conditions whose satisfaction they directly oversee without review by judicial authorities. Legislation encouraging greater responsiveness to local peoples' thresholds of nuisance has obliged police to interpret behaviours as anti-social that were not previously so regarded (Lumsden 2014). In six European countries citizens rank parents as having first authority for dealing with ASB. In five countries 'the community' or 'schools' are next, but in Britain it is 'the police' (Kaariainen 2007).

ASB is minor nuisance and disorder. This is increasingly forgotten, as shown by 2014 legislation allowing 'secure' tenants of local authority and housing trust properties to be permanently evicted for ASB. The Anti-Social Behaviour Crime and Policing Act 2014 replaced Anti-Social Behaviour Orders (ASBOs) with 'Criminal Behaviour Orders' following conviction for any criminal offence. Breach is punishable by up to five years' imprisonment. Before the 2012 Olympic Games police imposed a dispersal zone around Stratford and the Olympic Park with powers to move on anyone considered to display ASB, including waiting near a rail station, wearing a hooded garment, or any behaviour officers considered annoying. In neighbouring Tower Hamlets, police targeted sex workers, the homeless and unemployed to help the Council 'drive them off-borough' (*The Guardian* 5 May 2012). Before the 2011 Royal Wedding a group wearing zombie outfits and heading for a 'zombie picnic' organized by Queer Resistance was arrested for wearing a disguise, despite police observing their avoidance of rioting anti-monarchists. Bandanas constituted 'disguise'. The grounds for their detention was the tautologous 'to charge'.

Penalty Notices for Disorder (PNDs)—on-the-spot fines—were introduced under the Criminal Justice and Police Act 2001 to provide 'swift and simple' response to ASB and reduce police and court workloads (Hallingan-Davis and Spicer 2005). Unpaid fines are registered on criminal records. By 2014, twenty-nine offences were punishable by PND. PNDs save ninety minutes of police time compared to cautions and 150 compared to prosecution. Cautions and prosecutions for the main offences—harassment/causing alarm, and drunk-and-disorderly—fell, but less than PNDs being issued, indicating net-widening to behaviours not previously punished. Subjectivity marks offences like swearing at officers (Grace 2014), or drunkenness, which reflect officers' judgement (in 60%, officers were sole 'victims'). PNDs require no admission of guilt and are not a conviction, discouraging recipients challenging them—the efficiency gain relies on a low rate of contest. Fines are uniform and thus harsher for the poor, homeless, and unemployed (51% of PND recipients). Payment by instalment automatically increases fines 50%. PNDs may be 'swift' and 'simple', but the pay-as-you-go approach to incivilities threatens police legitimacy.

Governments instinctively lunge for new legislation following high profile cases, as when the Crime and Justice Act 2014 was amended to automatically imprison on second convictions for knife possession following grisly knifings in London. However, government also enacted the Protection of Freedoms Act 2012 which restricted DNA sample retention, imposed a code of practice on CCTV and vehicle surveillance, restricted entry onto private land to pursue enforcement action, and repealed the stop-and-search provisions of the Terrorism Act 2000. So not all new legislation tightens the noose around the public's neck. An example is 'Clare's Law', after Clare Wood, strangled, then incinerated, by her partner, whose record of violence against women included kidnapping at knife point. The Domestic Violence Disclosure Scheme permits women to ask police to disclose whether their partners have an abusive past and police to proactively disclose information to a partner they think is at risk. As this suggests, policy and law are inadequate arbiters of individual cases and contexts. For that, we look to police.

When police arbitrate between law and cases they do so in a policy context configured by wider circumstances. The police mission in relatively stable polities is an enduring one, but the delivery of that mission reflects the challenges of the time. As police organizations seek to adapt to the challenges they are posed they adopt different strategies, some more effective than others.

Evidence of mistrials and policing scandals saw the Judges' Rules replaced by the Police and Criminal Evidence Act, whose codes of practice represent the principal criminal justice reform of the late twentieth century. While PACE was incorporated into the training curriculum and into understandings of police professionalism, training itself trundled on much as before. Those emerging from it confronted stern new tests of established practices and the newly embedded PACE. The long-running sore of frictional relations with minority persons and communities, particularly ethnic and racial minorities, grew more acute as Britain grew more diverse. The population itself became steadily more uncertain around diversity, with what we now call 'hate crime' sufficiently grave as to require its own label, and the emergence of vicious new dimensions of terrorism. Rioting, organized and quasi-organized gang crime, and ongoing conflict over stop-and-search, manifested a population ill-at-ease with itself as much as with the police. Politicians and legislators responded by conferring new powers no more fully considered than their ability to quell media foment over the latest scandal or crisis, with little attention to their latent or collateral effects. Like the public, the police perceived change all around them, but the means by which they sought to respond proved as slippery and uncertain as the problems they sought to solve.

3

Twenty-First Century Policing?

Policing's contemporary socio-political context presents economic challenges, shifting demographics, rising public expectations, and the emergence of the internet as a social space. The police response emphasizes protecting the vulnerable and focusing on highest-risk offenders (CoP 2015: 17), policies that must negotiate an organization conditioned by past challenges and working practices, and made uncertain by conflicting pressures on senior managers.

Managerialism and Organizational Structure

Classic police management took the form of *post hoc* review of operational performance. Her Majesty's Inspectorate of Constabulary (HMIC) conducted individual force inspections and 'thematic reviews' across forces. Inspections highlighted good and poor performance. Thus, the year 2000 inspection of Essex Police found that human resource strategies had not improved since the last inspection and that management quality varied, but praised a 10% reduction in crime (HMIC 2000). Inspections gave a sharply detailed but retrospective idea of challenges facing force managers. In 2013 government curtailed the scope of inspections and demanded they be more 'accessible'.

The emergent managerialism of the 1980s and 1990s shifted financial authority to chiefs and corresponded with a growing consumerist approach to public services (Davies 2014). The landmark 2002 White Paper (Home Office 2002) advocating management reforms and 'modern' employment terms was driven by only 9% of recorded crime resulting in conviction (HAC 2002). A new Standards Unit would spread best practice. Chief officers would henceforth undergo appraisal. Respondents to a Home Office consultation wanted more community engagement,

Professionalizing the Police: The Unfulfilled Promise of Police Training. Nigel G. Fielding Published 2018 by Oxford University Press more visible and accessible police, and more local input in setting priorities (Home Office 2003b). The Home Office (2004b) announced Neighbourhood Policing (NP) would be rolled out nationwide, with communities getting more say. A national non-emergency number would be introduced. Under 'national occupational standards', sergeants and inspectors would receive training in managerial skills. Direct entry to senior rank would be introduced. Much of this came to pass, prominent reforms under New Labour being national occupational standards and Neighbourhood Policing, including community consultation (Home Office 2004c).

After several years of tightening performance management, government and senior officers began to question it. The Flanagan Report (Flanagan 2008) pursued reducing bureaucracy while improving public accountability. Flanagan resolved these contradictory ambitions by recommending reducing information recorded about all but the most serious crimes; replacing stop-and-account forms with receipts; standardizing crime report forms across forces; and strengthening local accountability. Flanagan had caught the tide of opinion. The Home Office immediately scrapped stop-and-account forms, streamlined stop-and-search forms, piloted handheld devices to record stop-and-search, introduced standard crime recording, and dropped the reasonable suspicion criterion where violence was anticipated or weapons-carrying was suspected. The last New Labour white paper promised 'report cards' assessing policing's quality locally, quarterly Basic Command Unit (BCU)/public meetings, and a simplified complaints system (Home Office 2009).

Flanagan, and Louise Casey's review of crime and communities, led to a 'Policing Pledge' stating what citizens could expect of police (Home Office 2008). A year later thirty-three of forty-three forces fell short of Pledge commitments ('requiring remedial action'), two consistently failed, and just eight were generally compliant (HMIC 2009c). Stations were not open when advertised; websites showed stale information, including officer names; 17% of non-emergency calls elicited no action; NP teams missed police/public meetings; few forces offered opportunities to discuss complaints; only two had translated the Pledge to other languages; and a commitment to answer all emergency calls within ten seconds was regularly breached.

In 2010 the Coalition, supported by the 'anti-bureaucracy champion' Jan Berry, scrapped the Pledge, proclaiming that under austerity forces must focus on law enforcement (Berry 2009). Despite having originated in the preceding administration both localism and cutting bureaucracy became favourite Coalition themes. Berry's final report identified as 'barriers' to police reform: complex accountability and confused governance; over-reliance on numerical performance and productivity measures; burdensome inspection/audit; inconsistent leadership, poor risk management and an institutionalized blame culture; skills shortages, including managerial; insularity; fragmented and dysfunctional systems and processes; uncoordinated commissioning causing duplication; acting before fully understanding problems (Berry 2010). It is difficult to imagine a harsher assessment.

Police and Crime Commissioners

Government's solution to the problems was to impose Police and Crime Commissioners (PCCs). While many looked askance at this, or at least the bumbling way in which it was done, the police authorities they replaced had an unimpressive record. HMIC found only fifteen 'adequate' (HMIC 2010c). They dealt satisfactorily with short-term local priorities but planning, budgeting, and scrutinizing serious crime and counter-terrorism policing were ineffective. Most were not proactive, were confused over chiefs' remits and were overly fearful of encroaching on chiefs' independence. Some 93% of police authority members (realistically) said the home secretary, not the public's representatives, had final decision in any disputes. Even when an authority voted against an intervention or policy it usually went ahead, as with issuing plastic bullets and CS gas (Millen and Stephens 2011). Not exactly a hard act for PCCs to follow, but an indication of what good police governance requires.

Even for Conservatives, alone in championing PCCs, it was not a unifying or high profile issue. PCCs were added late to their 2010 manifesto and then forced into the Coalition Agreement. Passage into law was fraught. Parliament was alarmed about politicizing operational decision-making and wanted guarantees on operational responsibility and impartiality (HAC 2011c). The Lords rightly deemed Policing and Crime Panel powers 'sharply limited'. They could only make 'recommendations' when PCCs sacked chiefs, and had no role in suspension. On 15 September 2011 the Police Reform and Social Responsibility Bill replacing police authorities with PCCs passed on a tied vote (222–222) in the Lords.

Candidates faced 'huge deposits, unclear eligibility rules, vast electoral districts and high campaign costs' (Garland and Terry 2012). Some 89% of the public (Gilmore 2012), and the Association of Chief Police Officers' (ACPO) president, were concerned about politicization. Campaign slogans included 'Let's keep local politics out of policing' (Peter Williams handbill, September 2012). Only 11% of voters claimed a good understanding of PCCs' role, nearly half expected no change, 45% that policing would get worse, and only 21% intended to vote (Gilmore 2012). Average turn-out was 14.8% (5.49 million in total). Numerous polling stations went unvisited. Ignorance of PCCs' brief—to link police and public—was a large factor (Loveday 2012); others were there being no London PCC election, little national news coverage, and candidates' largely indistinguishable platforms. Some 192 candidates stood for forty-one forces (both London forces being excluded). Labour and Conservatives contested each post, Liberal Democrats twenty-four. The Green Party refrained. The lowest turnout in peacetime history gave victors an average mandate of 7% of the electorate, ranging from 8.3% (Dyfed-Powys) to 3.3% (Hampshire). Sixteen Conservatives were elected, thirteen Labour, twelve Independents, and no Liberal Democrats. Of successful Independents, eight were former police. Of thirty-five females, six succeeded. There were no ethnic minorities. The election, PCC/staff wages and operating expenses cost over half a billion; each vote cost £85. A post-election ComRes poll found 38% had never heard of PCCs, with a large majority unaware how to contact them (Loveday 2012). Of those who had not voted, 79% said they were unaware of the election or not interested. The 2016 PCC election passed similarly, an average 22% of electorate troubling to vote.

PCCs took office in November 2012, becoming responsible for policing priorities, appointing or dismissing chiefs, public consultation and £8 billion in force budgets. With annual salaries of £65,000 to £100,000, PCCs are formally accountable only via annual reports and the ballot box. PCCs prepare annual strategies and priorities in Police and Crime Plans and disburse community safety grants. New PCCs uttered gung-ho declarations of 'zero tolerance', un-evidenced assertions that 'drugs were being dealt in every school', and promised they would 'make the prisons build loft extensions' (this in a county with England's lowest crime rate).

PCC's Police and Crime Plans declare their authority over chiefs, are liberally illustrated with photos of beaming PCCs, and seldom contain an endorsement or any direct input by the chief. They proliferate targets (disguised as 'measurable objectives', 'priorities' etc.) despite there being only one Home Office target—crime reduction—which is itself seldom mentioned. A 2014 survey found that 82.2% still did not know who their PCC was, only 35% supported PCCs, and 23% opposed them (Survation 2014). As to bringing police and public closer, results were unpromising, with 31% saying their trust in police had declined and 62% seeing no change.

Many voters will not have been alert to PCCs' substantial budgetary and commissioning powers, some added post-election. The official PCC election leaflet referred only to 'deciding how the budget will be spent', without specifying what budget or choices there were (Electoral Commission PCC Leaflet 2012). Asked to rate PCCs one year on, 64% saw no impact on crime reduction and 9% thought PCCs had rendered police less effective (YouGov 2013).

The Conservative thinktank 'Policy Exchange' recommendation that PCCs oversee local justice, including probation, has effectively, if quietly, come about, with 'local' reimagined as 'regional'. PCC budgets fund Crime and Disorder Reduction grants and community projects, with no obligation to maintain existing services like Victim Support. Community projects generally focus on education and diversion but large grants have been awarded to fire services for safe driving campaigns, the NHS for raising awareness about infection from drugs, county councils for e-Safety conferences, and residential trips to holiday destinations for 'disenfranchised young people' at-risk of offending. Boundaries around the obligation to promote 'public safety' are vague. Initiatives overlap with probation or youth services. PCCs have merged Community Safety Partnerships or de-prioritized them, arguing that detecting crime is more popular than prevention (Lewis 2013). For community consultation PCCs rely largely on formal meetings long known to be unrepresentative.

Whitehall has taken a more prominent role than envisaged due to ambiguous legislation (Chambers 2014). There remain concerns over Police and Crime Panels' (PCP) limited powers, contradictions inherent in their 'critical/friend' model of scrutiny, problems where PCPs and PCCs are not politically aligned, and PCCs' ability to constrain PCP scrutiny (Lister 2014). Panels can suspend PCCs who commit crimes, and veto chief constable candidates, either appointing the reserve or proposing another, but PCPs lack authority to hold PCCs to account (Bailey 2015). To exercise their power to veto precepts proposed by PCCs a two-thirds majority of the panel is required, and PCPs cannot set an alternative. Nothing requires PCC staff to give evidence to panels or disclose their briefings of the PCC. The Independent Police Complaints Commission (IPCC) investigated four cases of illegal PCC actions in the first year, plus inappropriate expense claims. For their part, PCCs of forces whose officers were involved in the Plebgate scandal attacked IPCC rather than calling their forces to account. Police operational independence is protected in law. Presently nothing else holds PCCs effectively to account.

PCCs may have a deputy and assistants for portfolios like equality and diversity. Sixteen PCCs immediately appointed deputies paid £65,000 (equivalent to full PCCs; Loveday 2013). West Mercia's appointee was the PCC's campaign manager, both being recently retired cops. An unedifying episode occasioned by PCCs' freedom to appoint assistants at will was Kent's appointment of a seventeen-year old girl as 'Youth PCC' on £15,000. It soon emerged that she had recently sent racist and sexist 'tweets'. She resigned in tears from what some may regard as officially-orchestrated child abuse. The first official dismissed by a PCC was in Middlesbrough. Despite only four months left in the police authority chief executive's contract, the PCC immediately replaced him with a friend, Mr Chicken, saying this was no different to action by any 'senior politician', demonstrating rather clearly the politicization of the office. A chief's unsuccessful court action against his PCC's decision against automatically renewing his contract signalled reversal of the power relationship of chief to police authority. PCCs were now principal and chiefs the agent. Chiefs' 'direction and control' of forces was replaced with exercising managerial and operational discretion 'to assist the relevant PCC to exercise the Commissioner's functions'.

The Gwent chief's open hostility to the PCC system resulted in her PCC (former president of the Police Superintendents Association) sacking her. Appearing before the Home Affairs Committee she claimed bullying and condemned anyone having 'so much unfettered power', a position that well-described her own former privilege. Parliament announced an inquiry into PCCs' role, effectiveness and powers. ACPO president Hugh Orde said there were insufficient checks and balances on PCCs' 'huge' powers. While judges ruled Lincolnshire's chief's suspension by his PCC 'unlawful, irrational and perverse', another sacking, Avon and Somerset, stood. The Home Affairs Committee (2014b) recommended independent mediation for broken PCC/chief relationships and a national register of PCC's interests.

The PCC concept emphasizing localism along with volunteering and a smaller state reflected themes prominent in Cameron's 2006 'policing revolution' speech (Brain 2013). Here were the seeds of PCCs' amateurism and ad hockery. Making things up as PCCs went along was only collateral damage because PCCs were essentially a device to enable Home Office police reforms, bypassing resistant chiefs. This is not to deny PCCs' power, since the office fuses both representative and governance functions (Brain 2014: 41). A representative body—the police authorities—albeit not directly elected—was replaced by a single individual. Even a mayor has to work with an elected council. With Strategic Plans passing to PCCs went any democratic input on strategic matters.

To some the premise that police exist to apply the law impartially is unconvincing, and political alignment of PCC's and government only the most obvious form of police/State collusion (Turner 2014). While Turner sees accountability and operational independence as myths, these doctrines give critics their best prospect of holding police power in check. They may be meant as no more than rhetorical tools, aimed at voters who regard accountability as something more than a price-comparison website, but a rhetoric casting accountability and independence as meaningful still gives critics some purchase. Even a force actively intervening in favour of a bourgeois notion of order marked by systematic inequalities is a contingent resource to be influenced if not actually steered.

Most commentators readily acknowledge repressive public order activity, inappropriate surveillance, corrupt investigative practice, discriminatory stop/search and the rest of the long list of police delicts. The division comes over whether this is an inevitable consequence of the present structural arrangements comprising the political economy of contemporary criminal justice. The plausible reasons for police malpractice, corruption, and misgovernance lie in poorly drafted legislation, lax regulation, incompetent practice, and personal prejudices. These are all things that citizens can do something about. If instead the failings of police practice are determined at the structural level it is hard to understand why anyone conducts research on the police, as these failings would be inherent in the relationships between the institutions of governance. It also cannot explain why, after being called to a war memorial where vandals set fire to wreaths on the 100th anniversary of the outbreak of the First World War, responding officers later returned to scrub the memorial clean because they thought it no more than the decent thing to do (*Daily Express* 30 July 2014).

Manning (2010) encapsulates democratic policing as procedurally fair, balancing coercion and service, and not aggravating existing inequalities or damaging the position of the disadvantaged. Where these conditions obtain, police play a legitimate part in democratic societies. The test of accountability is exactly whether it is able to influence, and change, what police do. By this yardstick the police have long failed, *inter alia*, to act effectively to make stop-and-search less racially discriminatory. This tells us that accountability mechanisms are flawed. It does not, however, tell us there is no point in accountability.

The former 'tripartite system' notoriously lacked public engagement and balance. Chief constables were long dominant, with periodic exertions by the Home Office. Police authorities were the weak party, ineffectual in representing the public. PCCs replace the ineffectual with the dangerous. Politicians' rhetoric about PCCs being fully accountable because they are elected is scarcely worth rebuttal. Hardly anyone voted, even in their inaugural contest. Several years in, hardly anyone knows who they are. Their public meetings go unattended, and their pronouncements vary from the bizarre to the nakedly political. They were introduced with no clear brief, taxpayers' money is aimlessly thrown at them, and they are entrusted with an efficiency and amalgamation agenda that has resisted implementation for over fifty years. There are some impressive PCCs, but as the link between public and police the system is farcical. In the US it is sensible to have directly-elected chiefs because there is no equivalent of the Home Office. In Britain the result is to have delivered governance wholly into the hands of politicians. Chiefs are neither in a position, nor the right job, to represent the public interest. The idea that the public can get rid of bad policies by waiting to vote a PCC out is fanciful. We are left with politicians *manqué* and central government running police governance, with the public not even in shouting distance.

Managerial Agendas

Structural criminal justice reform was an early, sustained Coalition priority. Within four months it abolished the Court Boards in England and Wales, the Legal Services Ombudsman, the Victim's Advisory Panel, the Youth Justice Board (YJB), the Serious Organised Crime Agency, and the Security Industry Authority. The Police Advisory Board, Police Negotiating Board and Police Arbitration Tribunal were all 'rationalized'. Closing the YJB was a decision unrelated to its performance (Public Accounts Committee 2011) and Parliament forced restoration. HMIC (2010d) sought to accommodate 20% cuts in police budgets by identifying weaknesses in planning and suggesting more collaboration between forces (HMIC 2011a). Police were heavily divided over the case that government made for a professional body (HAC 2013). Government wanted an 'inclusive' professional body, opening senior positions to non-police and widening training providers (Home Office 2011a). Its board would balance police and 'independent' membership by including—PCCs.

Targets and KPIs

Despite the Coalition's turn against Key Performance Indicators (KPIs) and targets, they were quickly reinstated by PCCs. Euphemisms like 'priorities' skirted Home Secretary May's insistence on the single target of reducing crime. Certainly targets based on single-indicator public satisfaction measures misrepresent opinion (Myhill et al 2011; Shilston 2011). However, rather than measures of the several dimensions of legitimacy and procedural fairness advocated by Myhill et al (2011), the 178 new targets set by PCCs were narrowly crime-focused—Norfolk police had to reduce violent and sexual crimes at specified times in particular parts of specific towns to no more than 450/year.

Recruits thus enter a performance-managed environment whose problem is measuring the things that actually matter. Performance measures most affecting the frontline have long existed; unofficial arrest quotas have featured since the days of the Bow Street Runners. This does not mean recruits can be indifferent to systems like Activity Based Costing, which records how officers spend their working time and informs cuts in officer numbers. The Police Federation (2014) found a 'culture of fear' resulting from 'draconian' and unrealistic performance targets. Managers were responsible for a 'bullying culture' around competency action plans. Officers reported that 'every month we are named and shamed with a league table by our supervisors'. The unsubtle Scotland Yard response referred to 'doing more with less'.

Amalgamations and mergers

HMIC's 'Closing the Gap' (2006) was seen as the starting pistol for mergers. Its drivers were wide differences in forces' capability and capacity, finances, and effectiveness against organized crime/terrorism. Larger forces had better capability and resilience. For example, forces lacking specialist murder units could be overwhelmed by a single hard-to-solve murder. However, on HMIC's own evidence two large forces fared badly, and some small forces met the standard due to effective management.

ACPO was split over amalgamation versus regional collaboration. The Chief Police Officers Staff Association worried about impact on chiefs' conditions of service. HMIC nevertheless insisted that reorganization was 'inescapable' and forces should have a minimum of 4,000 officers. The options were: collaboration; lead force for specialist capabilities; lead regional force; federation of forces; and creation of strategic forces. HMIC preferred the last, with federation the runner-up. The strategic force option reduces forty-three into around six super-forces. In 2005 Home Secretary Charles Clarke had invited police proposals for strategic forces in each region. When John Reid replaced Clarke, policy changed. Although mergers were 'ultimately the right way' more discussion was necessary, but Reid approved the planned merger of Cumbria and Lancashire. However, parliamentarians knew their differing council tax precepts could not be reconciled. On the day Reid made his statement the Lords voted to prevent mergers unless police authorities requested them. The Home Office withdrew its notices of intention to merge. The accompanying ministerial statement excluded the 'strategic force' option, highlighting instead collaboration or the lead force model, with an additional option of shared administration. The latter emerged most clearly from the merger fiasco. It drove, for example, enhanced collaboration between Sussex and Surrey police. Organic rather than scripted change is the current state in the game of critical mass. Mergers were in effect seen off by localism. Conservative and Liberal peers wanted police authorities to have the final say, not a central government organ, HMIC. Whether this was to do with democratic control or more instrumental concerns is moot, but the case of Cumbria and Lancashire, divorced before they reached the altar, suggests that instrumentalism featured.

Official encouragement to collaborate continues. Guidance to chiefs and PCCs includes a model decision process and governance design (Home Office 2012c). Forces should deliver at least 10% of their work through collaboration. PCCs have a legal duty to collaborate for efficiency's sake. HAC (2014c) endorsed the Warwickshire/West Mercia 'alliance' and Surrey/Sussex collaboration. Government insists full mergers should be under one PCC and chief. This ignores the 'net donor problem', where a force perceives resources committed for collaboration will be deployed solely in its partner's area. The government's position was unrealistic: forces should 'understand that a collaboration may not provide equal benefits in all parts to all participants or in total but is sometimes necessary for the greater collective good' (Home Office 2011a). Negotiating collaboration involves other problems. Chiefs set the style of force management and are strong personalities who can take opposing positions. Integrating Human Resources requires identical promotion criteria and processes. Procurement and complaints processes need alignment. One force involved in such a negotiation identified several thousand different processes and working policies requiring alignment. Collaboration needs to carry PCCs too. All this against ongoing budget cuts.

In their organization and structure forces have proved resistant to change, particularly in ways affecting ordinary officers. The principal recent innovation, Neighbourhood Policing, is analogous to quality circle manufacture, where small teams take holistic responsibility. Neighbourhood Policing struggles against policing's accustomed reactive approach and, being intensive of human resources, is vulnerable to cuts during hard times. NP is still based on territorial units, despite increasing impetus to move it online. Similarly, rather than prompting a rethink of how police relate to geographical area, station closures under austerity have simply seen officers re-sited in nearby libraries, hospitals, and supermarkets.

The National Policing Improvement Agency (NPIA) and ACPO explored 'workforce modernization' prior to the austerity period, piloting assigning officers to roles consonant with their skills and training. However, the pilots changed aims while underway, savings estimates were undermined by not taking account of absence, turnover, or abstractions, and initiatives unconnected with the pilots were not factored out, inflating success measures (Chatterton et al 2009). Workforce modernization continued but talk of meeting public expectations ceased; modernization was about austerity.

Technology

Policing has long inspired forensic innovation. The 1888–1891 Whitechapel murders associated with 'Jack the Ripper' prompted the earliest crime scene photographs, and a murder off St Martin's Lane in 1961 resulted in the first detection using Identikit images (Ackroyd 2001). However, contemporary technological innovations focus on managing working environments rather than directly assisting officers (Manning 1992). Online terminals in patrol cars and handheld devices promising faster response simply increase message traffic volume without improving effectiveness and service delivery (Haarr and Hultsman 1997). Computer-aided crime mapping and analytics become just another tool around which officers continue much as before (Manning 2008). Analysts report extensive mapping for descriptive representations but little for problem-solving (Weir and Bangs 2007). Analysts mostly provide illustrations for reports rather than identifying causes of crime problems or evaluating interventions. Only 29% of analysts report crime mapping being used regularly in operational decisions, 25% said it was seldom or never used.

In large US forces with integrated information systems, analysis in Compstat-type meetings is 'quick, querulous, and concrete' with 'an implicit pressure ... to do something, to have done something, or to plan to do something quickly', and the 'basically undirected and entrepreneurial work of patrol officers' goes unchanged (Manning 2008: 41). Dialogue in Compstat meetings is not analytical but constantly diverted by the riveting anecdote and reminiscences. Meetings are so skilfully orchestrated by technicians that they become entertainments, with cartoons shown in intervals while new crime scene visuals are loaded. Manning (2008) found neither work with the public nor citizen-suggested initiatives were discussed. No crime analysis training occurred. Trend analysis was stymied by historical data being on obsolete and incompatible systems, forming an 'archaeology of systems lying on top of each other yet not linked' (ibid: 150). Technologies are undermined by being 'back-fitted to the extant structure and traditional processes of the police organization' (ibid: 83).

A daunting 'affordance' of new technologies is their use in child sexual exploitation. The Child Exploitation and Online Protection Agency (CEOP) received 2,500 reports of exploitation in its first year (CEOP 2007b). Regular officers have a direct role on behalf of CEOP in detecting child trafficking, most for sexual purposes but also domestic labour (CEOP 2007a). Children's services, and the immigration authorities, assist in assessing missing-child cases for signs of trafficking, assistance whose importance is heightened by CEOP's chronic understaffing. An automated database was implemented in 2014 comparing pornographic images of children on seized computers to stored images, reducing duplication of effort in cataloguing images and identifying where they were taken from their GPS stamps. A 90% workload reduction was trumpeted. However, a similar system rolled out in 2003 was abandoned in 2011 due to lack of trained staff following budget cuts. Bright ideas around technology can also end up adding to frontline work. Satellite tracking of sex offenders requires 'standalone exclusion orders' that cost £42/day to monitor per offender. Police gain little useful information and 58% breach their order (Shute 2008).

The police record of technology procurement is poor. Surrey Police spent £14.8 million replacing their ageing criminal intelligence computer system before abandoning it unused in 2013. The business case was on grounds of tailoring to local needs but an inquiry found generic systems used by other forces were perfectly satisfactory and could interoperate, unlike Surrey's flop. The project 'was beyond the in-house capabilities and experience' of the force (OPCC Surrey 2014). The chief constable who commissioned it, Mark Rowley, ACPO's lead for business efficiency, was by then a Met assistant commissioner. Rowley was moved from overseeing technology and put in charge of counter-terrorism.

Technologies display 'mission creep' as their affordances are recognized. Experiments with Automatic Number Plate Recognition (ANPR) first related to traffic policing but found security applications (the 'Ring of Steel'—actually cameras—installed around central London after the 1996 Bishopsgate IRA bombing), and revenue generation (London's congestion charge) (Norris 2014). In 2002 'Intercept Teams' began arresting drivers ANPR flagged as unlicensed, uninsured, or wanted for crime. ANPR augmented surveillance capacity. Real-time pattern analysis notes how often driver A's vehicle is near driver B's, thus tracking 'associates'.

Data Protection law grants citizens the right to know what information is held on them. To submit a Subject Access Request (SAR), one must identify the likely source of information held. ANPR cameras belong to forces, and many are concealed. When journalist Steven Mathieson wanted to raise a SAR he had to submit a Freedom of Information (FoI) request to Devon and Cornwall Police to identify the camera. They refused, and the Information Commissioner rejected his complaint. An administrative tribunal upheld Mathieson's appeal and ordered disclosure. Police cited 'national security' and prevailed. The Information Commissioner's powers are confined to 'encouraging' disclosure (Information Commissioner 2007), and the Data Protection 'right' cannot be used because SARs require information that is refused.

This permissive circumstance was extended when police surrounded part of Birmingham with 150 large cameras mounted on tall masts. The Muslim community within was told it was for crime control but it emerged that the wiring was to Special Branch, not the police call centre. The equipment was for counter-terrorist surveillance. Exposure by *The Guardian* saw the cameras zipped into plastic bags, but they remained.

Police investigative powers must not impose inappropriate surveillance. The House of Lords (2009) warned that 'pervasive and routine' electronic surveillance was altering the relationship of

State and citizen, and undermining privacy. The UK has more CCTV per person than any other country, some four million cameras by 2008. Similarly the National DNA Database is the largest in proportionate terms in the world, with 7.39% of the population on it, compared to just 0.5% of the US equivalent. The Lords' concerns proved influential on the Coalition government, which enacted a Surveillance Camera Code of Practice in 2013, emphasizing 'surveillance by consent', with an independent Surveillance Camera Commissioner. There was an aspiration to 'streamline' the use of CCTV but no clear indication what that entailed.

It should involve rethinking CCTV altogether. Statistically-significant crime reduction effects are found in only two out of every thirteen installations at best (Gill and Spriggs 2005). FoI requests reveal that councils have covertly installed cameras in their properties to observe tenants. In one case housing services staff did not secure lawful authorization, and police viewed output in an open office with others present (*The Independent* 25 December 2014). The stated purpose was to deter criminal damage but an e-mail revealed police were using cameras to gather evidence of drug-dealing. It was claimed they were filming communal areas but footage showed they were pointing directly at the front door of particular flats. Police cannot sanction direct surveillance unless to prevent a crime punishable by at least a six-month sentence, and only with the approval of a magistrate. In the case in question the offences did not attract such a sentence and no magistrate was approached. The council described the breach of Data Protection law as 'council and police work(ing) in partnership to safeguard residents'.

Devon and Cornwall Police first used body-worn cameras (BWCs), in 2006. The Met acquired BWCs in 2014 to capture crime scene evidence, initially 500 amongst 31,000 officers. Firearms officers wear them in training, following public concern over the Duggan shooting which sparked the 2011 riots. As well as encouraging guilty pleas, cameras convey things officers find hard to express in written reports, like the state of frightened children at incidents, and have deterrent effects in disorder situations. US trials saw 88% fewer public complaints after BWCs were introduced and 60% fewer occasions where officers used force (CoP 2014). Police adhered more to guidance, spoke more courteously, and most felt protected against unjust allegations.

However, BWC only modestly increases the proportion of detections resulting in charges; 81% with BWC against 72% without (ibid). Data storage demands mean cameras cannot run constantly, affording scope for claims of selective recording wherever officers control recording (Bear and Rieken 2014). Practicalities also intrude: recording floor or ceiling, difficulties operating controls, and bad light. BWC provides only a 2-dimensional view and compromises officers' motor skills during incidents (Wyllie 2016).

Randomized control trials (RCTs) find that where officers do not control when cameras are activated use of force is reduced but where they control cameras the reverse is true (Ariel et al 2016). However, the same researchers found a 93% annual decrease in complaints against officers using BWC compared to before its introduction (Ariel et al 2017). Breach of procedures fell and suspect behaviour improved. A further RCT found the odds of force being used fell 50% with BWC but the effect was concentrated on the use of open hand tactics (physical restraints and non-compliant handcuffing) rather than the more aggressive forms of force (e.g. dogs, Tasers, batons, pepper spray), where there was no effect (Henstock and Ariel 2017). All these options now require officers to file lengthy 'use-of-force' reports, which may deter use of force as much as being on camera. Moreover, a large fraction of cases where force is used are indifferent to any deterrent effect of cameras because suspects are intoxicated or psychotic. Authoritative RCTs involving very large samples of officers find very small average treatment effects on use of force and civilian complaints, neither of which reach statistical significance (Yokum et al 2017). The complex picture from these RCTs suggests the need for precise definition of 'force' and strict adherence to it by forces without the gaming that often affects police reporting, and also suggests that BWC increases reporting of low-level force that formerly went under-reported. Thus, BWC may solve a relatively minor problem but at considerable expense, not least by implanting the belief that technology counters the excessive force that reduces police legitimacy and can trigger riots.

Blunderbuss technologies

Like their public, British police take pride in being an unarmed force. This does not mean forces have no armoury. Guns are available in Armed Response Vehicles, Tasers are in general issue, and officers with machine guns patrol transportation hubs. The 2005 shooting of Jean-Charles de Menezes exposed a non-statutory 'shoot to kill' policy emanating from ACPO. Police dispute there being such a policy but what is indisputable is that the SAS trains firearms officers to shoot suspected terrorists in the head, with the deputy chief of the Civil Nuclear Constabulary conceding that such shots generally kill (*Daily Telegraph* 1 January 2016). Nevertheless, officers on routine patrol are not armed beyond truncheons. In this, Britain remains unusual. Terrorist atrocities in 2017 had the National Police Chiefs' Council (NPCC) considering two weeks' firearms training for all officers.

Like the routine issue of guns, the view is long-established that the use of water cannons is alien to British policing. Police believe they are ineffective and dangerous, as likely to hit bystanders as rioters, and capable of blinding, as happened to an elderly passerby during a German riot. However, in 2014 the Met commissioner's request to purchase second-hand German water cannons was approved by then-mayor Johnson. Five of the six largest police authorities recorded their opposition, a view shared by incoming PCCs, former Met commissioners, and the London Assembly. Home Secretary May said 'the way we police in Britain is not through use of water cannon [but] ... through consent of communities'. Johnson's approval was seen as jockeying for advantage over May to replace Cameron as Conservative leader. Johnson obligingly offered to have himself shot by water cannon to demonstrate their safety. In 2016 footage emerged of the machines rusting unused in a police training centre.

Tasers were initially only carried by firearms officers but in 2007 the Home Office extended their use. Tasers fire darts into the body releasing five second bursts of electric current causing involuntary muscle spasms, auditory recall loss, and blocking of new auditory information for at least an hour, mimicking resistance (Kane and White 2016). Once targets collapse, handcuffs are applied. Despite legal classification as non-lethal, serious injuries and deaths occur (Terrill and Paoline 2012); in one gruesome case a man doused with petrol burst into flame when tasered. The Home Office monitors operational effectiveness, injuries, and patterns of use in seven categories (Drawn, Aimed, Arced, Red Dotted, Drive Stun, Angled Drive Stun, Fired). In 'drive stun' mode the weapon is pressed against the body, causing incapacity through pain rather than electric shock. The highest level use (Fired) occurs in a fifth of incidents. Most common use is 'red dot', where the aiming laser appears on the body.

Children and vulnerable people have been tasered, including a 14-year old with learning difficulties. In 2012 a blind man received 50,000 volts in the back when Lancashire police mistook his white cane for a samurai sword. No officer was disciplined. Bristol police tasered their own race relations advisor, mistaking him for a suspect (*The Guardian* 21 January 2017). Judah Adunbi serves on Bristol's police advisory group and a Crown Prosecution Service (CPS) community panel. Roughed up by officers, Adunbi, 63, fell backwards on his head and a WPC tasered him in the face while prone. A neighbour who videoed the attack protested but officers said 'he was trying to fight us'. The film shows the officers initiating the attack. Paralysis convinced Adunbi he was dying. The WPC ordered him to get up despite paralysis. Charges of assault and threatening behaviour were later dropped. Adunbi endured similar treatment in 2007. He said 'the first thing they should have done is come to me in a polite manner'. Few cases of misuse involve risk to officers, often featuring handcuffed suspects or non-offenders (Stinson et al 2012). While firearm authorizations fell 14% between 2009 and 2014 Taser use increased 232% (*Police Foundation Newsletter* March 2013), suggesting tasering happens where weapons were not formerly deployed. Training is often only two days, against six weeks for firearms officers.

Social media, cybercrime, and DNA

Police use of social media (SM) is maturing. Smartphone 'apps' let citizens track their neighbourhood officers, find the nearest police station and next consultation meeting, track the police helicopter, and vote on policing priorities. Facebook is used to post messages about specific crimes (Lieberman et al 2013) and Twitter for dialogue. An early success was quashing rumours about police activities during protests outside the deputy Prime Minister's office in 2011 (D. Waddington and McSeveny 2012). Networked applications like Video Skype can deliver advice to the housebound 'face to face' (Mason 2013) and social media 'tension-monitoring systems' monitor cyber-neighbourhoods (Williams et al 2013). Investigators mine data using federated and meta-search engines like *Dogpile* and people-search engines aggregating open-source information about individuals, like *Pipl*. Police use SM to: Publicize (e.g. a successful initiative); Advise (e.g. on crime prevention); Inform (e.g. recognizing signs of grooming); Warn (e.g. terrorist alerts); Appeal (e.g. for missing persons); and Engage. Communications officers from five forces with a combined population of 8,089,200 offered case study examples of each function but emphasized engagement (Fielding and Caddick 2017). They saw SM as having transformed police/public engagement, not least because frontline and senior officers were increasingly initiating or joining SM-based dialogue with the public. SM 'reach' is measured by message forwarding. An informal tone/style increases the odds of forwarding (van de Velde et al 2015), as does including web addresses and hashtags (Suh et al 2010); communications teams monitor forwarding. Technology's affordances have downsides. Social media accounted for half of anti-social behaviour (ASB) complaints by 2014. Officers dealt with six a day, but many are as trivial as 'unfriending' someone on Facebook. Deciding which to investigate poses a new test of officer discretion. The College of Policing (CoP) provided training to 6,000 frontline officers.

Technology is only as capable as its users. Police failed to identify online tension indicators before the 2011 riots, could not integrate SM information into riot control planning, and lacked software to distinguish rumour from fact (Silverman 2013). Police computer forensics focus on child pornography, terrorism, and murder, without addressing cyber-fraud or analysing the petabytes of CCTV data held (*The Economist* 13 August 2011). City of London Police is national cybercrime lead. Their fraud bureau refers 25% of cases to local forces, the rest not being investigated (BBC Radio 4, World at One, 30 September 2014). Since 55% of arrests overall result from arrest at crime scenes or identification by victims/witnesses (National Audit Office 2010), which is impossible in cybercrime, crime prevention advice-giving is the main frontline requirement.

The Criminal Justice Act (CJA) 2001 permitted police to take and keep DNA samples from anyone charged rather than only those convicted. The CJA 2003 extended this to anyone arrested for an imprisonable offence, even if not charged. By 2009 the database held 4,859,934 samples, four out of five from males and 7.3% from Blacks, disproportionate to population share. By 2010 a third of young black males were on the database. Between

1998 and 2009 there were 182,000 detections relating directly to a DNA match and 122,000 related crimes were solved by admission. But 40% of crime scene profiles are not matched to a suspect profile, and DNA convictions cost an average £16,042 per case (Doleac 2016). The Protection of Freedoms Act 2012 legislated destruction of fingerprints and DNA taken from those arrested for or charged with a minor offence if a charge is not brought or there is an acquittal. For those charged but not convicted of a serious offence, fingerprints and samples are retained for three years, extendable to five. Samples from convicted adults are kept indefinitely.

German police collected DNA at the scene of six murders over a fifteen-year period, believing the same woman was responsible for each. Some 12 million euros were spent trying to track her down until they realized that the DNA came from an innocent worker at the factory making DNA swabs. The leading British mismatch case was that of Raymond Easton, arrested at home in Swindon for a burglary in Bolton on the basis of a DNA sample found at the scene that matched his on six points. Easton had late stage Parkinson's disease so advanced he could no longer walk. Police went ahead with prosecution. It was thrown out when the samples were compared at a further four points of identification and failed to match. New super-sensitive DNA techniques make such mistakes more likely. With Low Copy Number profiling a single cell is enough, rather than the previous 200, increasing risk of error. There are also concerns about how careful police are to minimize contamination. Frontline officers must avoid destroying or contaminating possible samples or allowing cross-contamination of traces from suspect and victim but solo first-responders can hardly avoid stanching a wound for risk of contamination.

Predictions about technology's future impact on policing are highly unreliable. One authority pronounced it 'science fiction to look to a time when police officers on patrol have a tiny camera or microphone in their hats or lapels' (Edwards 1999: 266). Police bodycam pilots began within five years. IT has undoubtedly facilitated frontline work but has not transformed it. For example, CCTV supplements calls from the public when dispatchers direct officers. This is not transformative, and its Achilles heel is the investment in operator effort; when 800 Met Police officers were assigned to review CCTV footage of the 2011 riots it was sustainable only for a day. Some predict that in the course of the twenty-first century people will increasingly be 'chipped' (Haggerty 2008), initially offenders and welfare recipients to discourage alcohol or drug abuse. Apart from criminal and terrorist surveillance, monitoring could enhance the safety of the vulnerable, but enforcement still relies on physical interventions.

The New Challenges of Law Enforcement and Order Maintenance

The twenty-first century has seen an increasing concern with police treatment of vulnerable people. Understandings of what constitutes vulnerability have widened, with associated legal changes, including broadening abuse, harassment, and assault to include verbal as well as physical forms. Occupying marginal positions in society has been recognized as a form of vulnerability, with police initiatives to engage 'hard to reach' groups. This does not mean that harsher attitudes do not endure. Politicians' rhetoric around 'workshy' claimants was followed by criminalizing trespass, and the Legal Aid, Sentencing and Punishment of Offenders Act made squatting in vacant residential premises punishable by imprisonment and fines up to £5,000.

A scandal illustrating the intersection of several contemporary concerns—vulnerability, community, ethnicity, childhood, sexual mores—was the 2014 child exploitation cases in Rotherham and Rochdale. In Rochdale, children in care homes, largely girls, were systematically sexually exploited over decades by men of Asian heritage. Girls aged thirteen or younger from dysfunctional families or with chaotic lifestyles were groomed. They received drink, drugs, and seemingly genuine affection from their 'boyfriend' but were then handed from one man to another for sexual purposes. This was often willingly entered into, and the girls persisted in regarding the men as friends and protectors. Some testified that the sex generally happened when they were not drunk or drugged. Frontline officers' role was to find and return the children to Social Services when care homes reported them missing; officers knew the areas they frequented and addresses used for sex. Rape of 'innocent' girls engendered vigorous response but 'scrubbers' were willing participants and of no interest, bar avoiding complaints that could cause publicity; children were returned to care homes when officers happened on them. Government had set a priority on community cohesion, and managers feared racism accusations. Publically acknowledging that the crimes were culture-specific risked breaching fair trial provisions under the Human Rights Act 1998 (Akhtur 2014). Social Services officials connived in avoiding complaints, suppressing at least one official inquiry, and ignoring appeals by parents who suspected the truth.

At Rotherham, 1,400 children were involved over ten years. The Jay Inquiry commissioned by Rotherham council found 'blatant' failures of political and police leadership, given growing evidence of the problem from 1997 onwards, notably when a Home Office researcher discovered what was happening. Council officials instructed her to redact her fieldnotes, declaring she had exceeded her brief. Her manager promised to act immediately. Nothing happened. The researcher's contract was not renewed. The director of Social Services subsequently became PCC. When exposed, the council said it had 'lost' reports of internal inquiries into the crimes and no other copies existed; disappearance of case files was attributed to a laptop theft but police found no signs of a break-in. Police and CPS procedures in place since 1998 were disregarded until 2007, when CSE became a force priority. Frontline officers adopted a child-centred approach and managers began coordinating with Social Services. When disclosure of information about child sex offenders in communities was piloted it 'sharpened up' child protection work by giving officers explicit guidance (Kemshall and Wood 2010) but guidance cannot guarantee appropriate action.

Domestic abuse

Domestic violence (DV) is a pervasive social ill, accounting for 15–20% of all arrests and victimizing 1.2 million females annually (Home Office 2013a). On average, a woman dies from it every five days in England and Wales. Moreover, virtually all 'honour' killings occur in domestic contexts; officially averaging about twelve annually, the likely number is much higher (HAC 2008). In 2013 a new definition of domestic violence lowered the age of victimization from eighteen to sixteen. The public puts domestic violence in its top three crime concerns, above burglary (ONS 2013). Experience of domestic violence (including threats), sexual victimization, or stalking is reported by 36% of people, but 13% of women and 9% of men a year suffer multiple attacks, severe injuries, and multiple forms of violence (Walby and Allen 2004). Women in low income households are three and a half times more likely to suffer domestic violence than those in middle income households (men are one and a half times more likely).

In 2014 the home secretary announced an imprisonable offence of 'coercive and controlling behaviour'; victims' charities said this was hard to prove and better enforcement was needed, not new laws. Only sixty-one people nationally were charged in the new law's first six months. Domestic Violence Protection Orders (DVPOs) were introduced in 2014 immediately barring offenders returning home or contacting the victim. Previously victims only received immediate protection if police charged perpetrators or time-consuming civil injunctions were obtained. DVPOs are followed by application to magistrates for protection orders barring return for between fourteen and twenty-eight days. A pilot study found DVPOs were viewed positively by police and victims, and reduced domestic violence (Home Office 2013b).

Like other domestic violence initiatives, protection orders rely on research long taken as conclusive, which found that mandatory arrest was the safest course of action when a partner used violence. Sherman's Minneapolis Domestic Violence Study found that mandatory arrest deterred repeat offending for an average of six months (Sherman and Berk 1984), leading most US States to adopt it for misdemeanour assaults (acts unlikely to cause serious injury). Sherman's later Milwaukee Domestic Violence Arrest Experiment raised doubts, finding that where abusers are poor, unemployed, and black, arrest increased recidivism (Sherman 1992). Problems delivering procedural justice were implicated (Paternoster et al 1997). Sherman et al (2002: 5) then concluded 'mandatory arrest laws ... are unwise and should be repealed'.

When Sherman later followed up women from the mandatory arrest experiments he found them disproportionately likely to die prematurely from post-traumatic stress disorder-related medical conditions (Sherman and Harris 2015). Those whose partners were jailed were 64% more likely to die young than those whose partners were not removed from the home; amongst African-Americans it was a remarkable 98%. Stress associated with long-term relationship problems is a causal factor in coronary heart disease and other life-threatening conditions.

In Britain mandatory arrest is unpopular with officers and complainants (Hoyle and Sanders 2000; Rowe 2007). Both want arrest decisions to rest with officer discretion. However, there are 'alarming and unacceptable weaknesses' in initial investigations, with a confused approach to arrest, and poor understanding of 'positive action' (HMIC 2013a). A third of victims said they felt no safer and some did not feel they were taken seriously or believed. Some officers lack knowledge, skills, and supervision. Under austerity, domestic abuse units were restructured and centralized, creating unsustainable workloads and removing support and supervision.

The amount and effect of training on responding to domestic abuse is inadequate. Initial training should emphasize DV being core business, with regular in-service training thereafter. Two-thirds of DV involves repeat victimization; CoP should disseminate case studies on targeting repeat perpetrators (Home Office 2013a). But established thinking and organizational imperatives obstruct change. For instance, effects of work to improve police understanding of LBGT people subside quickly, recreating vulnerability through churn (continual turnover of staff) and new priorities in a constantly changing organization (Moran 2007). LBGT groups cannot even compile accurate lists of liaison officers due to transfers and the role being an unfunded add-on. Six years after each London borough was required to have a liaison officer, police call-handlers had no knowledge of them (ibid: 423). Officers' own problems negotiating gender, race, and sexual orientation, and limited personal experience of discrimination, obstruct support for people with protected characteristics (Dick et al 2014). HMIC inspections on public protection, domestic abuse, and child sexual exploitation indicate that training has not yet delivered a significant and sustained change in practice.

Mental illness and learning difficulties

Police treatment of the mentally ill or learning-disabled is a longstanding concern, but has latterly been taken more seriously. Police spend 15–25% of their time dealing with people with mental health problems. Some mental illnesses increase tendency to violent resistance to arrest (Mulvey and White 2014), and numbers of mentally disordered offenders classed as 'restricted patients' receiving supervised treatment in the community have risen from 499 in 2008 (MoJ Statistical Bulletin 1/09) to 5,218 in 2013 (Health and Social Care Information Centre 2013), but police are not automatically notified. Of 1,052 such patients discharged between 1999 and 2005, only 7% reoffended, but 2% committed violent and/or sexual offences and 1% committed grave crimes.

With an average two and a half hours spent dealing with each call involving the mentally ill, police often request other agencies' assistance but seldom receive it (Short et al 2014). The 2014 Crisis Care Concordat committed the signatories to police custody never being used in the event that mental health services were unavailable, and to police vehicles not being used to transfer patients to hospitals. Both practices continue. In 2014 mental health nurses were placed in police stations, initially in ten force areas, to identify mentally ill/learning-disabled people and advise police and call-handlers. National roll-out was promised but even the pilots were understaffed.

Only 37% of officers have received training on Autism Spectrum Disorder (ASD), just 42% are satisfied with their interactional competence with sufferers—a view shared by people with ASD—and both agree that training tailored to specific police roles is needed (Crane et al 2016). A large fraction of people who regularly interact with police have functional difficulties with speech, language, and communication (Bryan 2004). Half of incarcerated young offenders score significantly below acceptable standards in speech and language competence, such that it obstructs rehabilitation (Bryan et al 2007; Snow and Powell 2011). There is no clear training route for such understandings to reach frontline police.

Organized crime

Organized crime changes character over time, reflecting the opportunities afforded by contemporary commerce and demand for illegal services. Thus, target-hardening and improved security have reduced armed robbery but new opportunities have grown up around people trafficking (Hobbs 2013). During 2012 there were 2,255 known victims of human trafficking, up 9% on 2011, comprising 1,607 adults, 549 children and 99 age-unknown (ECPAT 2014). Sexual exploitation (35%) and labour exploitation (23%) were most prevalent. Two were trafficked for organ harvesting. The Home Office piloted providing accommodation and support for trafficked females while they decided whether to assist authorities. Not one arrest or prosecution resulted. Tensions flared around the different brief of police and immigration officers (Taylor 2006). Funding made no allowance for investigative time. The initiative was abandoned. Beyond established missing persons procedures, training and resources are sparse (Webb and Burrows 2009).

The public does not see organized criminality in terms of specific offences; it thinks any crime can be 'organized' (Bullock et al 2009). The public adds extortion, protection rackets, counterfeiting, and paedophile rings to the crimes HMIC considers 'organized'. Organized crime groups are more opportunistic and function more chaotically than the Mafia stereotype (Hopkins and Tilley 2011). In only 2% (thirteen cases) of non-terrorist homicides was a group with a recognizable structure involved, being better characterized as gangs. The pattern of typical victims being males aged 18–29 is even stronger in homicides linked to organized crime and a far higher proportion of victims and suspects are black. Local organized crime chiefly involves gang activity and drug supply (Home Office 2011b), where problem-oriented, community, and hot spots policing all out-perform traditional reactive detection (in that order; Wheller 2013; Braga 2007). A number of forces lack trained officers to address gang and gun crime (HMIC 2010a).

Community Policing

Critics who dismiss Community Policing (CP), seeing CP officers as 'empty holster guys' (Skogan 2008), are ignorant of its history. CP emerged following research showing that increasing police resources could not stop crime rising. 'Police needed a public that would notify them of crime, identify likely suspects, undertake self-protection, and mobilise informal opinion against potential law breakers' (Bayley 2008: 13). Police in Flint, Michigan, instituted what later became known as Community Policing. Robert Trojanowicz's programme there was promulgated to senior police and policymakers in 'Executive Sessions' at Harvard between 1985–1988 whose principles were (a) CP aims to control crime; (b) public engagement is a mechanism, not the objective; (c) CP is research-based.

Critics argue that CP is simply a circumlocution obscuring the reality of officers' authority to discharge non-negotiable coercive force (Klockars 1988), or that its principal function is legitimation, particularly after policing scandals (Waddington 1999). Where the public is accustomed to harsh policing, CP media campaigns, symbolized by posters of smiling police, cannot overcome enculturated distrust (Akarsu 2014). Underlying the elusive nature of Community Policing is the elusive meaning of 'community'. It is a 'free-floating signifier' (McLaughlin 1994), an idea of 'extreme vagueness' (Pease 1994) that is at once the site of governance, the mode of governance, and the intended effect of governance (Clarke 2002). Others see CP as a process in which police and partners selectively mobilize discourse that makes government resources flow (Schofield 2002). Its potential for 'democratization of security' is matched by one for 'a politics of nativist vengeance and moralizing authoritarian communitarianism' (Hughes and Rowe 2007). Cultivating local responsiveness can encourage obnoxious sentiments like Islamophobia or counter-productive policies targeting teenagers and minorities (Loader 2005).

The conceptual cross-currents are muddied by the proliferation of agencies involved, each with specific axes to grind. Each receives and regurgitates 'community' differently, leaving partner agencies talking past each other. Community safety partnership agencies negotiate their own politics, creating conflicting representations of communities deeming the same neighbourhood both 'unitary' and 'diverse' (Hughes and Rowe 2007: 323), making partnership work a slippery task for officers. The proliferation of auxiliaries—Specials, Police Community Support Officers (PCSOs), wardens, municipal staff, private security, citizen volunteers—regressively focuses actual officers on crime fighting (ibid: 325), vitiating training's emphasis on community. Neighbourhood Policing units increasingly carry bulk crime investigation responsibilities diverting them from cultivating community safety initiatives (ibid: 332). NP beats are enlarged beyond the plausibly local. National priorities displace local ones in response to contingencies like new forms of terrorism. Despite Home Office rhetoric, training does not prepare police to be 'community leaders'.

CP presents four main challenges: delayering the organization (cutting across hierarchies); professionalization (increasing frontline discretion to act as problem-solvers), democratization (securing public engagement and multi-agency partnerships), and service integration (aligning with other agencies' briefs) (Mastrofski 1998). It involves 'problem resolution, innovative resource deployment, risk management, downward delegation of authority ... participative management and client consultation' (RCMP 1992: 1).

It is unlikely that any force can deliver every element, but there is evidence that delivering even one can help. Take attuning CP to local events. A neighbourhood's horror at its first drive-by multiple murder afforded opportunities to improve community self-policing capacities (Carr 2005). Police helped residents develop responses ranging from shutting down a problem bar to campaigning against a condominium development and mounting a campaign to replace the corrupt governing body of a local school. A 'new parochialism' was promoted, selectively combining police and resident efforts. Instead of a whole-neighbourhood focus, Carr advocates supporting neighbourhood-based organizations representing the law-abiding. A UK innovation uses Neighbourhood Policing to foster restorative justice conferencing for petty crime and ASB, with dedicated Youth Intervention/ Youth Offending Teams liaising with relevant partners. Child arrests fell 59% between 2008 and 2013 by such means (Howard League 2014).

Crime and Disorder Reduction Partnerships involving police and local authorities conduct casework with drug users, hotspot initiatives like better lighting and CCTV, and provide crime prevention advice. Perhaps their principal contribution is information exchange about the community impact of offenders and their characteristics (e.g. family background, school exclusion, and whether they are vulnerable). Despite problems sharing data (Audit Commission 2008), partnership working can be effective (Berry et al 2011) and is supported by participating officers provided it has a pragmatic approach (O'Neill and McCarthy 2014). Officers who support partnership work also support offender reintegration (Kim et al 2013).

Public support and role

Police and public assessments of local crime and order problems, strategies, and CP, differ (Liederbach et al 2008). The public rates the importance of peacekeeping significantly higher than do police (Redshaw et al 1995). Fort Worth, Texas, had a strong, long-established CP orientation, including Neighbourhood Policing and a 2,600 citizen volunteer patrol. Citizens assigned more importance than police to ten of fifteen community problems, including disorder problems like unsupervised juveniles, public drunkenness, neighbourhood appearance, and homeless people. Officers saw law enforcement problems as more important. Citizens viewed CP as more important, with significantly higher importance for Neighbourhood Policing, citizen patrol, and mobile CP 'stations' (effective against high crime levels in very localized areas like single apartment blocks; Torres and Vogel 2001). There were no differences amongst officers by gender, age, rank, or experience, but minority officers were even less supportive of NP than white officers. Citizens were significantly more likely to believe that improving police/community relationships was important.

Citizens rate different CP activities discriminatingly. Investigating gangs and performing drug sweeps are prioritized highly, with little importance attached to neighbourhood clean-ups, removing graffiti, and abandoned cars (Webb and Katz 1997). Low ratings for removing abandoned cars and graffiti challenge a central feature of 'broken windows' logic. Unexpectedly, those with lower education rate these preventive CP activities more highly, suggesting the issue is not one of communicating the logic. Lower education correlates with poor housing, so the higher ratings may reflect immediacy of gang/drug problems and impatience to clean up neighbourhoods so it impacts on crime/disorder.

Delving into community ratings of neighbourhood problems suggests that while there is a measure of consensus across communities, there is significant disagreement amongst sub-groups about problem seriousness and solution utility (Bohm et al 2000). After all, the world would be a one-party State if every community agreed on appropriate policy. Bohm et al's sample site had one of the highest serious crime rates in the region, rampant with prostitution, drug houses, open sewers, absentee landlords, and a nearby prison steadily releasing ex-inmates into the mix. There was broad consensus about the area's problems, but significant disagreements about their seriousness. Not one of twenty-three social problems received a majority rating; dissensus was profound. The problems coming closest were drug dealing (43%) and bad area reputation (42%). However, officers shared consensus, with majority ratings (in order) being drug use and dealing (100%), robbery, prostitution, resident criminals, absentee landlords, abandoned houses. As to CP solutions, there was no strong agreement attracting a majority of residents; the highest was 50% agreement about demolishing crack houses. Nevertheless there was relative consensus on improving police services (bike patrols, building a local police station, more police, zero tolerance); community involvement in crime prevention; and more responsive politicians. Residents were much more optimistic about the community's ability to help itself; for instance, 96% said residents would take action if crack was being sold nearby but only 33% of police thought so.

A sensible focus for problem-definition is how perceptions of CP relate to crime fear. CP inhibits fear by improving perceived quality of life. While vulnerability does not affect this relationship between CP and crime fear, perceived disorder and dissatisfaction with quality of life in one's neighbourhood significantly increase crime fear (Roh and Oliver 2005). The higher the awareness of CP the less the perception of disorder and an unsatisfactory neighbourhood. Awareness of CP also increases satisfaction with police (Scheider et al 2003).

While a community policing approach is seen as an impetus towards professionalization (Burruss and Giblin 2014), organizational backing and frontline officer attitude are crucial. Full implementation of the Chicago Alternative Policing (CAP) programme, one of the most comprehensive CP programmes ever mounted, was hindered by officer resistance and a shift in organizational priorities, occasioned partly by cost and a new political administration (Graziano et al 2014). CAP's 'beat meetings' initially delivered real gains in police/public relationships and reduced physical and social disorder. However, the required resources displaced analysis of information from citizens, reducing effectiveness in problem-solving. CP increases public expectations and, without extra provision, takes resources from other functions (Kumar 2014). Drivers of actual citizen participation in CP are more focused and instrumental than crime fear and social cohesion (Randol and Gaffney 2014). Victimization, and esteem for local police, drive citizen participation, motivated by solving problems of immediate concern. Where police are unresponsive, support for vigilantism rises (Haas and de Keijser 2014).

Table 3.1 Responses to question 'Neighbourhood Policing is not "real policing"'

	%	N
Strongly Agree	3.3	76
Agree	8.4	194
Neither Agree nor Disagree	18.2	421
Disagree	46.4	1075
Strongly Disagree	23.8	551
	100	2317

Source: Metropolitan Police (2015) Cultural Analysis Survey, London: Metropolitan Police.

Some 70% of London police broadly favour Neighbourhood Policing (see Table 3.1). Gender and role affect ratings, with female officers, NP team members, and higher-ranking officers more favourable (Fenn 2016). Positive attitudes toward serving the public, openness to citizen involvement, and perceived organizational justice, had a direct positive influence on officers' attitudes towards Neighbourhood Policing as 'real' policing. The stronger their orientation to law enforcement the lower their orientation to NP.

Effectiveness

'High dosage' deterrence-based, sharply focused CP significantly reduces violent crime, while low/no dosage controls see no change (McGarrell et al 2010). The Humberside high visibility patrol experiment focused on personal robbery and alcohol-related disorder, with increased police/community engagement (Jones and Tilley 2004). High visibility patrols maintaining community engagement included extra public order patrols at weekends and continuing foot patrol to 10pm. Personal robbery fell 16% compared to a 5% increase across the force and 15% increase nationally.

However, obstacles are numerous, including officers cynically exploiting enhanced discretion. New York's C-POP (Community Patrol Officer Program) officers 'discovered' they were most needed 9–5 Mondays to Fridays (McElroy et al 1993). In a town granting CP officers flexible shifts and permission to take patrol cars home, CP officers said other officers 'really hate us' (Skogan 2008: 25). In Colombia senior officers see CP's emphasis on frontline discretion and community as threatening their power (Vasquez 2012). Across Latin America high turnover in ministers of the interior undermines CP and citizens customarily shun police (Fruhling 2012; Ungar and Arias 2012). Only the most conservative respond to community engagement, pressing for harsh crackdowns resulting in human rights abuses.

Conflict/transitional societies like Northern Ireland and South Africa (Ellison et al 2012) and post-communist European countries (Brogden and Nijhar 2005) are harsh ground for CP. Brogden and Nijhar cite myths of CP including: community; local accountability; professional use of discretion to solve problems; public support; promotion of informal social control; and CP creating organizational change. However, some of these assertions are contentious. The Japanese 'koban' system—emphasizing informal social control by relatives and neighbours—can certainly have an oppressive edge, but Brogden and Nijhar underplay cultural difference, which leads Japanese youths to accept interventions that Western youths might resist. Britons consider benefit to themselves when evaluating CP whereas South Koreans see CP as extending their commitment to the community (Choi and Lee 2016). Brogden and Nijhar's analysis of post-conflict and 'failed' societies relies on shallow evidence, contradicting their call for sensitivity to local history. Despite the challenges, Latin America has successes, particularly CP training collaborations with universities; graduates are agents promoting change. Civilian police staff are also advocates for CP (Ungar and Arias 2012). Using NGOs as go-between for police and community, exploiting their ties from working with the disadvantaged, has promise elsewhere. Brogden and Nijhar's theme that CP cannot help divided and deprived communities neglects evidence that even in the most disadvantaged communities some residents and businesses cooperate (Carr 2005).

Seeing CP as not 'real policing' contradicts extensive research on 'police vigour', the inclination to make arrests. CP officers are no more 'soft' (nor 'hard') than response officers. Tests of the influence of situational and community variables find that assignment to CP has no significant effect on arrest decisions (Novak et al 2002). An area's deprivation and population composition are not factors. Rather, the highly localized beat-level crime rate shapes arrest decisions and persistence of investigation (Sobol et al 2013). Because the strongest predictor of resident-perceived crime is violent crime in their immediate locale (Hipp 2013), officers are responding to what worries citizens most. Both CP and response officers respond most firmly where crime problems are significant. Local knowledge developed by officers extends their repertoire of techniques for managing disorder (Wood et al 2014). Using intelligence from community engagement to 'tune' interventions itself engenders public confidence and perceived well-being (Lowe and Innes 2012).

'Service-oriented' policing featuring visible patrol, community engagement, problem-solving and procedural fairness increases and sustains public confidence (Myhill and Quinton 2010). Societal differences in receptiveness to CP suggest tasks for training. French recruits are trained to understand policing as a dangerous job in an unfriendly, mistrustful environment (Cassan 2010). In contrast, values emphasizing communication as a core resource, and using force only as last resort, feature amongst Dutch and British officers. French training includes 'tips' like parking away from addresses to which one has been called lest a washing machine is dropped on the car from above, and characterizations such as 'relationship with the public? (laughter). It's non-existent!' When CP—'*police de proximite*'—was introduced its main tool was local public safety contracts following collaborative community safety audits. Commentators declared that, unlike 'passing fashion or the type of liberal thinking which underpins community and other types of neighbourhood policing', the French initiatives would endure because citizens were desperate for them (Monjardet 2000). But CP was hastily abandoned due to officer resistance, few applicants (despite 'day job' hours), and belief that a more open approach would increase reported crime, making police look less effective. There was no training for CP and communication skills were not recruitment criteria.

Goldstein's (1979) 'Problem-Oriented Policing' influences many constructions of CP. It involves: focus on problems of public concern; making effectiveness the main consideration; being proactive; starting by systematic, rigorous inquiry; fully using files and colleagues' experiences; grouping similar incidents together to identify the underlying problem; avoiding too broad a grouping; pursuing imaginative ('uninhibited') solutions; acknowledging policing's limitations; weighing differing interests when assessing solutions; readiness to take risks (Eck and Spelman 1987). It helps if officers regularly get input from community members, adopt an observant, discriminating approach, and work with partner agencies (Tilley and Scott 2012), bringing measurable gains in perceived empowerment of local publics and perceived effectiveness against crime (Turley et al 2012; Sozer and Merlo 2013). Dealing with underlying problems creates efficiencies, yet officers cite inescapable demands that continue while POP avenues are being explored, thus seeing POP as additional workload.

Neighbourhood Policing has a statistically significant impact on crime, public perceptions of police effectiveness against crime and disorder, perceived safety and public confidence in police (Tuffin et al 2006). In pilots of NP, ratings of local police as doing an excellent or good job rose 15% (against 3% in control sites), with significantly improved perceptions of police engagement. Evidence for NP causing these effects included the public accurately identifying targeted problems (e.g. less graffiti and vandalism), with no change in untargeted crimes. Regular foot patrol, street briefings, and 'have a say days', were all well-received. NP was launched nationally in 2005, again seeing particular gains in public confidence (Quinton and Morris 2009). Officer visibility rose (Table 3.2). There were positive changes at BCU level but not whole-force level, because implementation varied (Mason 2009; HMIC 2009d), as did public participation

Table 3.2 How often people saw a police foot patrol

Percentage of Responses	2006/07	2008/09	2010/11
More than once a day	2	3	4
About once a day	6	8	10
About once a week	18	22	25
About once a month	13	15	16
Less than once a month	22	21	19
Never	40	31	25

Source: Office for National Statistics (2014) *Public Perceptions of the Police and Police Visibility*, London: ONS.

(Bullock and Leeney 2013) and staffing levels (Casey 2008). Staffing fell under austerity.

Challenge for training

An irony of CP is that 'the "community" in "community policing" seldom includes officers themselves' (Sklansky and Marks 2008: 2). Against officers having a 'collective, deliberative voice' in CP, managers expect the frontline to raise complaints, not useful insights, and detectives fear losing power (Bayley 2008: 14). Managers believe frontline misconduct is more likely than rising crime to cost them their jobs (Skogan 2008). Yet Toronto Police successfully used cross-rank committees to evaluate and improve community policing (Bayley 2008). Where criminal intelligence and 'results' are forthcoming officers no longer see CP as career-limiting (O'Neill 2014).

Community policing places considerable burdens on junior officers: to engage with diverse communities and tailor responses to their problems, manage PCSOs, and develop interagency partnerships. They must do so with limited guidance. Since close supervision is infrequent, initial training is critical. It remains a prime site for learning skills of negotiation, cultural sensitivity, knowledge of social structures, analytical problem-solving, and project management skills. CP's crime prevention element requires knowledge of local demographics; crime trends, patterns, and *modus operandi*; and transferable solutions. Under austerity the trend is towards innovations like online community policing. Openness to such innovations is most strongly related to officers' support for real world CP (Bossler and Holt 2013).

Partnership work requires interpersonal competence, especially in dealing with those whose relationship with police is provisional or conflictual. Frontline officers need training that equips them for coordinating peers and specialists, and external parties. Carrying colleagues is as much a challenge as carrying the community. Communication skills alone are insufficient. In New York's CPOP, most officers were young in service and it was the compulsory first posting after police academy. Their indecisiveness disquieted both public and managers (Henry 1996). In Britain new officers who feel rule-bound, policy-driven and performance-measured are reluctant to use their discretion

(Brain 2009). Where managers reaffirm the value of discretion, an example being 'community resolution' encouraging officers to use their judgement in straightforward cases involving children and youths, restorative approaches prevail over arrests (Howard League 2014). Training must equip recruits to take independent approaches, with less reliance on supervisors. Given a crowded training curriculum, in-service training is also needed, via self-paced learning modules, distance learning, and trainer briefings when officers parade for duty.

When asked how to control crime more effectively, frontline officers spontaneously suggest CP components—enlisting public cooperation, addressing policing to local problems, encouraging community self-protection, and resolving petty disorder before it escalates (Bayley 2008: 13). Appropriate recruit selection, and training emphasizing communicative/interpersonal skills, are not the only factors in securing good CP. Commanders must secure strategic collaborations with local government and community activists, and provide continuity of commitment despite senior manager turnover (Wilson 2006).

Good CP requires dedicated resources, especially human resources (Fielding 1995), its successes can be hard to measure (Fielding and Innes 2006), and it is easily derailed by short-term demands (Fielding 2009b). However, the 'reassurance gap' that preoccupied senior officers in the mid-2000s suggests that if Neighbourhood Policing falters, the public will demand an equivalent. CP may indeed represent governance 'through' community, but when citizens are brought into the process there is scope to make ruling a more reflexive activity.

The turn of a century is often seen as a time for taking stock and for innovation. In law enforcement there was much talk of 'Twenty-first Century Policing' as a radical new departure but the irony is that police forces deepened their embrace of twentieth century 'modern management' based on Fordist principles of uniform service delivery and the strong leadership of the Chief Executive Officer. The epitome of the delusion that policing can be modelled on a management style developed for factory-based businesses was the principal structural reform of recent years, the imposition of Police and Crime Commissioners, a hybrid of the American city mayor and elected police chief grafted onto an entirely different constitution. Accompanying this ill-considered innovation was a managerialist agenda every one of whose main elements flickered briefly before fizzling out. So it was with the enthusiasm for Key Performance Indicators and annual targets that soon became so choking that a single supreme target was set before becoming lost in the confusion caused by the experiment with PCCs, finally disappearing altogether behind the cloak of austerity. Managers and politicians' fervour for force amalgamations likewise dwindled as the lessons of the Scottish move to a single force wafted South. 'Modern management' favours the technical fix. In policing this saw Taser use mushroom, the acquisition of never-to-be-used water cannon, and a flush of enthusiasm for body-worn cameras whose effects were as contested as any other panacea.

If the lesson of all this innovation is that policing remains policing no matter what the shock of the new, the same is true of the 'new' challenges of policing in the twenty-first century. Two of the major contemporary preoccupations—domestic abuse, and dealing with the vulnerable mentally-ill or learning-disabled—are 'discovered' social problems that, shamefully, have existed throughout policing's history, and a third, 'organized crime', is for the most part a good example of Yablonsky's 'near-group', opportunistic in the crime committed and as systematically-organized as a broken bottle. The conceit that the turn of a century is an instigator of change masks the enduring realities of policing and is well-represented by a final illusion, that community policing is an innovation, when it is actually what every right-thinking citizen has always described when asked what policing they desire. Policing is a stubborn social institution that shakes off froth in its daily performance, but both that and the pernicious effects of political interference and managerialist fads have inevitably marked understandings of police professionalism and, as we shall see, how to train for it.

4

The Contemporary Training System

Until recently the British police maintained a long tradition of requiring all entrants to undergo the same training and initial experience of basic policework. Now the taught element is delivered by a variety of 'providers', while newly-imposed 'direct entry' to the senior ranks has undermined common experience of the frontline. For many, the most tangible common experience is attachment with a tutor constable, not classroom training. Given direct entry and dissimilar 'pre-join' pathways, initial field experience and training may not retain their large place in an occupational culture that puts much emphasis on shared values and 'all being in this together'.

History of Training

Early in Peel's New Police, training was minimal. Having sworn an oath given by parish constables since the Middle Ages, recruits received top hat, frockcoat, baton, and cutlass, starting work the next day (Critchley 1978: 145). Instruction for London recruits comprised advice from senior constables and sergeants, two weeks of Drill and Sword Exercise, 'two lectures by a superintendent and considerable legal material to learn by rote' (Emsley 1996: 206), then a week patrolling with an experienced constable. Training rose to five weeks by 1890. Peel House, the first training school, opened in 1907. By 1920 training lasted ten weeks, featuring drill and rote learning of law, procedures, and regulations, but also first aid, self-defence, and report-writing. Later use of simulations was presaged by staging mock accidents (Emsley 1996: 206).

In the provinces nineteenth and early twentieth century training was on the job, with some borough forces arranging reading, writing, and arithmetic lessons by local teachers.

Professionalizing the Police: The Unfulfilled Promise of Police Training. Nigel G. Fielding Published 2018 by Oxford University Press

Elsewhere chiefs exhorted recruits to study the Police Manual at least thirty minutes a day (Emsley 1996: 207). The diligent kept notes about cases and applicable law for future reference. Published provision was popular where training was sparse. In the early twentieth century colleges offered correspondence courses for police. Sheffield's Bennet College advertised itself in the *Police Review* as 'the Policeman's University', and a nearby competitor was 'the Policeman's College' (Murrell-Abery 2003). Despite the Desborough Committee's recommendation not all forces appointed a training officer. Between the World Wars, training schools were established by six larger forces, also taking recruits from smaller ones.

By the 1930s all recruits underwent formal training before operational posting. Training's structure and content varied greatly, from systematic and comprehensive in the Met to cursory and basic in some provincial forces. Few small forces had their own programmes or training officers. Recruits often went straight to the beat, receiving training later, sometimes just ten days long. The Met's twelve-week programme was two-thirds legal/procedural rote instruction, one-third drill, self-defence and first aid. Recruits' heads were shaved. Fierce discipline encouraged submissiveness and discouraged individuality (Weinberger 1995: 28). Three new legal definitions were to be memorized nightly, up to the required 180. The first underscored the recruit's place: 'Law, as defined by Blackstone, is a rule of action prescribed by a superior which an inferior is bound to obey' (quoted in Weinberger 1995: 28).

Drill was less militarily oriented—recruits were not trained in assault—but featured self-defence, giving traffic signals, and the 'slow march', a gait commanding respect on patrol. Recruits looked to experienced constables, sergeants being remote and privileged. Arrest league tables were openly kept in cities; elsewhere, kudos lay in absence of break-ins, disorder, or traffic congestion. Constables who were subjected to assault were expected to handle it themselves; offenders could be beaten, but not charged. Officers learned to gauge how long arresting a drunk at the end of a night shift would take compared to the coveted automatic four hours' allowance for appearing at court the next day; if the calculation was adverse, the drunk was pushed over the divisional boundary.

Beats had 'fixed points' where constables must be at set times when sergeants might attend; citizens thus knew where to find police. The nineteenth century police/population ratio was 1:1,000 (1:700 in cities), 1:670 between the wars, 1:540 in the 1960s. From 1932, cars, telephone, and radio increasingly featured. Sub-divisions rather than beats became the administrative unit, shifting supervision from sergeants to inspectors, and mixing beatwork and patrols to make it harder for villains to anticipate police whereabouts. Police boxes (telephone booths) replaced fixed points, with officers calling supervisors rather than being visited; however, in 1933, 200 urban and 2,500 rural stations had no telephone. It was the car, not the telephone, that saw off classic beat policing. Cars began draining frontline capacity before the Second World War, not to reform frontline policing but to address motoring offences.

From 1948, an innovation from Aberdeen spread. Beats were pooled. Men divided into teams, each supported by cars. Teams could police their divisional area as they saw fit. Officers liked escaping the monotony of beat patrol and getting more crime action. It also saved manpower, appealing to managers. This initiated the move away from Rowan and Mayne's foundational emphasis on prevention and deterrence. The inevitable conclusion came in Kirby (Liverpool) in 1965. Foot patrol ceased, replaced by continuous patrol using cars with radios. Instead of their own initiative and local knowledge, officers were directed from HQ.

After the Second World War regional training schools and a national college for higher ranks' in-service training were established. Recruits attended Induction, then ten weeks' Initial Training Course at a district training centre (DTC), followed by short courses including Legal Procedures, and attachments with a tutor constable on the beat and other operational settings. At eighteen months the Continuation Course was taken at a district training centre. From the 1970s the approach to police training in England and Wales stemmed from a 1970 Home Office Working Party whose recommendations the Police Training Council accepted in 1973, but recruits still alternated formal (classroom) training with informal (experiential) training in postings, and forces still set curricula.

Recruit training 1983–2003

Up to the early 1970s training curricula had remained substantially the same for decades. Despite classes on 'Community Relations', 'Social Studies', and 'Public Relations', concern that training fell short regarding relations with minorities and community-sensitive policing led to a review (Police Training Council 1983) which resulted in major curriculum reform (MacDonald et al 1987). A thirty-one-week Modular Training Programme was proposed, elevating 'enabled learning' over instruction, and a core curriculum of research-based case studies of common policing situations to inform workshop/project sessions, bringing 'the street' to the classroom in a more exacting way than the war stories of instructors and lessening the division between classroom and experiential learning. The Modular Foundation Course inaugurated in 1989 was a diluted version of the proposal but was still resisted by trainers and senior officers who rejected the idea of the professional officer as a 'reflective practitioner' (Schon 1972). The student-centred approach threatened trainers' established practices—largely, the formal lecture—and troubled chiefs trained under the old system. Facilities enshrined that system, with school-type classrooms, parade grounds, and barracks accommodation suited to administering doses of training in remote locations isolated from communities. The fifteen-week regional centre residential course inhibited recruitment of those with family commitments (Centrex 2003: 9).

Given trainers' vehement rejection of MacDonald's model (described by one as 'a downright travesty in relation to how we work in the Service'; quoted in Murrell-Abery 2003: 57), the National Director of Police Training commissioned a review to 'make the necessary adjustments to the Probationer Training Programme'. It lengthened the curriculum to 'include subjects relating to policing matters'; formalized and structured the assessments; reintroduced rote learning of law and teaching to the test; allowed force training schools to offer training that 'reflected local needs' (Bray et al 1996). Thus, the first attempt to introduce adult learning to police training was stifled after seven years. As we will see, contemporary attempts to revive an adult learning approach have foundered as did MacDonald's model, not least because forces cannot provide the support required for adult learners as reflective practitioners.

By 2000 the strategic management of probationer training could best be described as unwieldy, despite a major review. 'Managing Learning' (HMIC 1999) advocated themes that were to become familiar: emphasis on lifelong learning, national standards for each rank and role, moving away from 'traditional classroom-based training provision', and 'professionalism'. Surveying every regional centre, it found that 'training is not properly targeted at those whose need is greatest; much of it is duplicated, poorly costed and not managed within a tight performance and accountability framework'. With about 6,000 recruits joining annually, force-level training 'result[ed] in expensive waste'.

At the time, 87% of training was by forces, the rest via regional centres, National Police Training (NPT), the Crime Prevention College, and external providers. None were linked, stakeholders were diffuse, NPT did not represent forces (which regarded NPT's curriculum as unaccountable), and training took too long responding to new legislation or policy (Home Office 1998b). A revised probationer training programme introduced in 1998 took forty-three months to implement. The steering group was 'ineffective' (ibid: 16), with confusion over who led it.

Forces varied in training policies and cherry-picked from the national training offer. NPT's director had no power to direct forces in any aspect of training; chiefs could ignore the training NPT designed. Force training was operating in its own cocoon. Most training departments 'acted as both "client" and "provider"' (ibid: 23), deciding for themselves what the force needed. By 1999 forces increasingly designed and delivered their own training, due to speed relative to NPT, accredited college provision, and an internal market enabled by financial freedoms under the Police and Magistrates' Court Act 1994. Forces began 'amending' NPT training that supposedly set national standards (HMIC 1999: 27). Tutor constable, sergeant, and custody officer training thus varied between one and fifteen days and refresher training largely disappeared. A third of sergeant training, and 17% of detective training, deviated from prescribed curricula. The Police Complaints Authority (1998) condemned custody officer training. Police Authorities were denied input to local training strategies (COLPA 1996).

Rampant localism undermined due diligence over the cost of training, with national provision running below optimum capacity. After forces failed to follow the prescribed method for calculating training costs the Home Office abandoned central data collection in 1993. Some forces stopped collecting data, others created their own system with different definitions. Fourteen could not even calculate direct training costs. Not one could fully calculate associated costs. The Committee of Local Police Authorities (1996) estimated that training and staff development accounted for 8% of total police budget, circa £500 million, but very large ranges featured in even the best estimates (HMIC 1999).

There was no agreement about how much training police needed annually. Forces varied in priority assigned to training, and could not agree what skills given roles required. Training budgets were not ring-fenced and were often first casualties of cuts. One force had eighty-eight different training budget holders. Some allocated training by demand until budgets were exhausted rather than by priorities. Many did not monitor classroom and/or accommodation utilization rates. Accommodation utilization was as low as 35%, averaging 67%. NPT's own budget was historical and unrelated to contemporary training need. Places on NPT training were allocated historically without assessing a force's circumstances. Some went without, obliging local provision. There was little consultation, notice, or flexibility over timetabling, so NPT places often went vacant or were filled by substitutes in irrelevant roles. Non-attendance was 20%, with high drop out. When chiefs gained power to set staffing against budget, extreme fluctuations occurred in recruit numbers so NPT could neither gauge the training staff requirement nor efficiently use facilities. Satellite sites had to be sourced ad hoc and without allowance in NPT's budget (Home Office 1998a), a serious problem since 60% of NPT business was recruit training. NPT's own sites could not accurately cost course delivery, lacked utilization data, and had no performance measurement (Audit Commission 1998). During the 1990s only nineteen forces measured trainer/student contact time, and only seventeen measured trainer/student ratio. Training did not declare explicit objectives and was seldom evaluated. In one force the officer responsible for course evaluations said he had boxes of them that 'don't go anywhere' (HMIC 1999: 109). Evaluation was weak at both force-level and NPT-level.

This was the context for HMIC's (1999) 'Managing Learning' initiative on common minimum standards within a national competency framework. It required 'professional standards'—expected performance by role and level—and 'educational standards'—accredited attainment markers like diplomas or degrees (Adler 1999). In 1997 the Association of Chief Police Officers (ACPO) and National Police Training (NPT) had developed a role-based competency framework using recommendations from working parties of officers from twenty-seven forces. Forces could develop local training provided it met common minimum standards and the national competency framework. Uncoordinated force-specific training could be squelched by providing better national curricula with input from forces. Local amendments could then be confined to enhancing core content. Consistency would facilitate transfers across forces and raise the status of trained staff. NPT gave way to Centrex, the Central Police Training and Development Authority, in 2001. Centrex authorized in-force recruit training.

HMIC's first comprehensive inspection of probationer training (HMIC 2002) was not reassuring. The learning requirement was obsolete and the means of meeting it were ineffective. Management lines were unclear. Training delivery was inconsistent and lacked quality assurance (the training role was often seen as 'a negative career move'; HMIC 2002: 78). Training in diversity remained deficient, including working with diverse colleagues. The tutor constable system was 'fragile': supervision was ineffective, selection criteria were lacking, and some were 'coerced' into taking the role (ibid: 80). Training varied from ten days to three, many tutors lacked investigative interview or diversity training, and the Centrex tutors course went unused. Probationers themselves sometimes 'trained' their tutor constable in new procedures (ibid: 81). Shortages were common, causing burn-out from taking probationers consecutively. Tutors and probationers were dragooned to frontline deployments, undermining learning from attachments and public safety when probationers worked unsupervised. Supervisors seldom received training for supervising and assessing probationers, leaving supervisor entries blank in Personal Development Plans and supervisor/probationer tutorials non-existent.

The uncoordinated, under-managed training system suffered overcrowded classrooms. Force training establishments were dirty and dilapidated. Indeed, after HMIC's report, stopgap measures were required to avoid prosecution under health and safety law. Placing drill at the outset of training infantilized recruits; boot camp routines undermined academic components. 'It is hard to see how [officers] can be inculcated with a readiness to exercise ... informed discretion when [they] are being barked at, marched about and treated like recalcitrant children' (Toch 2008: 63). The military style 'Passing Out Parade' coming at the end of the residential phase rather than the end of probation underlined the separation of classroom and on-the-job training. Exclusionary language and inappropriate conduct were extensive. Probationers from minority backgrounds were apprehensive on entering the police environment, but lacked support from trainers, tutor constables, and supervisors. Many recruits concluded probation with significant developmental needs. The assessment system was easily bypassed. Sometimes attainment was 'barely adequate'.

HMIC attributed the problems to failure at the highest level, chiefly the Police Training Council (PTC). Despite its constitution requiring biannual meetings it did not meet once between 2000 and mid-2002; one core committee did not meet for four years. Issues with major impact on training, such as training for auxiliaries, were discussed by the Executive but never forwarded to full council. Proliferating subcommittees blurred terms of reference and responsibilities. Subcommittee minutes from 1995 to 2000 reveal complacency, members believing no major service delivery failure was directly attributable to probationer training. The PTC Executive Committee dissolved itself in 2002.

Police training on both sides of the Atlantic underwent significant reform in the early twenty-first century, prioritizing the community role in response to public concern over the growing remoteness of police from communities. Radical change in the culture of police training was imperative. HMIC concluded that 'the current (probationer) programme is not wholly fit for purpose now, nor to support the police service of the 21st century'. DTCs ceased recruit and detective training in 2003, the year that saw undercover journalist Mark Daly expose everyday racism at a DTC. When District Training Centres closed training devolved to forces. Some still ran joint training centres. Centrex licensed these despite HMIC's damning assessment. Some forces gave recruits instructional materials while others did not, some refused to use nationally-provided materials, lesson lengths varied between forces, and trainers' calibre varied. Some classes had the same two instructors throughout while others had over twenty. A fundamental review of initial training in 2003 (Elliot and Kushner 2003) was the basis of contemporary standardized foundation training with national standards and a centrally-set syllabus.

'Managing Learning' (1999) and 'Training Matters' (2002) had been comprehensive, considered exercises in mapping a systematic approach to training, but were coloured by HMIC's centralizing agenda, forces slipping the noose by exploiting chiefs' new budgetary authority, and regular change at the top, with the National Policing Improvement Agency (NPIA) superseding Centrex in 2007. Ultimately HMIC, NPT, Centrex and NPIA presided over a fudge, a semi-managed, semi-market system of training and development. However, HMIC's reviews did engineer the move to a national competency framework and common minimum standards, which made explicit what was required of the competent officer. None of the organizations could guarantee uniform achievement of standards, but a baseline was a start. As we shall see, this did not mean the new system delivered an effective remedy, not least because it replicated the previous system's lack of systematic evaluation and monitoring.

IPLDP

With Labour's Crime Fighting Fund pouring in recruits from 2000, the Home Office had hurriedly reformed design and delivery of probationer training. Its Initial Police Learning and Development Programme (IPLDP) aimed to increase community engagement, strengthen accountability, and modernize the workforce (Home Office 2004a). It was to be tailored to force characteristics and needs but with accountability through national standards, accreditation, and quality assurance via the new Learning Requirement (Table 4.1). The Learning Requirement 'catered for individual learning styles and abilities' (ibid) and 'promoted professional excellence and ethical behaviour' (ibid). It was designed as a change instrument, defining forms of interaction and critical reflection through which recruits, trainers, and forces could secure legitimacy. 'The Student Officer is to both act competently and also learn something beyond the ingredients of immediate competence'. This corresponded with Glenn et al's logic and spoke to the service's yearning to be taken as a profession.

Table 4.1 Learning Requirement

The Learning Requirement:
* reflects the policing skills and competence rooted in established work-systems and anticipates new demands
* defines forms of interaction through which recruits, trainers and the Service can uphold law, instill community confidence and reflect critically on interactions.
* The Student Officer is to both act competently and also learn something beyond the ingredients of immediate competence.

Source: Home Office (2004) *IPLDP: Guidance for Chief Officers*, London: Home Office.

With the benefit of hindsight these provisions can be seen as rehearsing a system of fuller contracting out. We may consider IPLDP a halfway house between complete ownership and substantial divestment. Parts could be contracted to colleges or other providers, with NPIA administering funding. Force 'Professional Development Units' coordinated field tutors and assessors. Forces could collaborate with other forces, with NPIA, or deliver IPLDP solo. NPIA recommended a maximum trainer-to-recruit ratio of 1:16, and 1:1 with tutor constables in initial patrol experience.

During their first two years recruits undertake IPLDP, working towards the Diploma in Policing, with classroom training reducing in year 2. Much content is delivered through 'blended learning packages' via the National Centre for Applied Learning Technologies (NCALT) website. The Level 3 Diploma developed by NPIA and Skills for Justice replaced Level 3 NVQs in Policing as the national minimum qualification from 2010 and is administered through Ofqual's Qualification Credit Framework. The Diploma in Policing became the minimum mandatory requirement to join forces as a constable. Diplomas focus on IPLDP curriculum elements requiring accreditation. A Certificate in Knowledge of Policing is evidence of having satisfied the knowledge component of the Diploma.

IPLDP combines formal training (lectures, seminars, workshops and practicals), tutored patrol, and assessment of independent patrol, and is sharply differentiated from Police Community Support Officer (PCSO) and Special Constable training (Table 4.2). IPLDP starts with trainer-led sessions, followed by posting to Basic Command Unit and tutor constable. Case studies are used for group projects. Classroom learning is assessed by

Table 4.2 Initial Police Learning

Student type	Programme name	Description
Police constables	Initial Police Learning and Development Programme (IPLDP)	A two-year programme with approximately 35 weeks of supporting learning materials. Mandatory qualification: Diploma in Policing.
Police community support officers	PCSO National Learning Programme	Approximately 10 weeks of direct learning, normally completed over a period of six to 12 months. Non-mandatory qualification: Certificate in Policing.
Special constables	Initial Learning for the Special Constabulary (IL4SC)	Approximately 3.5 weeks of direct learning taken over varying timescales. This programme takes student officers to a point where they are fit for accompanied patrol. No formal qualification.

The National Curriculum for each programme is presented through learning outcomes contained in module specifications/descriptors. Forces can choose to use the national materials, locally developed materials or a blend of national and local to meet the outcomes of the programmes. Support, advice and guidance through the initial programmes is provided locally through force trainers, operational tutors, operational line managers and supervisors.

Source: Home Office (2004) *IPLDP: Guidance for Chief Officers*, London: Home Office.

essays, exams, learning contracts, and project work. The original twenty-three National Occupational Standards (NOS) grouped into twenty-two learning modules were later condensed into ten National Standards. They are periodically supplemented; in 2009 there were new NOSs on Criminal Investigation and Police Searches, Critical Incident Management, and Public Order.

IPLDP Phase 1 lasts three to five weeks, covering First Aid, Officer Safety (including 'safe interaction with the public'), Health and Safety Training, Professional Standards, Race and Diversity, basic technology applications, and Social/Community issues. Phase 2 introduces legislation concerning Community Safety Partnerships, along with local policing delivery and how police can impact upon community concerns. Recruits have a two–three week community placement in settings where conflict is not expected. Phase 3 provides the bulk of training on law, policy, and guidelines, with some local optionality. Real-life community situations are emphasized over in-depth legal knowledge in modules like Patrol, Theft, Burglary, Public Safety, Roads Policing, Neighbourhood Policing. Phase 3 concludes with declaration of fitness for Independent Patrol, which in turn concludes with 'Confirmation of Appointment'. Despite HMIC opposition recruits are attested on appointment and given full police powers. In Phase 4 recruits are expected to use the regular working environment to achieve competence. Protected learning time equivalent to thirty days is allowed. Performance evidence is included in a Student Officer Learning and Assessment Portfolio and assessed against National Occupational Standards and the Learning Requirement.

'Race and diversity' is intended as a 'golden thread' running throughout the curriculum, particularly placements, with a minimum of eighty hours' learning about community expectations and diversity of gender, age, disability, sexual orientation, and religion/belief. Placements should feature diverse groups—specifically ethnic minorities—but also reflect community composition, often mostly white. Different forces' standards for assessing community-based IPLDP components are undocumented. Beyond placements, community input extends no further than the Volunteer Witness Scheme, where citizens act as mock witnesses for student officers, uptake being such that few recruits experience it. The large role designated for Community Beat Managers to impart partnership work in Phase 1 has fallen victim to pressures on Neighbourhood Policing (NP). Since trainers struggle even to find suitable and willing community speakers one must question the aspiration to place recruits in grassroots community organizations, let alone such organizations contributing to training materials, as the Home Office desired. Some forces resist probationers taking their first posting in an NP role, with chiefs declaring 'we don't put junior or inexperienced constables into neighbourhood roles because they have got to take responsibility in the community … [O]ur junior officers join response teams' (quoted in *Surrey Advertiser* 7 February 2014).

Schools, hospitals, and charities predominate in community engagement placements. It is uncertain what aspects of community such placements can reveal. Understanding diverse groups is meant to spark reflection on recruits' own attitudes, informing coursework (Heslop 2011b). Placements in schools, community centres, or hospitals partly reflect recruits having powers of arrest without knowing how to use them, but the need for 'safe' environments (conveniently not needing supervision) restricts exposure to community tensions. In the second year of training recruits take a 'more challenging' placement with hard-to-reach community groups (Home Office 2001c). Heslop's sample responded positively to the first ('safe') placement, for example, reporting 'intense experiences' working for four days with Drug Dependency Unit (DDU) clients. Given the expectation of confronting one's own attitudes, a recruit whose sister was an addict thought she would learn little at a DDU but after asking an addict if he wanted children and hearing him say he must first conquer his addiction, she realized she had assumed that addicts were amoral (Heslop 2011b: 335). However, after seven months she had largely forgotten the experience. Her revelation about stereotyping occurred in an environment 'completely alien to how she might interact with drug users in her "real" working life' with addicts swearing and spitting at her.

Brief placements early in training may be well-timed to challenge attitudes, but not to affect operational work. Telling experiences may occur in a four-day placement, but the flow of incidents on a busy shift is such that what may yield a telling insight if reflected upon passes in a blur. The blur of work that does not permit reflection is the locus of acquiring the police role, and those with whom one shares it shape one's views more than any short placement. Moreover, placements need to emphasize things useful in operational work. A recruit first placed in a Jewish community centre, with his second placement a Drugs Intervention Programme (DIP), wryly observed that he had still not encountered a call demanding knowledge of Judaism, but he now policed an area with drug crime and the DIP placement was useful—' "on my second community placement I was thinking about policing" ' (Heslop 2011b: 338). Community placements have a supplementary utilitarian role but are unlikely to instil awareness that one's values are neither universal nor diminished by recognizing those of others.

IPLDP has been subject of little research or evaluation beyond debates on developing links between training and higher education (HE) providers (Peace 2006; Wood and Tong 2009). When IPLDP was introduced it did not include an evaluation programme. Curriculum like unarmed defensive tactics, and first aid, went unvalidated. Across 190 modules, only one concerns crime prevention (HMIC 2012c). The Adult Learning Inspectorate (2005) evaluated IPLDP after its first year. IPLDP was introduced too quickly, with inadequate lead time to develop learning materials. Trainers, tutor constables, and supervisors were not fully trained and started the programme in confusion. Problems included quality assurance, and measuring effectiveness. Aims to tailor learning to individual needs were not satisfied (ibid: 3). There were no procedures for remedial work. Assessment protocols gave insufficient guidance on standards and trainers did not understand them. There were no procedures ensuring consistent experience across placements. Forces' budgetary provision for training was inadequate, particularly for assessment. Guidelines for Personal Development Portfolios were 'ineffective and inconsistent'. Students were not exposed to the full range of policing experiences. Value for Money was elusive because operational targets did not accommodate IPLDP. Supervisory support for tutors was inadequate because they did not grasp IPLDP. Many tutors moved to other postings without replacement. Staff/student ratios were high and increasing. Despite original commitments to chiefs (Centrex 2003: 9) there was no accreditation of prior learning or experience, so no means for early specialization. Students were ill-prepared for simulations, and left to apply complex theories to practice without preparation. The NOS were inadequate to instil Community Policing (CP) competencies. If CP really is to be a 'golden thread' binding training, placements must be more diverse and assessment of recruit engagement must be more systematic.

The Adult Learning Inspectorate (ALI) evaluation presciently identified several enduring issues. Accommodating individual learning needs, effective assessment protocols, criteria to facilitate comparison of experience between placements, budget pressure robbing from training and tutoring, incomplete or non-existent supervisor input to PDPs, misalignment of performance measures and IPLDP learning, and neglect of Accreditation of Prior Experiential Learning (APEL) all remain pressure points. Further, positive recruit views on cultural awareness, equality and diversity training fade quickly, with ALI reporting 'disparity between the ... problem-solving/neighbourhood approach of community engagement ... and the accepted culture of short-term targets for reducing crime through arrest' (ALI 2005: 12).

'Vastly different' commitment to training was an early sign of problems that simply adopting National Standards struggles to solve. The assessment protocol is regularly violated, with inconsistencies between forces, and students waiting months for their marks. Some lack study space or equipment. Daily de-briefing quality, and consistency between assessors, stand unchecked. Student performance goes unobserved, and competency assessments in learning plans are completed by students themselves rather than tutors/supervisors. Progress towards NOS goes unmonitored, without guidance on developing portfolios, leaving many ignorant about writing the reflective statements required by their learning plans (Alcott 2012). Training begins without formal learning needs assessments, so plans are based on self-declared needs or idiosyncratic tutor observations. Community placements are a surprise for which some are unprepared. Recruits are daunted by university-type essay requirements, dislike wearing uniform, and do not expect residential training. Bad probationary experience is a resignation risk factor. Of those who resign 42% said training failed to meet their expectations (Cooper and Ingram 2004: 18); failure of training to meet expectations accounted for 68% of those who resigned while still probationers, and 40% found their tutor constable 'worse than expected' (ibid: 19).

Similar problems mark training internationally. Despite 90% of US police agencies reporting incorporation of CP by 2000, the San Jose training model, developed before CP existed, remains in widespread use (Chappell 2007). US field training thus remains focused on law enforcement. The model does include 'human skills and communication skills' that could capture dealings with a diverse community, but Field Training Officers (FTOs) complete forms on the same tenets by which they themselves were evaluated as rookies (ibid: 500). Attempts to update the model to reflect CP have failed due to the 'subcultural preference toward traditional policing', with FTOs emphasizing the mechanics of arrest, handling police vehicles, and armaments. The more recent Police Training Officer Program (the 'Reno Model'), specifically designed to accommodate CP, is based on an adult learning approach but formal evaluations and daily 'narratives' by Reno FTOs feature radio and dispatch, attitude, driving and parking, geography, officer safety, policies and procedure, assertiveness and investigation skills, with little or no discussion of CP or racial/

ethnic sensitivity. Across reports on sixty-five recruits Chappell found three mentions of CP, the longest being twenty-two words (ibid: 498). 'Decision making' relates largely to 'parking tactically' and investigative procedure, with scant attention to problem solving. There is much evidence of FTOs hammering 'strong officer presence' (ibid: 507). 'Instructed to be more aggressive and take control' was one note. FTOs did not advise how to temper such qualities or attune demeanour to citizen response.

All training programmes evolve, and IPLDP now stands in the different circumstances of a pre-qualifying system. Skills for Justice, which promotes better criminal justice standards, reduced the 'burdensome' assessment package in 2009 (Skills for Justice 2009), although community placements continue as before. By 2017 Skills for Justice no longer listed policing amongst the fields it supported, showing the logo of the obsolete ACPO on its legacy Police Standards pages, and fifty of its police role profiles were being rewritten by the College of Policing (CoP). Tellingly, evaluations of the quality of service delivered by those trained under IPLDP find no difference to non-IPLDP colleagues (Alcott 2012). Complaints alleging discrimination still relate substantially to deficient training in diversity (IPCC 2014a). Because the next major change in police training was motivated by fiscal crisis, we will never conclusively know how well the system operating from 2005 to 2011 worked.

The Neyroud Review 2010

In 2010 the new Coalition Government set out its police reform agenda (Home Office 2010). The big ideas were elected Police and Crime Commissioners (PCCs) and replacing national targets with PCC's local Crime and Disorder Plans. Significantly for training, NPIA was to be phased out. The essential context was recession. While officials spoke of a new 'golden thread'—connecting local, national, and international policing—the real ligature was fiscal constraint. The Conservative-led administration was not just out to control the cost of policing but to reduce police numbers, curtail perquisites, and impose bottom drawer civil service pet projects, like annual fitness tests. Eventually recruitment freezes became general, but not before policing's mix of local, regional, and national governance created a period of confused uncertainty, with some forces honouring offers made, others reneging, and differences between forces in how half-completed training was treated.

To Peter Neyroud, NPIA director and former Thames Valley Police chief, fell the task of reconciling the professionalism agenda with the demand for police to 'do more with less'. The underlying principles of his fundamental review of how professional standards could be advanced were familiar icons of public sector management. Policing was to be 'democratically accountable', 'evidence-based', 'nationally and internationally coherent' (counterbalancing Westminster's accent on localism), and 'capable, competent and cost effective' (Neyroud 2010). Drawing on research literature on leadership and training, the creation of a Police Professional Body (PPB) was the Review's first pillar, others being 'Building Professional Development', 'Developing Senior and Strategic Leadership', and 'Delivery of Leadership and Training'. The chartered PPB would set national standards, qualification frameworks, and training approaches. It would simplify standards by retaining only the 'really important ones and jettisoning what has become a welter of unnecessary and bureaucratic guidance' (Neyroud 2010: 11). ACPO had turned against NPIA guidance, and Neyroud's PPB featured an Executive Board with non-police members, and a Council of Chief Constables without ACPO's 'convoluted' governance structure (ibid: 16).

Under IPLDP there had been a considerable overhaul of the curriculum, substantial moves toward standardization, and cautious but tangible roles for mainstream further and higher education institutions. The qualifiers in the previous sentence ('considerable', 'moves toward', 'cautious but tangible') reflect the evolutionary nature of the changes. The Neyroud Review was a sharp contrast. It proposed that would-be constables would obtain a new Police Initial Qualification *before* being attested. It would be prerequisite for membership of the professional body. Routes would include coming from other occupations or having 'high quality degrees'. In-force classroom training would go. Instead, at their own expense and risk, would-be entrants would seek tertiary qualifications. Simultaneous service as Special Constables would 'reinforc[e] the public service ethos' (i.e. unpaid labour). Forces would commission delivery of qualifications from PPB-accredited providers. Commissioning most training and curtailing in-force training promised large savings on facilities and staff.

Despite fanciful reference to 'the post-industrial globalised 21st century' making geographical policing, and its accompanying culture, obsolete (ibid: 20), the Review largely focused on baseline training for territorially-based frontline officers. The Review's 'guiding principles' were resolutely domestic and offered proposals characteristic of Westminster understandings of professionalism and how to achieve it. If not actually parochial, it gave limited attention to other systems of training. The main comparator was not international police training but English nurse education.

The account of professional status was surprisingly thin: 'a police career is still viewed as more challenging than most. This long-held assumption supports a professional approach to leadership development and training in the police' (Neyroud 2010: 31). Naturally, a definitive interpretation of professionalism was not the central objective. The assumption was probably that its meaning and value were obvious. However, what one might expect of a review that sweeps away established training and its supporting practice guidance would be a systematic, thorough evaluation of research evidence on what constitutes good training. The *words* 'systematic' and 'evidence base' appear, but the Review relied on 'Rapid Evidence Assessment' (REA), essentially a pressured literature review using narrow search terms. The Review provided no account of how the synthesis of evidence was done (e.g. how contradictory findings were resolved).

Five REAs were used: 'What works in leadership development', 'What makes a great police leader', 'What works in training and development approaches', 'What works to change professionals' behaviour', and 'What works to implement guidance'. One suspects the terms in which these titles are couched says something about their sophistication, a view reinforced by the conclusion that 'great police leaders change their style to fit the task at hand', which does not seem altogether revelatory. In fact NPIA had already done the two leadership REAs, so the Review's original evidence amounted to three REAs conducted in six weeks all told.

What does the 'What works in training and development approaches' REA tell us? It found that 'the evidence base on effective training was very limited across all sectors' (Wheller and Morris 2010), which may surprise education researchers. Drawing largely on healthcare and teaching, the REA found that training integrated with practice is more effective than pure classroom instruction (per Van Maanen 1973 and Fielding 1988b), 'simulation training' is promising (following MacDonald et al 1987); and that peer syndicates assist learning (following Becker et al 1961). While the REAs did not produce anything *wrong*, they did not offer anything *new*. Nor can REAs offer anything more robust than regurgitating the literature. Moreover, they are silent on professionalism—what it consists of, how to impart it, and why it is better than the status quo. The Review itself noted that training already included practices that fared well in the REAs, like simulation and scenario-based learning. While sincere and substantial, the Review's inescapable context was recession and an administration questing to take on the police. Despite its policy significance, it did not provide new insights into whether training worked or why its reforms were improvements.

One should not perhaps have expected more. In a turbulent policy environment it was pragmatic to float the professional body idea and let others craft it subject to sentiment. Thus 'a professional body, in the right form, would provide … clearer standards, a service-owned qualification framework, greater focus on professional development … and a more productive relationship with other providers' (Neyroud 2010: 45). What 'the right form' might be remained sketchy. Broadly it would have 'an inclusive membership across the police service' (to practice, officers would have to be members; Neyroud 2010: 47) and 'independence' while 'accountable to government' (ibid: 48), ideally with a Royal Charter. Retirees could hold membership; their tendency to reappear as civilian staff or training consultants would continue.

Presently, no police service in the world has the status of a chartered profession. Chartered bodies can litigate, regulate service delivery, and enjoy powers analogous to those of companies. The PPB's Independent Strategic Board contained police staff associations, HMIC and NCA, an unusual construction of 'independence'. PCCs plainly had an interest in standards, hence their place in the PPB's Executive. However, government strongly favoured preserving the operational independence of the office of constable. Neyroud was anxious to reflect this by keeping the PPB separate from local democracy. Local government had no representation on the Executive Board. The channel for the PCC interest would be an Independent Scrutiny Board chaired by a PCC and advising the Executive. Like the US Police Executive Research Forum (which has a 'member at large' seat for non-US citizens), Neyroud wanted international representation on the Executive. In practice the PCC interest is served by having a PCC on the Board, and there is no international member.

The Review concluded with a financial analysis. The most conservative estimated saving on 2009/10 costs was £40.1 million and the largest was £530.7 million where all forces opted for the full pre-entry model. In the 'pre-employment' model, students enrol on a fee-paying degree course and are not police employees, getting practical experience as Special Constables. After graduation they apply to forces without guarantee of acceptance. Under the 'post-employment' model, recruits complete a foundation degree incorporating the IPLDP and National Occupational Standards but funded by a force. Despite parliamentary criticism of the former system's ambiguity over whether NPIA guidance was binding on chiefs, Neyroud conceded a 'comply or explain' framework allowing chiefs a 'locally defined approach'. Chiefs are only required to have due regard for Authorized Professional Practice when included in a Code of Practice. They also decide what qualification to require—a tertiary qualification, police qualification, or experience as a PCSO, Special, or police staff (Home Office Circular 001/2014).

Contemporary recruit training and Continuing Professional Development (CPD)

The move to individualized pre-qualifying training coincided with setting up the College of Policing. It seeks to maintain the hallmark of the centralized system, that all are trained to the same standard under a nationally approved curriculum. On standards and training CoP is also responsible for non-territorial forces like the British Transport Police.

Prior to the pre-qualifying system a scheme linking the study of criminology with police training had been launched, providing the knowledge component of IPLDP. CoP emulated this with the Certificate in Knowledge of Policing (CKP) in 2013. By 2014 there were sixty approved CKP providers, thirteen being universities. Chief constables decide whether to require recruits to have the CKP. The Met requires that candidates complete all other recruitment processes first. Qualifying training often involves former officers. For instance, the director of Education Support Associates Ltd, which trains in the Police Law and Community curriculum, formerly led a force's Learning and Development unit. After completing CKP, would-be recruits undergo interviews including role-play scenarios at CoP's national assessment centre. There is considerable attrition despite progressing through pre-join training because recruits lack practical understanding of working conditions.

Around eight HE institutions offer two-year foundation degrees in policing. Curricula mirror IPLDP with some topics in more depth. A foundation degree reduces initial training from twenty weeks to three. Since students pay fees and subsistence, pre-join training costs forces far less. For example, 600 foundation degree graduates produced by Cumbria University and University of Central Lancashire between 2008 and 2013 saved forces £10 million (Robinson 2013).

Requiring recruits to have undergraduate degrees customarily alarms some, although Essex Police first sent selected officers to the University of Essex in the 1960s. When New Labour mooted it the Police Federation chair responded 'police officers needed to be practical rather than academic' (*Sunday Telegraph* 13 September 2009). Expressing similar scepticism, the first officer to head an Oxbridge college (her alma mater) said 'some people believe that you can't have an education and common sense ... Our police officers are best off with both. That's not to say it should become an exclusively graduate-entry profession' (*Times Higher Education* 24 November 2016). An experienced constable did not find his Management degree necessary, albeit useful in paperwork and IT. When first posted he 'had to learn how to talk to people simply and effectively, with fewer of the long words and padding out needed in essays, and I had to learn when talking wasn't working and I was going to need to use force' (Anonymous 2017: 28). In 2014 CoP's head of research dismissed any suggestion of making policing a degree-level profession, citing cost. In 2015 CoP announced that future officers must have degrees.

From 2020 all recruits in England and Wales must hold a degree either through an apprenticeship funded by the recruit's force, a specific policing degree 'as in other professions', or a graduate programme funded by the force (CoP 2016). The curriculum for the Higher Level Apprenticeship Scheme for police includes Evidence-Based Practice and research awareness, criminology and sociology. Announcement of the Police Education Qualifications Framework (PEQF) acknowledged that policing attracts people of all backgrounds, many of whom see it as a 'vocation', thus casting 'vocation' and 'profession' as distinct, if not actually counterposed (CoP 2016).

Despite headlines about a graduate force, the PEQF that emerged from consultation differed from initial proposals by emphasizing work-based learning as the route to attaining the education level for confirmation. Promotion criteria reflect this approach. Newly-promoted sergeants will take a twelve-month higher-level apprenticeship in leadership and management and not be confirmed until completion. A similar qualification applies to inspectors but at a higher standard. New superintendents will complete an MA/MSc 'apprenticeship'. Applicants for Assistant Chief Constable (ACC) must possess a Masters.

The PEQF means that recruits and those promoted mostly learn on the job. This may ease the issue of paying to qualify without guarantee of employment, but it further complicates the 'bitty' nature of the pre-join arrangements. Moreover, daily exigencies have always displaced both recruit training and CPD, and with ongoing austerity this is unlikely to improve. Participants will be at different stages at any one time, with variable competencies. The new system does nothing to resolve the issues of mentoring, progress monitoring, and supervisory input that plague IPLDP, and CoP must design new courses and convert variable experience into standardized accreditation levels.

Of 3,045 responses to CoP's PEQF consultation, 80% were officers. Only 46% favoured the new system, with 32% opposed and 21% undecided, but thirty-eight of fifty-two responses by 'organizations' (mostly forces) favoured it, with one force against and thirteen undecided. Since officers were more divided than forces PEQF may be contested. The only majority response (at 74%) was for accrediting existing experience, which suggests that three-quarters of officers, staff and auxiliaries only accept the system if it rubber-stamps what they already do. The fact that only 45% agreed there should be multiple routes into policing while fully 40% disagreed and 15% were undecided demonstrates the resilience of the belief in all starting with frontline constable experience. With CoP's Leadership Review floating the idea that 'in future some basic powers may be bestowed on ... [direct entrants] from day one of their careers' (CoP 2015: 33), and put against twenty-three out of twenty-six policing organizations favouring multiple entry points, one might forecast substantial friction between bosses and practitioners. As to the HE element, none of the fourteen universities responding to the consultation were research-led, which sits uncomfortably against the Evidence-Based Policing approach CoP says is its underpinning.

The value not only of initial training but of ongoing competency development has long been recognized (Kanter 1983). Research-led universities are more engaged in CPD for police than foundation degrees and CKP, for example, Liverpool, partnered with Merseyside Police, offers CPD on decision-making, criminal behaviour, police powers, public order, and gang crime. CoP favours structured, formal CPD. Decoding this, universities derive third stream income from CPD but 'formal CPD' requires independent, quality-assured assessments. Universities prefer CPD without the accreditation overhead. The revenue-bearing and 'accredited learning' elements of CPD are in tension.

Structural contradictions are not the only issue. Like initial training, the Achilles heel of CPD is its lack of integration with practice, in which the key agents are not the learners but their supervisors. Taylor (1911), the originator of 'scientific management', believed that most competencies were acquired by direct personal observation but inefficiencies occurred because supervisors/managers did not analyse the required competencies, despite job analysis beginning with Socrates (Primoff and Sidney 1988). Professional learning requires an interactive relationship between learner and object of study, in which the object of study can be modified, not just the learner. It recognizes the internal dimension in how practitioners construe competent practice but without discounting the importance of externalities (Bhaskar 1998; Fletcher 2017). While understandings of competence involving learning from predecessors are important, professional learning acknowledges that managerial evaluations and systematic evidence about given practices are also germane. If the agenda of the last fifty years of police training has been standardized national provision, those in charge have created a system that reinforces the idea that learning is something that is done to you rather than construing and supporting learning as a collaboration between learners, instructors, and supervisors.

A contested curriculum

While recession drove training to a 'recruit pays' approach, the Coalition's 'bonfire of the quangos' challenged the training curriculum and body of professional knowledge. Rather than reflecting professional complexity, there being 400+ items of NPIA 'doctrine' (guidance) in currency represented 'clutter' in the policing landscape. Even NPIA director Neyroud judged it of 'varying quality'. Proliferation and duplication reigned, e.g. six different firearms manuals. Moreover, doctrine is seldom evidence-based but a distillation of practice-based experience, a codification of what is seen as appropriate by curriculum-writing teams of officers and trainers. Thus, the police knowledge base largely reflects what police already do, not what research evaluates as effective. However, Neyroud's review was more exercised over doctrine's extent and the apparatus required to produce, approve and promulgate it. Participants had ninety-seven meetings a year and ten NPIA staff sat in meetings full-time (Neyroud 2010: 74). This issue diverted attention into streamlining the status quo.

Under the previous system, recruits' first year focus was training, with little availability for frontline duty. Here we see the appeal to a cash-strapped government of Neyroud's approach. Rather than the opportunity to go professional, it may have been increased availability for duty that attracted ministers. Moving to a 'recruit pays' model was not unproblematic. Some 65% of Neyroud's survey respondents were hostile, with comments like 'if you want the best people for the Job you have to invest in their training. Otherwise you will get people who can afford to fund their own progress over those better candidates who cannot' (quoted in Neyroud 2010: 84).

Neyroud's claim that pre-entry qualification has 'been recognised to ... widen participation and increase professionalism' and 'strengthen learning support and inclusion', lacked evidence. The Australian scheme cited included guaranteed police employment on qualification, unlike in England and Wales. The Review sought to resolve the jumble of central and local force training via the pre-entry qualification, capped by a 'national pre-join Police Initial Qualification'. Believing that this is a marker of professionalism equivalent to medicine and teaching confuses form with substance: one cannot practice medicine with a foundation degree.

Adopting a new system was an opportunity to end the exercise of the full powers of the office of constable by inexperienced probationers. Instead the Review 'encouraged a significant number of recruits [to] pre-qualify in independent patrol' (Neyroud 2010: 86). This rather contorted reference to Special Constable postings moves inexperienced frontline service to the period before normal attestation. Thus, the public is served by officers who are not only unqualified but have different levels of 'professional' knowledge. Neyroud was explicit that a principal benefit of the Special Constable element was 'a substantial increase in visible presence on the streets while the potential recruits are qualifying'. This author once gained entry to a sold-out music festival by donning a high visibility jacket, baseball cap and Dr Marten boots. That no more made me a security guard than the festival-goers who mistook me for one (the real curiosity was actual guards treating me as their superior). A 'visible presence on the streets' is not the same as knowing what to do when more than a clothes horse is required.

The Review struggled with fundamental questions about knowledge levels. Curriculum levels lurch from postgraduate degree to kindergarten. At one point it aims to raise constables' understanding of statistical meta-analysis to grasp 'What Works', at another it addresses 'numeracy [and] literacy'. Yet the Review included a blistering declaration that education providers must adopt a 'more employer-led approach to learning, to include scheduling of courses and assessment approaches', a retrograde take on professional education. Universities do not consult commissioning bodies about timetabling, and if the service wanted to discredit professional education from the outset a good way to do so was to interfere with assessment.

The declaration that 'the new world' will be 'one of national frameworks and local flexibility' (Neyroud 2010: 89) represented continuance of the local variation that dogged previous systems. Under the guise of 'suiting a range of life choices' no effort would be made to identify the right approach amongst part-time study, distance learning, or learning police-relevant knowledge within a wider qualification. The only exertion of consistency would be the national minimum standards. Training's deficiencies remain. HMIC (2013b) cited knowledge deficits in the legal basis for use of stop-and-search powers; skills in establishing and recording reasonable grounds for suspicion; how best to use powers to prevent and detect crime; and understanding the impact that such encounters have on community confidence and trust. Probationers practice on live case evidence files. Prosecutors find schedules of evidence and disclosure files commonly omit vital information, a longstanding problem (Plotnikoff and Woolfson 2002). Police themselves call for better training and guidance.

Developing one's beat is not taught in training. It can be done in frontline officer forums that review decisions and public complaints, involving rookies in debate about the meaning of good policing (Muir 2008) but a fractionated mix of pre-join classes and Special Constable assignments affords no such opportunity. Training's emphasis remains on exerting control and enforcement-based solutions, rather than interpersonal skills and how to deploy them (Graham with Karn 2013: 3). Given the many police interventions involving juveniles and young adults, training in interpersonal skills and competencies is obviously important (Engel et al 2012) but no training specifically addresses dealing with the 18–24-year olds. Both in IPLDP Mark I and IPLDP Plus there is little training in managing encounters with minorities or de-escalating conflict situations. Opportunities to learn how youth workers engage youth are lacking. Recruits dissatisfied with training and initial service cite being ill-prepared for interacting effectively with young adults.

Official exhortations about 'doing more with less' offer few grounds to expect improved basic competencies, let alone professionalism. Moreover, some see no need. An example was a Greater Manchester Police communication skills course; 600 frontline officers received fourteen hours' training in interacting with crime victims. One subgroup received an extra day involving role play actors whom they interviewed about a crime, with personalized feedback. The training improved politeness, body language, and attunement to differing norms of cooperativeness. Before-and-after surveys with officers and victims found victims were more satisfied with the trained officers, reflecting the procedural justice theme that fairness closely affects public cooperation (Jackson et al 2012a) and feelings of shared moral purposes (Jackson et al 2012b). However, the Taxpayers' Alliance lambasted the training, saying good manners and communication skills should be entry requirements.

Many will say policing's reality cannot be reproduced in classrooms. Thus, training customarily features operational postings.

If learning sessions and patrol experience are interleaved, realistic simulation and video stimulus material can prompt those encountering difficult circumstances to articulate what they have encountered such that other learners, and trainers, can use their own experience to suggest ways to learn from it. However, this is unlikely in a system where colleges and private businesses deliver the curriculum. They are unlikely to have capacity beyond teaching narrowly to NOS, and are likely to focus on price.

Training Needs Analysis (TNA) in professional education differentiates individual, workgroup, and organizational levels, which we might equate in evaluating police training to individual recruit, training programme, and community measures of effectiveness (Table 4.3). TNA encourages forces to consider links between roles and functions when setting training requirements and enables officers to self-assess competency development linked to organizational objectives. However, rich diagnostic competency matrices like Kent's, covering 700 roles, are little use if training does not mesh with rostering. The best case for TNA is wasted training. Blatant examples include training on topics for which

Table 4.3 Indicators and Measures for Evaluating Police Training

Individually focused
Complaints against probationers/early service officers by the public
Numbers of internal complaints
Retention rates
Rates of transfer to specialist functions
Absence due to work-related health problems
Numbers with post-secondary Further Education qualifications
Numbers with Higher Education qualifications
Training programme focused
Community input to training
Independent evaluation of Personal Development Plans
Community focused
Types of placements taken under IPLDP
Integration of placement learning into tutor constable attachment

Source: The Author.

there is no identified need; generic training not attuned to individual priorities; learned skills not used; and performing a role for years before training in it, potentially embedding poor practice. A driving course used an unmarked 'hot car' on country lanes but most participants drove marked diesels in cities. Two years' tutor constable training was given to officers never allocated probationers. A force trained over 100 officers in child protection but needed ten. Some 306 staff trained in an online crime information system never subsequently logged on.

The widely-used Kirkpatrick (1975) training evaluation model examines: Reaction—participant ratings of learning intervention; Learning—changes in knowledge, attitudes and skills; Behaviour—changes in job performance; and Results—changes in organizational effectiveness. But evaluations seldom attempt to measure changes in behaviour. Evaluators instead focus on 'effects' during training and at its close. The Home Office National Evaluation Strategy has a micro dimension to measure skill changes but it is demanding and forces continue to use Kirkpatrick. Training is evaluated on cost, and there is cultural resistance to evaluation (Gibson 2009).

Systematic training evaluation involves capturing structural and processual dimensions (Fielding 1988a, 2009a). The structure and organization of police training is inflected by wider socio-economic and political conditions such as austerity as much as is the process that recruits negotiate in developing a working personality within an incoherent semi-marketized system. Present prospects for the professionalizing project of the police confront uncongenial structures and processual obstacles.

Auxiliaries

Police Community Support Officers (PCSOs), the principal British police auxiliaries alongside Special Constables, were introduced under the Police Reform Act 2002. In 2015 there were 12,649, 45% being female and 9% Black and Minority Ethnic (BME), considerably larger proportions than police officers. Because the responsibility—and funding—for PCSOs was originally shared between forces and local authorities, troublesome organizational arrangements have been reflected in incoherent training arrangements. Formally, PCSOs are uniformed civilians employed by PCCs under chief constable direction.

Until PCCs were introduced they were funded by Home Office Neighbourhood Policing grants matched by forces, councils, and business. Now PCSO funding is included in overall police budgets. Public concern endures about variation in powers and uniform (NPIA 2008). From 2010 forces increasingly replaced PCSOs with regular officers, following public criticism of inadequate powers that varied between forces.

There is no set recruitment system but normally a fitness test and criminal record vetting. Training varies by force. The Met provides six weeks' training, elsewhere from four to eleven weeks. Training includes operating police radios, report writing, handling evidence, appearing in court, dealing with crime scenes, gathering intelligence, legal powers, race/diversity, human rights, use of force, self-defence, directing traffic, and first aid. There are written exams and class quizzes, a minimum five week posting with a 'tutor PCSO', and twelve months' probation. Before confirmation recruits must complete an NVQ. Original training was hastily prepared, with some relating to offences not yet legislated. Diversity training was too theoretical; scenario-based training was needed. Pre-course reading was 'impenetrable' (Johnston 2007). Most NOS for PCSOs are common with those for constables (Merritt 2007), yet PCSOs have no promotion structure, specialisms or overtime (Merritt 2009). High turnover matches weaknesses in training and supervision (Cooper 2006).

Standard powers include the right to confiscate alcohol in public places; issue fixed penalty notices for anti-social behaviour (ASB); and seize drugs. Discretionary powers include the right to detain people suspected of offences; issue fixed penalty notices for disorder and graffiti; search those suspected of carrying dangerous items; and stop cyclists without lights. Amongst concerns, removal from beatwork to cover other duties has joined poor training (*Police Foundation Newsletter* March 2014).

Initially, entry standards were lowered to boost numbers quickly (Johnston 2006). At joining, nine-tenths of PCSOs thought they were well supported but this fell to a third after a year, with worries over lack of safety training (Johnston 2007). Supervisors were plagued by disciplinary problems. PCSOs used racist language to other officers because they thought diversity training only applied when with the public. PCSOs were dissatisfied and bored with security patrolling (e.g. at rail stations). Only 10% of regular officers rated PCSO quality 'good'. PCSOs netted trivial offences, leaving regular officers following up things they formerly excused.

PCSOs should not be deployed where confrontation is likely, a high degree of discretion is required, or a high risk of harm to others applies (ACPO 2005). They can detain for thirty minutes awaiting a regular officer for any offence 'that appears to have caused injury, alarm or distress to any other person or to have caused loss of or any damage to any other person's property' (Merritt 2009: 388). However, there are no provisions for cautioning or other arrest procedures, including search, and it is unclear what happens if police exceed thirty minutes in responding. Force (including touching) can only be used if the local authority has approved. Detainees can simply walk away where this is not the case. The legal status of an admission of guilt to a PCSO is unclear. Identically-uniformed PCSOs from different forces may have fundamentally different powers. These variations, and limited training, engender public wariness when PCSOs are given main responsibility for NP, as in South Yorkshire. Regular officers afford considerably greater reassurance than PCSOs (Rowland and Coupe 2014). The important point for training is that for the police constable the community role is important but not exclusive, whereas for the PCSO the community role is their *raison d'être.*

Detective Training

Selection for CID represents horizontal mobility seen by many as a promotion. For much of the twentieth century detective training was entirely experiential. Understanding the criminal milieu was central (Hobbs 1988). Hierarchical rank relations did not prevail, but, under pressure to get confessions and detections, detectives were competitive, and did not easily share information. In-force training lasting twelve weeks focused on law rather than skills (Morgan 1990). Advanced investigative training was delivered centrally.

Preparation for criminal investigation occurs after pre-qualifying training. A National Investigators' Curriculum defines the learning requirement from Professionalising Investigation Programme (PIP) Level 1 (constable) to 4 (detective chief superintendent). Selected constables undergo six weeks' initial detective training for accreditation at PIP Level 2. Core Investigative

Doctrine for the initial detective curriculum involves a curriculum designed by practitioners and piloted with experienced officers. Lesson plans, learning objectives, trainers guide, and visual aids are issued to force training centres. Learning outcomes and resources are provided locally under license (NPIA 2010). Forces can provide local contextualization and market their programme to other forces. The rigour of licensing has been questioned, including the realistic risk of revocation.

The six weeks' Detective Training Centre programme largely duplicates material that junior detectives receive earlier in short courses, because their required portfolio of previous training experience is ignored. In some forces high volume topics like burglary, robbery, and even firearms are covered in a single afternoon. Few now want detective postings, boosting the workload of those who remain, and direct recruitment of detectives to make good the shortfall means that entrants who fail are a pure waste because they have no uniformed experience. Criminal law remains prime, with little on investigative skills, and where forces rely on CoP material tutors are not motivated to craft their own or draw on their own knowledge (Tong 2017).

PIP does improve investigative decision-making (Fahsing and Ask 2016). However, CoP has little affected senior detective training, with programme design and content changing little. A case study-based 'Senior Investigating Officers Development Programme' is delivered over three weeks, comprising a homicide investigation exploring practical, legal, managerial, and diversity issues. This is followed by a one-week course using HYDRA, an immersive distance learning system. Successful completion leads to PIP Level 3 accreditation. Prospective child abuse investigators take a specialized two-week programme. Despite a well-developed national curriculum, many junior detectives and even trainers are not aware of the principal guidance or how to source it (Fox 2013). The Murder Investigation Manual was last revised in 2012. There is an insidious but widespread concern that guidance could be used against officers in court if lawyers show they deviated from it.

A principal resource for investigative interviewing techniques is the Home Office 'PEACE' model (Planning/preparation (P); Engage/explain (E); Account (A); Closure (C); Evaluation (E) (Clarke and Milne 2001), involving cognitive interviewing and 'conversation management', which emphasizes active listening to stimulate recall (Shepherd and Griffiths 2013; Koehnken et al 1999). PEACE features facilitative, balanced opening questions, periodic summaries, explanation of legal considerations, rapport building, open questions, and avoidance of leading. Good interviews display depth, structure (eliciting accounts in logical sequences), opportunities for free recall, and minimal interruption (Clarke and Milne 2001: 56). Fullness of accounts is criterial.

In practice, the elicitation and construction of confessions, effects of participant awareness of being recorded, and the leverage suspects and interviewers seek from using laughter are prominent (Carter 2011). 'Utterances ... of no benefit to the suspect can be used by officers to secure the admissibility of the interview as evidence, claims to knowledge that contradict the suspect's version ... can yield a confession, and laughter can be used ... to circumvent rules' (Carter 2011: 1). 'Minimization' avoids realistic words to describe the crime (semantically distancing suspects from involvement), proffers rationalizations for committing the crime, and obscures the consequences of confessing (ibid: 139–41). Much of this contradicts approved techniques and training.

None of those recently completing Tier 1 IPLDP interview training apply the full Cognitive Interviewing procedure, suggesting it is too complex for early training (Dando et al 2009). Experienced investigative interviewers deviate from guidance because they believe they know what constitutes key evidence (Krahenbuhl 2009; Cederborg et al 2013). There is a highly significant positive correlation between perceived effectiveness of techniques and frequency of use (Oldershaw 2013); least used were 'change perspective techniques' (telling what was witnessed from another's perspective) and 'temporal order' (telling stories backwards). The more experienced the investigator the less responsive to training encouraging open questioning (Powell et al 2014), enabling legal challenges over non-neutral or oppressive questioning. Officers investigating child abuse use closed questions for: suspect identity; meaning of terms children used to describe genitals; whether penetration occurred; suspects' intent/motives; timing/location of abuse (Guadagno et al 2013). Approved techniques and training are supplanted by the needs of case-making.

They are also supplanted by changes in case-making itself. Criminal investigation is increasingly 'anticipatory' (not reactive to incidents); 'actuarial' (using statistical risk prediction);

'bureaucratic' (with set resource allocation); and 'intrusive' (using surveillance and technologies) (Mac Giollabhui et al 2016). Surveillance employs covert observation and methods of deception. These approaches conflict with core principles of frontline policing and with the emphasis of training. Since detective tradecraft involves restricting access to information and working in rigidly-divided, mutually-exclusive units, direct entry to the detective role, initiated by the Met in 2017, denies investigators a grounding in policing's core values, threatens accountability, and challenges democratic police professionalism.

Supervisor and Management Training

The national police college for in-service training of higher ranks founded after the Second World War had a Special Course for accelerated promotion. A Senior Staff Course for middle-ranking officers aiming for senior rank was introduced in 1962, a training programme for command officers in 1965, and a Fellowship Scheme in 1979. Senior rank cannot be held without attending the Senior Command Course, and promotion regulations prescribe the Accelerated Promotion Course. Dissatisfaction with this training is regularly expressed. There was no training needs analysis and the programme went unevaluated for many years.

CoP's 2015 review of leadership training commended a more collective model of leadership and conceded that training in 'soft' skills vital to leadership is often first to cut in hard times. Leadership was a prime issue in 'establishing the elements of a formal profession' (CoP 2015: 7). Subordinate officers model their behaviour on supervisor priorities and expectations (Engel and Peterson 2014). Sergeants who prefer crime fighting and emergency service impart such views by their tone in making and following-up assignments. In change programmes like Chicago's CAPS, sergeants' scepticism about public collaboration in problem-solving was a serious obstacle, tainting frontline officers (Toch 2008). The more often supervisors commit integrity violations, the more often do those they supervise (Huberts et al 2007). Yet role-modelling is neglected in training would-be supervisors (Camp et al 2013). Role-play and close feedback on performance in simulations are effective pedagogies for supervisors (Schafer 2009) but 63% of sergeants have no role-specific training (HMIC

2008a) and national standards for sergeants have not been evaluated (Giblin 2011).

Sergeants' pivotal role means they have to attend to both frontline perspectives and managerial policies. They bear the practical brunt of supervision and are the conduit for organizational policies (HMIC 2008b). Yet role profiles lack clarity of purpose and consistency across forces, with evidence of fundamental skills gaps and many finding workloads unmanageable. Variation undermines appropriate selection, a cohesive identity, and a focus for skills training. Officers testify that training for frontline supervisors ('arguably the most important level at which to establish leadership skills') is a 'development-free zone' (CoP 2015: 31). Competencies and selection are covered by a National Police Promotion Framework whose main elements on law and procedure, and criteria evaluating temporary promotion, are identical to the previous 'Ospre' (Objective Structure Performance-Related Examination) standard condemned by HMIC (2008a).

Strategic Command Course pedagogy features scenario exercises and placements. However, secondment of chiefs to a non-policing organization is not always achieved (CoP 2015: 27). In 2012 the requirement that chiefs have experience in another force was removed and HMIC lost its role in such appointments, together forming a decided swing to the local, to which national standards for senior ranks are CoP's corrective. The curriculum covers leadership, ethics, partnership, 'transformational management', and evidence-based policing. Until 2013 'professional policing skills' (e.g. running misconduct hearings, covert and human intelligence operations, effective command strategy) also featured but this has disappeared in favour of producing graduates able to lead any public sector organization. Higher training treats police management as generic management. Neyroud (2010: 108) deemed post-SCC follow-up 'haphazard' and 'hopeless'. Evaluation is based on testimony from successful completers (Kodz and Campbell 2010). There are clearer effects of training on successful participants' knowledge than on behaviour change or organizational performance.

Competing discourses about traditional law enforcement, standards and professionalism are found across Europe, despite the European Police College's efforts (McClellan and Gustafson 2012). The Bologna Process encouraged EU-wide provision of undergraduate and Master's degrees in police training and education (Jaschke and Neidhardt 2007). The Scottish Institute of Police Research (SIPR) founded in 2007 involves twelve universities, Police Scotland, and the Scottish Police Authority, and hosts an Executive Seminar series, practitioner fellowships, postdoctoral fellowships, co-funded PhD places, and a postgraduate Diploma. SIPR's research has security business input and is aligned with Scotland's Strategic Police Priorities. The longstanding German police university has civilian and police staff, and an emphasis on research-mindedness (Jaschke 2010). A six semester BA/MA Security Management programme educates security staff of large firms alongside police (Jaschke 2014). Aligned training across cognate sectors may be more effective than assuming police management is the same as managing any public sector body.

Direct Entry

The historic precedent for direct entry at senior rank, Viscount Trenchard's scheme at Hendon Police College, produced 197 graduates who immediately assumed inspector rank. Rank and file officers hated it, and the scheme was not revived after wartime suspension. The stated reason was that police should be led by people who understood frontline demands from direct experience. An alternative view is that civil servants feared a cadre of highly-educated officers inclined to fight their corner against government.

The 1962 Royal Commission on the Police compromised between reintroducing direct entry and insisting on entry as constable. The Graduate Entry Scheme included a 'Special Course' through training, and accelerated promotion. The compromise did not mollify the rank and file, nor did it satisfy those looking for a highly-educated elite to professionalize the police. Graduate Entry became the Higher Potential Development Scheme, which has failed to attract highly-qualified graduates and offers too little mid-career development (Grint and Holt 2011). Perhaps less so for the mis-named Fast Track, whose three-year pace is the same as an undergraduate degree in, say, accountancy, at the end of which employers expect to get an accountant. Promotion to inspector comes three years *after* completing the programme, with an interim promotion to sergeant.

Substantial changes came in 2014. Following the Winsor Review an accelerated promotion scheme from constable to inspector was introduced, with direct entry to superintendent rank, including by foreigners. Winsor promised that people on 'work experience' would not lead public order or firearms operations. The Met advertised for direct entry superintendents in 2014. Of 360 expressions of interest, 249 were male and 85 from ethnic minorities. Most were managers (135), with 91 professionals and 58 public sector workers. There had been concern that hardened ex-Army officers would predominate. Quite the opposite. Selection interviews revealed that applicants liked office environments and worried about operational roles. That was the exact point of the formerly long-established insistence on a single point of entry.

Thirteen successful candidates (out of forty) became superintendents, fewer than expected. There were nine men, four women and only two BME. Historically the police service performed well in senior officer diversity. Only 13% of senior police have an independent (fee-paying) school background, compared to 44% of 'leading people' (Kirby 2016). Fully 60% of top military ranks went to independent school, 63% of leading lawyers. The former single point of entry encouraged promotion on merit.

Direct entry superintendents need not hold a Certificate in Knowledge of Policing. Training, mostly in-force, covers each rank from constable to superintendent in eighteen months, including some patrol; the Met commissioner described it as 'a sheep dip'. The training is also supposed to nurture existing competencies; given that the scheme exists to secure skills not found in forces one wonders where the instructors for that are found. Trainees prepare personal development plans, one of the weak points in IPLDP. Job advertisements emphasized leadership experience but training includes leadership skills.

Direct entrants must grasp the operational environment, handling police/public conflict, balancing interests in divided communities, managing a mixed workforce of civilians and sworn officers, and legal knowledge. This is a considerable ask. The Met's direct entry lead admitted 'the Met will want to tap into their skills from day one' (*The Guardian* 23 May 2014). Given superintendents' command role, the crash course providing their training, and budgetary pressures which mean forces need to deploy them immediately, direct entry poses a considerable risk. Superintendents often manage upwards of 500 people, with big budgets and geographical areas.

The relationship between force training departments and the successive bodies responsible for centralized elements of training has been one of constant friction. Training has long operated on semi-market terms, worrying National Police Training, CENTREX, NPIA, and now CoP about local compliance with nationally-approved guidance. Cost has driven force training delivery, materials and trainers' calibre vary, and effort is duplicated. Cost also motivated the move to 'pre-join' training. The disconnect that the 'pre-join' scheme caused between being trained as a police officer and actually being employed as one has dissolved into an even more uncertain selection and training system in which policing is to become an all-graduate occupation but one where prior experience will somehow qualify officers as graduates. If training—recruit, in-service, and managerial—is to spearhead professionalization, the curriculum, pedagogy and delivery mechanism has to work both from what policing is in the eyes of the police and from what policing needs to learn from its critical friends in the education and research community. Presently in the UK the pieces are on the board but the players have yet to agree coherent rules.

5
The Experience of Training and its Aftermath

With a sense of the structure of training and the way it has conditioned the training curriculum in mind we are in a position to consider the forms of pedagogy it represents and the evaluations that have been made of it.

Pedagogy

Knowledge, beliefs, and values grow in dynamic inter-relation. Adult learning theory is informed by the learner-as-agent approach, where educators-as-facilitators nurture learning in an 'andragogic' pedagogy (Knowles et al 1973; Rogers 1983). To this is added the emotional and social elements that make learning part of socialization (Lave and Wenger 1991). These elements are particularly important to professions through their role in learning *in situ* in a 'community of practice'. Matters are not as glib as the 70% of learning being from experience claimed by the 'organizational learning approach' (Jennings 2014), but experience is more influential than formal pedagogy, particularly where attitudes, inclinations, and skills matter. Indeed, informal learning is more significant and effective than formal learning across many occupations (UKDA 2015).

The andragogical approach structures learning through 'learning contracts' setting achievement levels for each stage. If police training has two pillars, here we see the origin of the Personal Development Plan pillar. The long legacy of rote learning represents the second, in the form of National Occupational Standards (NOS). The enduring dominance of the 'instructional systems design approach' manifests in the imprint of NOS across the programmes of the 'authorized providers', and the constricted higher education (HE) contribution. The unequal contest between an instructional approach and a learning approach can be expressed in the same terms now as police trainers dismissed MacDonald's andragogic model in the 1990s, something 'forced on (us) by a bunch of academics' (Murrell-Abery 2003: 56).

The instructional systems design approach produced a set curriculum whose mechanistic learning was directed to passing formal examinations (MacDonald 1982). Its stimulus/response model offered little scope for student initiative. It mandated pedagogy based on continuous, standardized repetition of material treated as fact. After two to three-year postings, instructors returned to operational policing. Justified as ensuring they maintained operational competence, it ensured they stuck to the script. There was little career return in innovating, which might lower pass rates. Thus, regardless of incumbent, the same easily-delivered model ploughed on. Answers were always either right or wrong, the instructor was the expert, classes, not individuals, were the learning unit, and policing was the invariant application of rules.

MacDonald's modular framework involved more interactive learning, more self-learning, and real attempts to interweave street experience with the classroom. This was not, as some trainers and chiefs perceived, an attempt to disrupt or question policing, but to promote more *continuity* between classroom and field (Vuorensyrja 2013). Legal/procedural knowledge was integrated with interpersonal skills via case studies and scenarios. The scenarios' credibility would spark 'aha' moments amongst learners, consistent with attempts to engage with policing's ethical, legal, and political dilemmas in community policing, intelligence gathering, and organizational leadership (Waddington et al 2013).

The experiential learning approach understands that training integrated into routine practice is more effective than classroom teaching alone (Kolb 1984). There is evidence from teacher education that Continuing Professional Development (CPD), particularly collaborative CPD, improves teachers' practice and student outcomes. Factors boosting collaborative CPD include using external experts, peer support, reflection and experimentation (like the Initial Police Learning and Development Programme's (IPLDP's) personal portfolios), self-appraisal of needs, and sustaining CPD over time. Simulation-based training scores over classroom teaching on knowledge gains, critical thinking, and confidence. Classroom training alone is ineffective in improving skills or changing behaviour. There is no robust evidence either way for learning technologies and virtual learning.

A Rapid Evidence Assessment (REA) on embedding professional behaviour identified eleven robust studies, ten being systematic reviews, all from healthcare. Approaches included issuing guidelines and learning materials; conferences; online reminders; audit and feedback; outreach visits by trainers; opinion leaders facilitating sessions or disseminating guidelines; and peer-led small groups. Active approaches scored over passive ones and peer-led small groups created sustained change. Combined methods encouraging active participation were most effective. Reminders were effective when delivered at critical times, and when requiring response. Issuing guidance and publications—central training's stock-in-trade—neither changed behaviour nor outcomes.

Recruit training for Community Policing

Initial training remains critical because thereafter in-service training competes with workplace exigencies. Introducing new practices like Community Policing (CP) is a case in point. Training under budget pressure can vitiate innovations (Skogan 2008: 29). One US city introduced CP with no training at all. Officers were required to do CP as overtime and figure out what to do from the initiative's name ('Neighbourhood-Oriented Policing'). Other cities offer one, or two, days' training. In Canada, CP was delayed two years while command staff argued over what CP meant in practice (Deukmedjian and de Lint 2007). Where recruit training is seen as a means to reform the force's approach consistency is important. Canada adopted a training model promoting Problem-Oriented Policing (POP) and partnership, the CAPRA model (Clients, Acquire information, Partners, Response, Assessment). Recruits learnt about gathering and analysing information, developing partnerships to share workload and secure cooperation, and evaluating interventions as 'case or incident managers' (Deukmedjian and de Lint 2007). However, the middle ranks would not cede operational authority to the 'empowered frontline'. So a 'Shared Leadership' programme promoted direct dialogue between supervisors and frontline. This was the programme's undoing. Frontline officers aired thousands of employment grievances, and managers stonewalled. CAPRA was abruptly abandoned by executive fiat. The Solicitor General imposed a national strategy in which CP was reconfigured as Intelligence-Led Policing (ILP), making the CAPRA cohorts' skills irrelevant.

Glenn et al (2003) found recruit training highly deficient in inculcating skills and values necessary to appropriately reshape officer discretion. Training focused on what officers do 10% of the time—law enforcement—and on the technical rather than the interpersonal. Under 3% of US basic training time was spent on problem-solving and scenarios requiring communication and reasoning (Bradford and Pynes 1999). Despite training incorporating human relations as early as the 1920s—covering racial, religious, and ethnic conflict; how social problems relate to crime; and preventing crime (Radelet 1986)—how to work in communities was read off from rote-learning of law, telling recruits that community problems were solely addressed legalistically. While successive presidential commissions recognized this, decades passed until Trojanowicz and Bucqueroux (1994) advocated anchoring training in CP, moving from technical skills to problem-solving. CP skills required 'inculcating ... a sense of society and community' (Palmiotto et al 2000). The Palmiotto syllabus spans four working weeks. Week 1 covers Philosophy of the Police Department ('co-activity with community', 'trust community', 'customer-based policing'); Department Organizational Structure; Socio-Economic/Political Composition of Community (including victim characteristics by neighbourhood); Cultural Diversity of the Community (including hate crimes); and Police History. Week 2 covers Police Operations (including police/community relations); Police Mission (including 'long-range goals' and 'professional orientation'); Police Culture (including 'understanding police cynicism and police myths'); Police Discretion; and Police Misconduct (seven types, including sex on duty, corruption, and excessive force). Week 3 covers Police Ethics (including analysing ethical dilemmas); Problem-Oriented Policing (including 'Broken Windows', and 'resources'). Week 4 covers Crime Prevention (including 'environmental design' and 'situational crime prevention'); and Community-Oriented Policing (including evaluating CP strategies and 'future and long-range implementation'). The Diversity segment is allocated sixteen hours, with the other Week 1 and 2 subjects running four to eight hours. Weeks 3 and 4 subjects are twenty hours each.

Evaluations of curricula redesigned to embrace CP find that highly educated recruits, and females, fare better than in the traditional curriculum but overall, recruits perform similarly on assessments to counterparts receiving traditional curricula (Chappell 2008). Chappell's specimen curriculum involves a problem-solving model, scenarios, and tailored learning materials. Many sessions start with a scenario to stimulate groupwork, followed by a 'lessons learned' lecture. The curriculum 'rewarded a more educated, empathetic recruit' but minorities did particularly poorly (Chappell 2008: 51).

Imparting values of diversity has a poor history in police training; effects are mild and short-lived (Bull and Horncastle 1986; Gould 1997). Where delivered in-service, resistance increases with service length. Gould assessed CP training for recruits and experienced officers. Recruits were positive about the training and its relevance but experienced officers vented anger about communities not understanding what police wanted to accomplish, supervisors being out of touch, and CP not being what society wanted police to do. There was a clear relationship between service length, attitude to diversity, and hostility to CP training, the latter representing the attitude 'nobody cares about us so why should we be trained to care about others'.

In Britain, while overall Black and Minority Ethnic (BME) satisfaction with police has improved, young BME males in poor communities retain negative attitudes relative to other-race peers (Barrett et al 2014). Minority community liaison officers are often integrated into their community but not into mainstream policing (Foster et al 2005). Community and race relations training lack systematic reinforcement, for example, through appraisals (Craig et al 2010).

Recruit training for conflict situations

Curriculum design to impart interpersonal skills for conflict resolution must address negotiational tactics, provision of mediation, and sensitivity to cultural, ethnic, and racial differences. Both attitudes and skills help avoid excessive force. Crisis intervention training measurably increases effective non-violent resolutions

(Pearce and Snortum 1983), particularly through enhanced ability to defuse overwrought emotions (Bandy et al 1986).

Many maintain such training is vitiated by hierarchical organizations discouraging neophytes' initiative and creative problem-solving (Hodgson 2001). However, if rule-following is a trait of such organizations, a rule discouraging force unless as last resort would be a start. Hodgson depicts North American police academies as total institutions, more boot camp than college, with set bedtimes, 'personal hygiene habit' checks, and room inspections. 'You run 'til you're sick, you lift weights till you're sick, and you engage in hand to hand combat until you can't stand up', Hodgson writes of a Royal Canadian Mounted Police (RCMP) programme modelled on the British cavalry (ibid: 535). There were echoes in the former regional training centres but this does not describe present British practice. Moreover, Hodgson's account of how regimentation encourages aggression and indifference to due process is thin, amounting to a reference to criminal subculture learning theory and a sudden 'thus, for police officers, violence is a learned value' (ibid: 536), with no rationale for how recruits equate to delinquents lacking effective informal social controls. This leads to the unsupported assertion that 'police officers who shoot and kill a suspect are usually held in high regard within the paramilitary structure and will receive an enhanced level of occupational prestige and status by way of promotion and/or notoriety' (ibid: 537). More nuanced accounts maintain that regimentation's effect is to drive recruits together to survive a gritty and boring experience by subtle forms of resistance and gallows humour (Van Maanen 1989). The issue is not stultifying hierarchy but tensions with more hardened officers, a more direct cause undermining interpersonal conflict resolution training.

The US Department of Justice (2017) blames poor training for Chicago police regularly using 'unjustified, disproportionate and otherwise excessive' force. People posing no threat were shot with guns/Tasers and 'retaliatory force' was used against sassy children, Blacks, and Latinos. Avoiding undue force requires training in physical defence and control tactics against resistance or aggression. This training attracts much criticism and controversy (Kaminski and Martin 2000). Without national standards, provision varies considerably, in the US ranging from 10 to 148 hours' defensive tactics training (Strawbridge and Strawbridge 1990). Empty-hand person control and self-defence methods began superseding truncheon training in the 1970s, with martial arts instruction increasingly prominent despite no evidential basis. Methods effective in police gyms and with mock assailants prepared to tolerate pain for demonstration purposes do not necessarily transfer to the street. Copyrighted martial arts 'systems' nevertheless emerged and were purchased with little evidence of effectiveness, consideration of the training time required, or allowance for human motor performance limitations (physical lag times, attention, stress effects on fine motor skills). Consequently, training was ignored in real situations, with officers reverting to clubbing people over the head. Another failing was that the first step in gaining control is application of a joint lock hold, which, if resistance continues, is met by applying pressure to the joint. Resulting pain may bring under control a sober opponent but many are drunk or high, impairing pain response. Officers then increase pressure, causing tissue or bone damage, enabling excessive force claims when the citizen sobers.

Latterly training drawn from sports psychology and exercise physiology has been preferred. As few techniques as possible are taught (e.g. a handcuffing method effective whatever the degree of resistance and the subject's position), gross motor skills (using large muscle groups) are preferred because fine motor skills deteriorate first under stress, and training environments mirror the street. Some 72% of participants find arrest and control tactics easy to learn and 54.5% easy to remember, but only 31.4% find them easy to apply to resistant subjects (Kaminski and Martin 2000). Only 24% find unarmed defensive tactics useful when assaulted. Over half found the training for defence against multiple unarmed assailants wholly inadequate. Training helped with verbal tactics, locks and holds but not baton controls, pressure point controls, firearms, or multiple assailants. Thus, at least half of officers find arrest and control, and defensive, tactics easy to learn and remember but difficult to use on resistant or assaultive suspects. The more aggressive the citizen, the less effective the trained tactics. Yet, as discussed later, one officer group consistently delivers effective policing without excessive force—females.

Police learning

The instructional systems model assumes learning is an individual process involving 'acquisition' (Heslop 2011a). Yet learning in placements and operational postings involves participation alongside others, not simply acquiring factual knowledge. In operational postings 'immersion in the social, cultural and emotional aspects of work are not merely factors that influence learning (but) are central to it' (Heslop 2011b: 330). The question is how to combine this and individualized acquisition such that the lessons of formal training endure. The evidence favours careful integration of classroom, experiential, and online learning. However, there are problems with content as well as pedagogy. National Standards and the Integrated Competency Framework's (ICF) machine metaphors and binary distinctions (e.g. theory v. practice) comprise a hidden curriculum undermining problem-solving and community focus (White 2006). Training presently ignores the distinction between syllabus and curriculum—discrete knowledge components are learned, but not the values motivating them. Conceiving of National Occupational Standards as the route to professionalization dooms the enterprise; no script can provide a complete behavioural paradigm for the situated contingencies of police practice.

The prospect that training for professionalism will embrace anything more attentive to social divisions and community-building seems remote. A rather stilted emphasis on 'diversity' and 'different cultural values' is as much as can be expected. That is the unconducive ground that higher education institutions amongst the College of Policing's Approved Provider list inhabit, even when providers obligingly start from police 'best practice' (Bryant et al 2014). Pre-join training delivered by a mix of police forces, private companies, further education colleges and universities is reflected in textbooks with an uncertain blend of 'training' and 'learning', largely authored by ex-officers (Rogers et al 2011). ICF's behaviourist form of scientific rationality is the perfect complement to constructions of policing purely as control. The ICF cannot accommodate things it cannot measure, even if society values them. Since 'you didn't do enough' is hardly answered by 'I gave you the common minimum standard', ICF-based training leaves officers without answers to aggrieved citizens (White 2006: 390–1). Training preferring curriculum (*qua* ethical/moral values) to syllabus would enable a more convincing response. That approach was actually taken in IPLDP's early design, which contrasted a 'framework of common values' and a 'framework of qualifications' (Elliott and Kushner 2003) but the

Home Office rewrote it such that the Learning Requirement was absorbed into the behavioural competencies, leaving the ICF the only word on delivering ethics in training. We might consider what a competency framework syllabus that only permits one response tells learners about the organization's real view of diversity, or what its inclination to learning styles discouraging active engagement with ideas implies about its commitment to professionalizing service delivery. As Heslop (2011c: 299) encapsulates it, training remains 'a set of normative practices in search of a curriculum'.

Interestingly, when probationers fail, instructors cite immature learning styles—low commitment to self-development, resistance to personal change, and/or poor problem-solving, alongside unrealistic expectations, low integrity, and arrogance (Jones 2011). Despite some recruits' educational calibre, few respond positively to didactic instructional styles, strongly preferring more interactive styles (Murrell-Abery 2003: 152), consistent with improved problem-solving and critical thinking (Kooi and Palmer 2013). Recruits value preparing Personal Development Profiles (PDPs), which spark thinking about policing and how they are adapting to it. They criticise supervisors' lack of interest in PDPs. But epiphanies can occur. They run the gamut from elation to anger, but are sharp features in probationers' learning. Their principal resource in negotiating epiphanies is other learners. Trainers are not a primary learning resource due to their role in assessments. Probationers draw on 'networks of practice'—informal peer learning groups, like those found in medical and legal education 'syndicates'. Groups are fluid, being task and topic focused (Murrell-Abery 2003: 310–15), yielding cumulative tips gathered from different sets of peers.

Thus, although training incorporates the management of behaviour and attitudes into its accustomed focus on regulatory knowledge while remaining fixated on didacticism and tests, probationers themselves show the orientation to self as adult learner that differentiates professions from occupations. For trainers enjoying a trainer-centred rather than learner-centred system, and tutor constables largely pursuing their own operational concerns, the principal feature of probationers is that 'every decision they make is a liability' (ibid: 337). Such trainers are unapproachable and probationers do not even try, but, where tutor constables are less uncharitable than the one quoted, probationers set great store by the words and guidance of those they yearn to respect as their 'professional companion'. Moreover, tutor constables testify that they are sometimes aware their shift is pursuing a course of action inconsistent with training and want to change it but fear being accused of 'only' doing so because they have a probationer (ibid: 348). Officers are not unthoughtful about established practice or opposed to change. For many years the backstage areas of police stations have harboured sealed boxes for anonymous notes suggesting improvements to forms, procedures or working relations. The culprit in limited learning support for probationers is not lack of reflectiveness but of recognition, reward, and allowance for time invested.

Socialization

McNamara (1967) and Van Maanen (1973) pioneered the longitudinal study of police occupational socialization. McNamara highlighted disjunction between training and the street. Van Maanen conceptualized different socialization stages (notably the idealist anticipatory stage and the 'shock of reality' stage around first patrol). The first UK longitudinal study contrasted the salience of formal and informal socialization, and the conflict in the latter between recruit idealism and experienced officer perspectives (Fielding 1988b). Van Maanen in the US, Fielding in the UK, Monjardet and Gorgeon (1992) in France, and Chan et al (2003) in Australia, found idealistic commitment gave way to disillusion during socialization.

Conti (2006) described three identity stages that aspiring applicants navigate: 'civilian', 'contestant', and 'anticipatory recruit'. Background checks, physical ability tests, psychological evaluations, and interviews each contribute to fashioning moral identity. Civilian identity is progressively suspended as stages are successfully passed. The wider point is that policing is an identity, as distinct, say, as priesthood (Skolnick 2008). Skolnick's (1966) early conceptualization featured a working personality revolving around exercise of authority (parallel to teachers), exposure to danger (parallel to soldiers), and pressure to produce (parallel to factory workers). This manifested in an attitude of tough-minded suspicion and predilection to use force. Training's prime role was keeping force lawful.

Some US forces give military veterans 10% bonuses on exams. Physical ability tests include 'holstering up' with a duty belt and rubber pistol, which recruits like a lot. Pistols are presented ceremoniously. Candidates then run a quarter mile obstacle course ('Getting to the Problem'), sprint for 73 yards, twice pull a resistant object to the ground, handcuff a dummy ('Solving the Problem') and drag it for 30 feet ('Removing the Problem'). Scores are given publicly. A Chicago policewoman's memoire describes candidates undergoing laser removal of gangland tattoos prior to the test (Gallo 2001). Applicants falsely claim scripture study and community work. One overweight candidate stuffed a wig with paper, raising her height and lowering her ostensible Body Mass Index. Once in, recruits' class ranking plays a large part in their self-esteem. What is universal here is that undergoing police training involves identity work.

Learning transforms imagined understandings of policing into concrete competencies and adaptations. As socialization proceeds a 'theoretical ethic' becomes a personal set of rules and conduct (Alain and Gregoire 2008). Alain and Gregoire surveyed Quebec recruits longitudinally. Training involved three years' technical college, followed by fifteen weeks' police academy. The college programme was half humanities, mathematics and sciences, and half criminology, law, CP, and emergency driving. Simulated situations using professional actors were timed rapid fire to sustain stress and promote a diverse repertoire of competencies. Competition was intense. Only 20% got into the college programme, and only 5% graduated. The successful thus expected rapid advancement, but three-quarters remained basic grade throughout their career. At the end of training, before this reality dawned, recruits displayed deep commitment, scored highly on ethical scales, and were pro-social about policing's purpose and their approach to policing (Alain and Baril 2005).

Within a year this succumbed to doubt and disappointment, particularly about CP. Yet their reasons for being police, featuring symbolic over instrumental aspects, did not change, consistent with other longitudinal studies. They remained strongly committed, and believed that promotion should flow from professional criteria not experience (94% v. 6%). As formal socialization gave way to informal, belief declined that formal training had prepared them for situations and citizen behaviour, with increasing perception that being efficient contradicted following rules. Awareness grew that those they routinely dealt with were alienated, disadvantaged and marginalized and that enforcing law caused resentment directed at themselves. This drove them into 'a professional culture and environment ... set apart from ... society, governed by its own rules and standards' (Alain and Gregoire 2008: 179). Even in the first year of training, only 40% thought police had sufficient legal powers, falling to 21% in early service. The 84% in year 1 believing CP was a good public safety strategy fell to 52%. The 34% averse to 'rocking the boat' rose to 54%. When it became legally mandatory to denounce fellow officers if one witnessed or heard about misconduct it drove a sense that civilians were anti-police (Alain and Gregoire 2008: 182). Those who agreed that officers should protect each other in misconduct allegations rose from 24% to 40%, those who disagreed with lying to save a colleague's position fell from 82% to 58%, and those agreeing with the use of street justice rose from 8% to 33%. Evidence across a range of ethical challenges indicated that officers moved from evaluating situations chiefly by reference to ethical principles to drawing on situated context. Their move into moral relativism paralleled growing disenchantment. The critical time for these ethical changes was early service, not the end of training.

Alain and Gregoire's work is powerful not only for its rigorous research design but for their conclusion that the ethical relativism emergent in early service, the move from monochrome to grey, does not mean harsh ethical positions will be taken for the remainder of recruits' careers but that they will respond to the contingencies that present themselves by attending to their situated context. The link between bearing attitudes associated with traditional police culture and propensity to use force is far exceeded by the strength of situational variables (Terrill et al 2003).

If situational features govern ethical response, in-service training should feature situated learning (Sexton and Denicolo 1997: 133). In a study of parallel cohorts of student nurses and police recruits it was expected that cultural socialization would be prime influence, flowing from desire for acceptance and imitation of role models. Nurses lacked opportunities to adopt role models because their training involved short attachments to specialist departments (ibid: 139–140). They had to gain rapport quickly, understand skills in use and personalities involved, then move on. They were thus less bound by group pressure to adhere to established norms. What they took away was sharp, strong views of good and bad practice by individuals. They were guided by the observed behaviours of experienced nurses, not patients. It was assumed this would be even stronger with probationer police, given that police culture is notoriously strong. However, officers proved far more preoccupied with their interactions with the public than with their colleagues, assigning acute salience to how they were treated. This accords with Alain and Gregoire's move into 'situation ethics'. The professional aspects of nurse training dominated nurses' early socialization, whereas during formal socialization police recruits were obsessed with peer relationships and passing tests. Once they 'hit the street', peer relationships were secondary, having already been negotiated. Experiences with the public were most salient (Denicolo and Pope 2009: 144), informing situated judgements. Taking this on board requires greater and more sustained trainer, tutor constable, and supervisor investment.

Wastage and Advancement

In policing's early period, recruit origins were 'field or factory or colliery' (Critchley 1978: 145). Although nineteenth century urban forces sought recruits from rural backgrounds, most were from cities (Shpayer-Makov 2002). They were attracted by 'respectability, warm clothes, and the opportunity for self-improvement', along with a pension (Critchley 1978: 145). Pay was below that of skilled artisans, hours were long, and discipline harsh. Turnover was high. Resigners were disproportionately the more skilled, from superior occupational backgrounds. Many of those who stayed were barely literate, even in the 1900s. Chiefs harshly suppressed union activity but granted improved pay, promotion according to merit, and subsidized leisure activities as they strived to curb wastage, particularly after the First World War. Paternalism was evident in selecting uplifting literature for police station libraries, and supervised leisure activities involving sport and healthy, strength-building pursuits. Socializing in pubs was sternly discouraged.

Only a quarter of Met officers in the early twentieth century rose above constable, disproportionately those from non-manual occupational backgrounds with better education (Shpayer-Makov 1991). The same was true seventy years later (Reiner 1978). From

1930 to the 1960s it took twelve years to make sergeant, and a further eight to inspector (Shpayer-Makov 1991). World Wars and the Great Depression depleted recruitment, accelerating promotion. Policing was a vehicle for working class advancement; humble origin was not a barrier to achieving high rank.

Following the early twentieth century police strikes, the Desborough Committee (1920) put pay 55% above the average industrial wage. Police fared well during the Depression, with free accommodation, good pensions, and job security (Weinberger 1995). While Steedman's (1984) Victorian police were regarded largely as members of the servant class, Weinberger's sample of recruits between 1930 and 1960 were not the farm labourers of the nineteenth century but sons of policemen, railwaymen, or postmen. In 1936, 54% of Met recruits had secondary education and 33% had school leaving certificates. After the Second World War, the dearth of men saw the pass-mark lowered on entrance exams. Standards did not rise again until the Royal Commission's 40% pay rise for constables in the early 1960s. Whether more educated men made more ethical and incorruptible police was a debate amongst senior officers but the calibre of recruits was tied to the state of the economy.

Desborough was a first step in the police claim to professional status. A 1930s plan for a national police college offering accelerated promotion to high risers and military officers was met with suspicion by chiefs and local authority worries about militarization. The plan fell on costs but revived under Commissioner Trenchard. He inherited a system where those seeking promotion had to apply in their first ten years. About half refrained, leaving a steadily ageing group with nothing but their pension to look forward to. To reduce constables' average age and improve promotion prospects Trenchard introduced a scheme whereby these men would get no pension but a gratuity after their ten years' service (Weinberger 1995: 17). A police college would train highflyers and graduates. After two college years they would be appointed inspectors. Hendon Police College opened in 1934.

Ordinary police hated Trenchard for violating their most deeply held article of faith, that the quality of policing depended on constables, not officers, and experience, not education. The Second World War came and the College shut, along with the short service scheme. Trenchard's accelerated promotion men blocked already sclerotic promotion prospects. Recruitment problems became chronic, as national pay fell behind the cost of living and the Second World War took police army reservists. The rule that only single men could join and that marriage was not permitted until four years' service elapsed was abandoned in 1939 but recruits increasingly regarded policing as just another job, not a calling.

During the Second World War police had a sixteen-hour working day, without time off during bombing. There was a complete ban on recruitment and retirement. After the war 10,000 recruits were needed. Although 9,000 soldiers returned to policing by 1946, wastage was high. Recruits were attracted by free accommodation during a time of housing shortages but resignations topped 2,000. By 1955 forces nationally were at least 10,000 short of established strength. Until the 1960 Royal Commission recruits were few, quality poor, and resignation high. Pay and promotion prospects were poor; after 1960 only 11% joined for pay, status or security (Reiner 1978). Cadet schemes were adopted nationwide in 1965, but wastage was high. In London, with wastage exceeding intake, team policing became impossible. Staffing troubles dominated the supposed 'Golden Age of Policing'.

The cost of recruitment and training makes premature resignation expensive. Relative to general labour market turnover (averaging 15%/year) the police rate is historically low, at 6%/year (Cooper and Ingram 2004). In 2014 the Met rate was 5.89% (MOPAC 2014) and the national rate 5.4%. But wastage is stubbornly high amongst groups the service wants to retain, women and ethnic minorities (Cooper and Ingram 2004). In London, voluntary resignation accounts for 42.38% of female officer wastage and 39.56% of BME wastage, compared to an overall rate of 24.03% (MOPAC 2014). Nationally, females were 1,359 out of the 6,904 resigners in 2014 (Home Office 2014c).

Females and BME officers are regarded as bringing emotional intelligence to their work (Brunetto et al 2012). For example, black officers display higher tolerance for negative demeanour in the interest of conducting stops routinely, whites being sensitive to 'disrespect' (Engel et al 2012). Emotional intelligence raises job satisfaction, perceived well-being, and engagement with organizational priorities. Organizational commitment moderates resignation intentions. Cooper and Ingram (2004) found that most joined for 'varied work' and public service, which were equally prominent in the 1980s (Fielding 1988b) and feature across cultures; Conti (2006) reported similar motivations amongst US recruits, as did Van Maanen (1973) some thirty years before. There is, however, high dissatisfaction with management. Surveys consistently find that many officers do not feel valued, and regard management as unfair and ineffective.

Over recent years BME officers have been twice as likely as white officers to resign. The rate of *dismissal* is also two to three times higher than for whites. The BME rate of dismissal in London, at 18.69%, is far above the overall rate of 6.6%, while females are dismissed at a rate slightly above the norm, 6.95% (MOPAC 2014). In 2005, officer turnover for females was 2.92%, hitting a low of 2.38% in 2010, but was 4.36% in 2014. BME turnover was 4.19% in 2005, declining to 2.13% in 2009, but rising to 4.35% in 2014 (MOPAC 2014).

Historically it takes longer for BME and female officers to gain promotion (Bland et al 1999). This is improving in London. Thus, 11.4% of applications for promotion to Sergeant were from BME people, they were 11.8% of those interviewed, and 12% of those selected (MOPAC 2014). Similarly, 21% of applications were by females, they were 23% of those interviewed, and 23% of those selected. However, BME and females fared differently at the move from superintendent to chief superintendent. The BME share of applications was 8.8%, against 24% by females, only 2.8% of those interviewed were BME against 25% for females, and of those successful 4% were BME but 33% were female. Denial of experience of specialist departments obstructs promotion. About twice as many whites as BME officers had worked in traffic, and three times as many had CID experience, despite similar age, gender, and length-of-service profiles.

Obstructed promotion and lack of rank-holders from one's own group can lead to resignation. Cooper and Ingram (2004) found there was not usually one decisive event but an accumulation. Some referenced unequal treatment, disputes with management or dissatisfaction with policies. Thoughts of leaving were prompted by lack of support (21%), organizational culture (20%), not feeling valued (19%), and relationships with supervisors (16%). Some 23% of resigners (27% of females, 13% of males) said they had been bullied; 40% of women and 10% of men claimed discrimination. Both female and BME officers disproportionately cited bullying/discrimination.

But minorities are not interchangeable. BME resigners have fewer years' service than other resigners, suggesting that, relative to women, they are less willing to tolerate objectionable behaviour (Cooper and Ingram 2004). Males and females have similar promotion aspirations in early service, even controlling for family obligations (Fekjaer and Halrynjo 2012), but gender differences appear when seeking promotion; 17% of women (against 5% of men) note conflict with domestic commitments (Holdaway and Parker 1998: 52). Parental and marital status strongly influence women's stress but little affect men; the 'second shift' of domestic responsibilities is a stressor and resignation factor (Kurtz 2012). Women feel they must work harder than males to achieve parity of acceptance and face difficulty working the hours required to secure promotion. Senior officers on promotion boards perceive lack of career-long commitment. Women report significantly less supervisory encouragement yet shun equal opportunity grievance procedures, citing ineffectiveness and fear of reprisals. From early service to getting ahead, supervision and organization are consistent obstacles to diversity and professionalism.

Evolutionary change has marked the police training of the last five decades. It is a more humane experience than before but less so because of planned change systematically delivered and more so because, reflecting wider society, intolerance and brutishness is less tolerated and the needs of minorities are at least better understood, if not effectively accommodated. Training is not 'the sharp end', and still affords opportunities to reflect and to debate. But these require nurturing, facilitating and exploiting, and the pressures of the job, aggravated by austerity, constrict what regular officers with crucial roles in drawing out the lessons of training can do. Key parts of the curriculum are impeded, including the delivery of useful placement experiences, briefings about contemporary communities and appropriately-attuned interventions, the way in which training for conflict situations is construed and provided, and, above all else, the input of experienced officers to the personal development plans and other discursive elements that enable and shape the reflective practitioner. These troubles are the more acute for the minorities whose recruitment could give policing a more representative face, and their dysfunctional effect is bluntly manifest in minorities' higher rates of premature resignation and lesser prospects for promotion. Diversity is a mark of professionalism because it signals equality, fairness, and legitimacy, and the signals also influence not only the majority group amongst officers but the public too. The problems that impede training's effectiveness make bleak the prospects for addressing the daunting range of occupational hazards and organizational troubles that we look to training to correct.

6

Does Training Produce Professional Policing?

Corruption, Misconduct, and Complaints

Officer performance indexes training's impact and effectiveness. The customary focus is on deficiencies and delicts. Misconduct is always more than an individual matter because of policing's symbolic and instrumental roles in governance (Fielding 2005). The UN (UNODC 2006) classifies police misconduct into: Corruption; Physical abuse; Prisoner mistreatment; Evidence manipulation; Unauthorized disclosure of information; Extortion; and Sexual misconduct.

Corruption

Corruption is as old a theme in policing as the need for policing itself. Fielding's Bow Street Runners were soon ensnared in corruption, congregating with 'villains' in taverns and receiving stolen property. Public anger over police corruption followed the 2011 revelations of officers allegedly receiving payments for leaking information to *News of the World* (NoW) journalists about missing schoolgirl Milly Dowler before her body was found. HMIC launched an inquiry into abuses of power in police relations with the media (IPCC 2011a), including relations between NoW editor Neil Wallis and the Met's Director of Public Affairs over a contract for media advice, and allegations that a former Assistant Commissioner secured employment for Wallis' daughter. After extended sick leave, Commissioner Sir Paul Stephenson resigned, citing Wallis as a major factor. From the Brixton riots onwards police saw the media as a means to improve public perceptions and a modern form of accountability. The Leveson Inquiry into the wider NoW scandal concluded that police did not know where to draw the line.

The Independent Police Complaints Commission (IPCC) (2011a) nevertheless declared that police corruption was relatively rare in England and Wales, a view not shared by Transparency International, the anti-corruption organization that the Association of Chief Police Officers (ACPO) commissioned to assess police integrity following the NoW scandal. Until that scandal IPCC had never received a single referral or initiated any investigation into media-related corruption. Defining corruption as 'abuse of entrusted power for private gain', TI found significant variations in integrity procedures and corruption risk management across UK forces (ACPO 2012b). Budget reductions, pay cuts, and the drive for outsourcing all raised corruption risk (Transparency International 2011). In 2011, police disclosed 14,916 business interests, and, when senior staff leave, the civil service 'cooling off' period before taking positions with bodies that may gain advantage from their information and contacts is seldom imposed.

Concentration of both governance and executive functions in Police and Crime Commissioners (PCCs) is another concern (Transparency International 2012). Chiefs are formally accountable to PCCs, who focus on executive functions, leaving practical delivery of integrity programmes hanging. TI recommended citizen panels to scrutinize integrity programmes, as in the NYPD, questioning why forces do not have non-executive boards responsible for integrity like most businesses. British forces score poorly on anti-corruption reporting, particularly in engaging watchdog groups, NGOs, and the public in governance. While 89% of citizens expect police to be more honest than average citizens, 36% believe police corruption is fairly or very common (HMIC 2013b). Gifts and hospitality undermine public confidence, provoking suspicion of wider corruption (Prenzler et al 2013). Subcontracting requires systems to avoid risks around hospitality and information disclosure, with more training on integrity (HMIC 2011d).

IPCC (2011a) itself offered a defensive, even cringing, account of not prioritizing corruption. It had been preoccupied 'in its first seven years' investigating deaths and serious injuries in police custody and its 'small' research capacity was overwhelmed by discovering the extent of officers' sexual misconduct. IPCC thus relied 'predominantly on police forces to investigate [alleged] corruption' (IPCC 2011a: 11). Allegations suggested widespread granting of exemptions for traffic offences, sexual assault on vulnerable individuals, use of police computers to initiate such assaults, and the supply and abuse of steroid drugs; 15% of the 837 corruption cases referred to IPCC between 2008 and 2011 involved abuse of authority, and 9% misusing computer systems. Despite Leveson, journalists still tempt officers. Timothy Edwards, deployed at Heathrow, was imprisoned after receiving £22,000 from a newspaper for providing thirty stories based on evidence from the police computer over three years involving celebrities, drug smuggling, and aircrew behaviour. The subject of one 'smutty sex-laden scandal' story attempted suicide (*The Guardian* 6 June 2014).

Graft and corruption inevitably occur, as shown by international comparison with differently-staffed and differently-organized forces (Gottschalk 2011). In UK, police corruption does not top public concerns about crime but does corrode confidence (IPCC 2012a). From 2009 to 2012 forces recorded 8,542 corruption allegations. There are dramatic inter-force variations, from eleven referrals per 1,000 officers to none. Irregularity in evidence/perjury is most prevalent (3,758 allegations), then improper disclosure of information (3,521), and corrupt practice (1,263). While IPCC's independent corruption investigations have been increasing, the base is small—eleven in 2010/2011. Of 104 between 2008 and 2012, forty-seven (45%) were referred for prosecution. Of the fifty-one officers involved, eighteen were prosecuted, thirteen convicted and ten gaoled. Risk factors were inappropriate associates, financial insecurity, occupational dissatisfaction, and substance misuse.

Corruption of an altogether different order was exposed by Operation Tiberius, conducted in 2002 but only made public in 2014. The 'Adams family' syndicate had bribed serving- and ex-detectives and infiltrated Scotland Yard, gaining access to intelligence on surveillance, technical deployment, undercover techniques, and live investigations of rival gangs and murders. Officers and criminals jointly owned properties and racehorses. Officers participated in high volume drug importation and money laundering. Tiberius named forty-two serving officers and nineteen former detectives. Corrupt officers led investigations of gangland murders and organized crime, occasioning failed prosecutions. The police statement of a highly sensitive witness helping police pursue killers of a man who lost £1.5 million of ecstasy pills owned by the Adams family was found in the safe of a nightclub the family controlled. Tiberius's remedies were interestingly weak. They included combining corrupt officers into a single unit under a strong manager to keep an eye on them, and redeploying some to uniform. The Tiberius gangsters used Masonic contacts to recruit corrupt officers. Similar tactics emerged from the 2008 'Project Riverside' report on rogue private investigators. In 1998 the home secretary ordered police to declare Freemason membership but ten forces refused and the policy was abandoned.

'Noble cause corruption'—that committed in the name of good ends—appears to have little profile with IPCC. In such corruption there is a conflict between protecting communities by removing offenders from circulation and acting in accord with procedural law protecting human rights (Cooper 2012). Moralistic corruption occurs when the protector role predominates (Muir 1977). Default preference for the protector role reflects its unambiguously 'just' ends, whereas procedural lawfulness may involve letting criminals go free. Officers are also rewarded for good arrests much more often than for following procedural guidelines (Crank and Caldero 2000). However, one might ask why, if the moral bind is so strong as to cause moralistic corruption, it is too weak to deter economic corruption.

The relationship between frontline deviance and managerial/supervisory ties is also neglected. Punch (2009) rejects the 'bad apple' metaphor in favour of 'bad orchards' because individual corruption represents collective, institutional failure. Perceiving that their managers are fair raises officers' sense of their own legitimate authority. Where this does not obtain, occupational culture is a redoubt against 'unfair' management. Those founding their sense of legitimacy on occupational culture rather than on bearing organizational values of fairness bear more cynical and authoritarian attitudes and less inclination to support procedurally-just policing (Bradford and Quinton 2014). We need not discount moral values expressed by recruits to see that a force or unit displaying good 'organizational citizenship behaviours' can discourage both moral and economic corruption. Confidence in legitimate authority reinforced by managerial respect and engagement provides resilience against moral challenges and 'workplace uncertainty' (Colquitt 2008).

Misconduct

Other predictors of misconduct are largely individual characteristics; the only external variable influencing misconduct is violent crime rates (Eitle et al 2014). Straightforward dishonesty occurs steadily, although seldom as puzzlingly as the case of a chief inspector who committed fraud offences netting £11,000 (*Surrey Advertiser* 9 May 2014). With twenty years' service, Tanya Brookes bought goods which she returned to higher-priced outlets demanding a refund using forged receipts, wearing her police lanyard. She obtained heavy discounts on a luxury holiday by posing as a counter-terrorism officer, and falsely claimed against airlines for belongings supposedly damaged in transit. The jury discounted testimony that Brookes' frauds began after brain surgery (in one case she risked her career for £16) but her thirty months' imprisonment was later reduced. The 2013 case of a Firearms Enquiry Officer was particularly troubling. Over eight years he sold over 100 weapons surrendered to police (IPCC 2013). He received fifty-one weeks' imprisonment suspended for two years. As these examples suggest, the exceptional resources of power and authority that policing requires offer extraordinary temptations and can also cloak misconduct until it grows from nuisance to matters of grave concern. Instances include child pornography accessed on duty using police systems, sexual messages sent via force email, and police computers used to obtain information for sexual grooming. In 2013, 169 officers and support staff were investigated for predatory sexual behaviour, including rape, sexual assault, voyeurism, accessing indecent images, and indecent acts with a child. Many victims were vulnerable, having gone to police after other abuse. In the US, 41% of police sexual violence cases are committed by recidivist officers, averaging four victims every three years, with a pattern of moving across jurisdictions dodging allegations while maintaining police certification (Rabe-Hemp and Braithwaite 2013). An IPCC/ACPO report on police sexual misconduct concluded that more effective supervision was needed, including auditing IT use and work pattern records (ACPO 2012a).

Lacking official statistics, information has to be pieced together from court reports and misconduct proceedings. These suggest involvement at all ranks, and sometimes in concert. The most senior officer accused of serious sexual misconduct was Wiltshire's deputy chief constable, subject of complaints by thirteen different female staff, who killed himself during the inquiry into his behaviour. An inspector and two sergeants faced gross misconduct charges after a complaint from a pregnant black woman charged with arson that she was kept handcuffed in a police cell for eleven hours, stripped naked from the waist up, and assaulted, inducing labour ten weeks early. The 2013 case displayed elements of prejudice, blundering interpretations of policy, and diffusion of responsibility. Having decided she was a suicide risk her upper clothing was deemed a means of self-strangulation and three male officers rushed into her cell, ripped off her T shirt, cut her bra off, and handcuffed her hands behind her back. When she was later rehandcuffed and said she could not handle it due to pain from the previous handcuffing she was repeatedly punched in the arm. Officers involved crossed several shifts.

The most notorious recent cases of misbehaviour relate to undercover policing. Mark Kennedy was engaged in such close 'surveillance' of environmental protestors that he sired a child with one of them. Four Special Demonstration Squad officers were similarly engaged between 1987 and 2007. Kennedy, a married man, spent seven years undercover, enjoying sexual relationships with at least two campaigners. The case gave rise to eight official investigations, including one by HMIC (Hogan-Howe 2011) that advised against the independent oversight recommended by ACPO, including its undercover operations lead. Hogan-Howe, later Met commissioner, defended internal supervision, which is retrospectively reported annually to the Office of Surveillance Commissioners. Why such a long operation was needed against pacifist environmental campaigners when undercover work is designated for counter-terrorism, major drug dealing, or importing firearms remains unanswered.

The problem with relying on internal supervision is that surveillance officers' daily routine is lying and supervision is lax. Kennedy claimed he had fully informed his managers, noting that his BlackBerry phone had a tracking device, and that his superiors had 'sanctioned every move I made' (*The Guardian* 15 October 2011). Appeal court judges quashed the protestors' convictions for trying to occupy a power station because crucial evidence, covertly recorded by Kennedy using a £7,000 specially adapted watch, had been withheld. The eight women who sued Scotland Yard after finding themselves in sexual relationships with officers observed that the government had failed to ban undercover police from having sex with surveillance targets.

The sex and surveillance cases were bad enough but the Met then made determined efforts to keep the victims' lawsuits out of court, including the bizarre argument that since undercover operations were subject of a 'Neither Confirm Nor Deny Policy' (NCND), trials would be unfair to the Met because it would be unable to respond. The lawyers could not produce any document confirming the policy and had to withdraw their objection. Their difficulty was unsurprising, given that Met senior officers, and covert officers themselves, had appeared on a BBC documentary called 'True Spies'. The Met was obliged to publish the undercover officers' names in court papers. In the 2013 High Court case on 'Whether Sexual Relationships Induced by Undercover Police Officers Constituted Degrading Treatment' (*AKJ and Ors v Commissioner of Police for the Metropolis & Ors [2013] EWHC 32*) the judge held that the NCND 'policy' did not provide immunity and that no evidence explained why the women's rights were outweighed by the public interest or protecting others' fundamental rights.

Further revelations emerged as the victims' cases went through the civil courts. An undercover officer who had been using a dead baby's identity disappeared overnight when his tour of duty ended. When the victim's searches got close to discovery police immediately transferred him overseas. Contesting the woman's claim for damages, the police line was that the relationship was willingly entered into. Since some undercover officers were married some may feel the Met chose to make itself party to adultery rather than admit wrongdoing.

It then emerged that the Special Demonstration Squad (SDS) had spied on the family of the murdered black teenager Stephen Lawrence. The home secretary added the Squad to the brief of the Ellison inquiry into alleged corruption, abuse of power and outright prejudice in investigations of Lawrence's murder. An advisor to Macpherson published a detailed account of legal manouevring by police that had undermined important lines of questioning and constrained the Inquiry's scope (Stone 2013).

Ellison concluded that it was possible that a detective in the investigation was corrupt. The head of counter-terrorism, Commander Richard Walton, was moved from his post having allegedly placed the SDS spy close to the Lawrence family. Walton, who helped prepare the Met submission to Macpherson, received from the spy 'fascinating and valuable' information about the Lawrence family that could provide police with a 'secret advantage' at the inquiry (*The Guardian* 6 March 2014). After Ellison, the home secretary announced a new offence of police corruption because the existing offence of misconduct in public office was inadequate against serious corruption. However, intelligence gathered by undercover officers remains on the National Domestic Extremism Unit database, which is not established under law. No policy governs its precise purpose or scope.

Infiltration is also used in drugs policing. Posing as an addict, Neil Woods would befriend addicts, buy drugs from their dealers, and then have all participants arrested (Woods 2016). Woods contributed to national guidelines for undercover operations but later regretted jailing destitute addicts, excusing himself because he then believed the end justified the means. Woods also claimed that when he informed on corrupt colleagues nothing happened because supervisors believed corruption was inevitable. Woods left the police after a breakdown, suffering from Moral Injury, a form of Post Traumatic Stress Disorder (PTSD).

An understanding of police misbehaviour should also include offences against colleagues. Fortunately few cases are as extreme as that of detective constable Peter Foster, who in 2012 hammered his wife Detective Constable Heather Cooper's head ten times with a baseball bat until she was unconscious before stabbing her fatally in the throat in front of their three-year old son in an argument about a missing baby changing mat. After burying her in woodland he sent messages from Cooper's phone creating an alibi. Once arrested, he claimed he killed Cooper in self-defence. She was on maternity leave after their daughter's birth. Having received a minimum seventeen-year life sentence Foster made several suicide attempts, eventually succeeding. A martial arts fanatic the judge described as an 'extremely dangerous individual' with 'a short fuse', Foster's case perhaps bears messages for police recruitment criteria, Foster having pre-joining criminal convictions.

A curious twist lends weight to that concern. Testimony that Foster committed suicide because of upset over another prisoner's suicide was given by Foster's friend Ivan Esack, another wife-murdering ex-detective. Esack stabbed his wife eleven times at her hair salon after she left him following a long history of serious domestic violence. Shouting she was 'a dead woman walking' and 'tick tock, tick tock' he attacked with such ferocity that the eight inch knife broke, with Esack telling a terrified teenage salon assistant 'she deserved it, the bitch'. At trial it emerged that Esack was a bisexual cocaine addict. Mrs Esack contacted police four times about abuse, the last a month before her murder. The judge said anyone forming a relationship with Esack would be in danger, describing him as 'controlling'. Policing is about control, but professional practice begins with self-control.

A case of workplace entanglements more mundane than those involving a Kennedy or a Foster but equally telling was that of Police Community Support Officer (PCSO) Kim Boichat, who wrote herself threatening notes in order to persuade her superiors that she was being bullied (*Surrey Advertiser* 14 October 2011), subsequently admitting to wasting police time. Boichat said she acted because previous bullying complaints were dismissed and ignored. Her mitigation statement said:

> The bullying was very underhand so that nobody would notice. I was always told to grow up and always told it was low-level and not worth taking any further. When I took it to my senior management, I was never taken seriously. I feel none of this would have happened if Surrey Police had done something when I first raised it.

Chief constables are not irreproachable. In 2012 Cleveland's chief Sean Price was sacked for gross misconduct. He lied to the IPCC about his role in the hiring of the daughter of the police authority chair and ordered a staff officer to do the same. The IPCC intimated that Price believed he had absolute authority and could order others to do anything he wished. Meanwhile the Dyfed-Powys chief constable was found to have misused the force computer system and corporate credit card, missing official meetings to visit a girlfriend. He resigned, avoiding misconduct regulations.

Some misconduct is nuisance aggravated by police status. Of 828 cases from 2009 to 2014 where police made racist comments online or asked crime victims to become Facebook friends, 14%

resulted in no further action and only 9% in resignation, retirement, or dismissal (BBC News 19 August 2014). Most were dealt with through supervisory advice. A larger concern is that of excessive use of force. An instance was the killing of Ian Tomlinson by PC Simon Harwood, tasked with riot control during G20 protests in London in 2009. Harwood, acquitted by a jury in 2012 despite a 2011 inquest verdict of 'unlawful killing', hit Tomlinson with a baton and shoved him to the ground. Tomlinson fell awkwardly, hit his head, and died. Harwood's disciplinary record included similar previous incidents. The Met attempted to keep Harwood's discipline record secret from Tomlinson's family, arguing that disclosing his string of previous complaints for excessive force, including punching, throttling, and kneeing people, and committing unlawful arrests, would breach his privacy. The Met was eventually instructed to tell the family's lawyers but it was kept from the inquest and jury trial. Harwood avoided disciplinary action by retiring from the Met. Rejoining three days later he then reapplied for uniformed posting. If vetting procedures and the disciplinary system have any purpose it is surely to prevent individuals known to be violent taking such deployments.

The option of resignation with no further liability has long been criticized. Misconduct hearings are employment hearings so if an officer resigns the hearing has no sanction. Between 2008 and 2012, 791 officers facing misconduct charges—including sexual assault, serious violent attacks, perjury, corruption, and fraud—resigned or retired, based on Freedom of Information (FoI) requests to twenty-seven forces (therefore an under-report). Pensions are unaffected even if there is a subsequent criminal conviction. Home Office guidelines encourage but do not require automatic dismissal/compulsory resignation for committing offences in service. Police trainers report academic misconduct including cheating and plagiarism (Stout 2011), suggesting a requirement to teach *academic* integrity in police training.

Complaints

Forces and HMIC use IPCC complaints data to monitor public satisfaction. Four main causes of complaint are unprofessional behaviour, criminal conduct, tortious action, and unacceptable policy (Smith 2004). Beyond regulating standards, complaints expose weaknesses and necessary changes. Complaints are rising internationally; New Zealand saw a 5% increase between 2004 and 2009 and New York City a 13% increase; however, they rose 36% in the UK. Allegations per year per 1,000 officers run at somewhat over 200 (IPCC 2012c). Appeals against outcomes and the proportion upheld have increased.

Before 1977 complaints were wholly dealt with by forces themselves. The Police Complaints Board (1977–1985) was meant to have greater independence, but queried chief officer decisions on complaints in only 0.4% of cases, then accepted almost all (Maguire and Corbett 1991). Under the Police Complaints Authority (PCA) (1985–2004) lesser complaints, including minor assaults, were subject of 'Informal Resolution', accounting for 35% of all complaints in 1998/9, plus 36% 'withdrawn or dispensed with'. Even the PCA chair criticized its limited independence, and pronounced PCA's own investigations tainted by 'excessive secrecy', being seen as 'an agent of the police', and lacking accountability (PCA 2001). Despite provision of civilian investigation managers and seconded senior police investigators from 2000 (Home Office 2000a) the system remained under-resourced; referrals actually fell 12% and 22% fewer officers were dismissed/resigned in PCA's last year (Home Office 2003 Statistical Bulletin 04/03). The core concern dogging confidence in the PCA remained police investigating police.

The Independent Police Complaints Commission became operational in 2004 (and was re-named the 'Independent Office for Police Conduct' in 2017). Its statutory brief is to increase public confidence and access, investigate complaints, recommend appropriate action by forces, and where necessary refer cases for prosecution. IPCC remains reliant on police investigators. Only complaints about officer 'conduct' (behaviour, language, actions, or omissions) are in frame (IPCC 2005), not operational direction or service standards. Replacing Informal Resolution, 'Local Resolution' allows for third-party (e.g. witness) complaints. Under 'Local Investigation' the force's Professional Standards Department (PSD) investigates; 'Supervised Investigation' sees IPCC supervise PSD investigation, in 'Managed Investigation' IPCC manages the PSD investigation, and 'Independent Investigation' is wholly by IPCC. Statements by any person in Local Resolution are not admissible in legal or disciplinary proceedings nor can outcomes be appealed (except on procedure). PSD decisions in Local and Supervised Investigations can be appealed to IPCC. Bar judicial review there is no appeal for Managed or Independent Investigations. Few complainants know anything about Local Resolution (LR), and some are told it is their only option (May et al 2007). Officers are ill-informed and cynical about LR, believing it biased towards complainants. Only half report any training. Contrary to IPCC advice, half of forces use frontline officers for LR. 'Desktop resolution'—handling complaints without recording them—still happens.

IPCC's move somewhat away from the police-investigating-police model garners more confidence amongst the general public, but not complainants. Police still largely staff investigations because IPCC lacks capacity. Understaffing causes long delays, aggravated by new responsibility for complaints against HMRC, the UK Border Agency, and the National Crime Agency (NCA). In 2009/10 alleged neglect of duty accounted for 24% of complaints, rudeness and intolerance 22%, and common assault 14%. About two-thirds of complainants were male and 19% were 18–29. Two-thirds were white, 6% Asian, 7% Black, but police failed to record ethnicity in over 20% of cases (HAC 2009b). IPCC was only able to start 106 independent investigations, an annual increase of just six (IPCC 2010). Local Resolution accounted for 41% of cases, Investigations for 36%, some 12% were withdrawn and 2% discontinued. Overall, 29% of appeals were upheld, due to: misinterpreted evidence (41%); inadequate information provided to complainants (27%); inappropriate decisions/action by the force (18%); clear indication of a case to answer (15%). In 22% of appeals, things the police committed to were not done. Fully 10% of LR appeal cases were found too serious to have been dealt with by LR (IPCC 2011b). IPCC received 33,176 referrals in 2013, a new high. Of these, just 5% were investigated by IPCC, 10% supervised by it, and fully 70% dealt with by the force in question.

The Public Accounts Committee (2009) found IPCC was working above full capacity, undermining formal quality control. IPCC was not monitoring follow-through on its recommendations and thus had no valid idea of their impact. The Home Affairs Committee (HAC) was also sharply critical, declaring '99 times out of 100' complaints involved 'police investigating police' (Home Affairs Committee 2010). Ex-officers still often investigated former colleagues. The average 269 working days to investigate a complaint 'does nothing to increase anybody's confidence', it was unclear whether inputs or outcomes were IPCC's performance measure, and complainant satisfaction was ignored. In 2013 HAC declared that IPCC was still not providing the powerful scrutiny needed to secure confidence. There were too few independent investigations, insufficient rigour in supervised investigations, and death and serious injury investigations were too slow. Even serious corruption was not automatically referred. Other criticisms were lightness of disciplinary measures; delaying high profile investigations under police pressure (as in the Jean Charles de Menezes and Ian Tomlinson cases); no external scrutiny nor checking if recommendations were implemented; insufficient and inadequate investigator training.

These are all different facets of the lack of full independence from police. In Northern Ireland the Police Ombudsman carries the role, and is, by statute, fully independent. Hard-to-reach groups particularly want an accessible system, including briefings on how to complain and allowing community representatives to act as proxies (Ipsos-MORI 2007). The NHS receives similar volumes of complaints. Its Patient Advocates explain the process, try to resolve complaints, and guide complainants if needed.

Recording complaints of racially discriminatory behaviour began in 1991, when there were forty-nine. This rose twelve-fold to 579 in 2000 (Bowling et al 2004). Substantiation was considerably lower than the 2% for all complaints. The IPCC report (2013) on the Met's handling of race discrimination complaints revealed substantial weaknesses in handling and response. West Midlands, Greater Manchester and West Yorkshire police were failing at every stage of discrimination investigations (IPCC 2014a). Of 170 discrimination complaints not one was upheld. These forces upheld 11–13% of overall complaint allegations but over 50% of discrimination alleged by *officers*. Yet complaints against fellow officers show the same pattern as complaints by the public (Harris 2010). Insufficient diversity training undermined initial decisions, seriousness assessments, Local Resolution and Investigation, outcomes, and communicating outcomes. Seriousness and officer history were not fully considered in 80% of cases. Decisions failed to weigh evidence for and against.

A police marksman was charged in 2014 with murdering Azelle Rodney, a young black man he shot in a car in 2005 on suspicion of intending armed robbery. IPCC initially found no case to answer. Claims that crucial evidence could not be disclosed were used to deny an inquiry for seven years. The eventual inquiry found Rodney was unlawfully killed. The marksman had been called a 'serial killer' by his manager (he previously shot two others dead), a remark inspiring a defamation lawsuit that yielded the marksman £5,000. Sometimes misconduct is aggravated by racial prejudice or ignorance. Like Rodney, black ex-paratrooper Christopher Alder was found by an inquest to have been unlawfully killed. CCTV showed him choking for breath while restrained by five officers who chatted and joked around him, thinking he was acting. He struggled for eleven minutes before dying, after which ape noises were heard on the recording. The officers were cleared of manslaughter and misconduct.

A small minority of officers account for a disproportionate share of complaints (Walker and Bumphus 1992); under 0.5% of LAPD officers account for 15% of excessive force complaints. Problem officers are typically male, young, and inexperienced (Brandl et al 2001). Like criminal careers, the 'problem officer' career features earlier onset, longer duration, and above average problem behaviours. Public complaints rise quickly, peaking at three years' service. Average officers get a public complaint every two years, with desistance in year nine. Internal complaints show similar trend but less volume, suggesting colleagues grant more leeway than citizens. Officers who attract public complaints also attract above-average internal complaints, their complaint career is longer, and in both complaint types a minority account for most problem behaviours.

Between 1994 and 2009 Tasmania Police saw 77% fewer complaints, having introduced enhanced recruit ethics training (including sessions from internal investigators), and improved complaint-handling procedures, including sessions for officers having above average complaints with internal investigators (despite ostensibly developmental rather than punitive aims, quotes suggest explicit advice on consequences, e.g. 'I think its time you sat down with the deputy commissioner and discussed your future') (Porter et al 2012). Since most complaints involve low-level misconduct, large returns are possible by such means.

Although surveys find that 77% of people say they would make a complaint if they were 'really annoyed' with an officer the reality is otherwise (IPCC 2006). Some 27% of respondents say contact with police had left them feeling 'really annoyed' at least once (Grace and Bucke 2010). Some 10% made a complaint, while 3% tried but failed. Of those who complained, 62% were very dissatisfied with how police handled it, 21% being fairly or very satisfied. The groups customarily having problematic relations with police—youths, ethnic minorities, the poor—are especially unlikely to complain. Predictive factors for those defeated by attempting to complain are being aged 16–29, being female, and being from an ethnic minority. Given that, due to frequency and type of contact, younger and ethnic minority people are more likely to have grounds for making complaints, there is a case for a more accessible complaints process. There is much evidence of officers being rude, abrupt, or asking irrelevant questions (IPPR 2009). Only 56% of complainants expect things to be 'right first time', and people are quite accepting of problems if the manner of police is appropriate (Hopkins 2010: 15). Most complainants simply want an apology, which officers are not required to provide.

Response to failures of service delivery

The other side of the coin is that incidents do not need to be serious to provoke public concern. Isle of Wight residents were offended by an illegally parked police van while officers bought sandwiches, with letters to the editor including 'as disturbing as it gets', 'arrogance of the police … in believing the laws of the country applied just to the public and not to them' and 'police … shouldn't use their position to their own advantage' (*Isle of Wight County Press* 28 March 2013). An elemental understanding of fairness surfaced. Inappropriate practices may reflect practical exigencies rather than insensitivity; initial training is critical. In the 2016 TV documentary 'Britain's rookie cops' seven recruits were followed from training school to confirmation in post. They were shown making mistakes, being corrected, and then implementing what they had learned. Senior officers noted that areas for improvement were part of fortnightly senior staff meetings on organizational learning and reflected a national drive to use evidence of what works and co-learning.

Some forces now provide training on selected integrity issues (HMIC 2013b). Yet measures imposed post-training have limited effect. The original Discipline Code was an awesome instrument, such that it was used only *in extremis*. Parliament instigated new misconduct procedures in 1999. Standards of proof in misconduct proceedings were reduced from 'beyond reasonable doubt' to 'balance of probabilities' and a Code of Conduct with fast-track procedures for serious cases and written warnings for minor incidents was introduced, but officers, including discipline staff, saw no improvement, investigations did not increase, charges per officer actually declined, and fewer cases reached an outcome (Home Office 2003b). Officers struggled to understand the Code's definition of misconduct, preferring previous, simpler definitions. They devised their own example-based working definitions, which were sometimes quirky or wrong. Officers saw the procedures as a mechanism for dismissal rather than reducing misconduct, thought the lower evidential standard unfair, and castigated delay and lack of communication. Some might consider it a success that officers wanted to avoid the new procedures, but avoidance of formal processes in the face of problems was exactly what brought the former system into disrepute. Evaluators concluded that complaints staff should work with training departments to educate officers about ethical standards, encourage active supervision, and strengthen reporting mechanisms.

Changes in how frontline work is regulated have an underlying importance because of the 'paradox of police discretion'. Baseline roles in hierarchical organizations are usually entirely subordinate. But this does not typify policing. The bulk of constables' work is not directly supervised. Often the only account available for their exercise of discretion is their own. Intermediate and command officers are ensnared in internal and external relationships with others to whom they are accountable. Consequently the lowest grade officers have greatest functional discretion—the 'paradox'. The problem of discipline codes is not procedural or related to legal considerations like standards of proof but to operational and workgroup realities. Officers are increasingly reluctant to use discretion for fear of sanctions (Heaton 2010). Police seldom appeal Crown Prosecution Service (CPS) decisions on prosecution; of 395,298 cases of pre-charge advice by CPS Direct between April 2015 and September 2016, police appealed 1,210. Nearly half were upheld, suggesting officers are cautious, as does the low rate of appeal itself. Effective exercise of discretion is a matter of balance. Officers need to feel able to use their own judgement but must be adequately supervised to inhibit idiosyncratic or biased judgement. Merseyside Police significantly reduced complaints with a peer referral scheme that focused on the immediate workgroup, confirming the value of accommodating rather than ignoring the paradox.

Deaths in or following police custody are a prime concern. Between 1998/9 and 2009 there were 333, with a falling trend, from forty-nine in 1998/9 to fifteen in 2008/09 (Hannan et al 2011). Whites were 76% of the 333, blacks 7% (above population share), Asians 5%, mixed race 2% and Chinese/other 1% (Table 6.1). A struggle or violence occurred in 29%, and 26% involved physical restraint. Ethnic minorities and those aged twenty-five to thirty-four were significantly more likely to be restrained, most often being held down. Restraint caused death in 5% of cases—twelve were white, three black, and one Asian. Four died from 'positional asphyxia'. In over four-fifths of cases no one present had first aid training and in only 4% had anyone present received refresher training. Some thirty-eight of the officers involved lacked training. Training should specify which techniques are unauthorized and how long someone can be restrained while prone. While death in custody trends are downwards, the proportion of suicides is rising (IPCC 2012b). Long detention is a risk factor (IPCC 2014c), with up to 4,000 annually held over twenty-four hours without charge (Home Office 2012b).

Following complaints over policing major public order events, HMIC sought to reassert accountable policing based on minimum force (HMIC 2009a). Recommendations majored on training. Common standards on using force were lacking, including training in shield tactics. Nineteen forces trained with intermediate and round shields, two with long shields, and one with all three. Some training included using the shield's edge against individuals, breaching standards. Training for situations involving batons and distraction tactics was neglected. Safety training and public order training were disconnected.

Diversity in the Police Organization

Across Europe, police forces lack diversity of gender, ethnicity, and sexual orientation, and diversity diminishes with rank (Van Ewijk 2012). British forces have grown slowly more diverse, with more women, minorities, and graduates. In 1981 there were 2,610 graduates but 7,409 by 1988 (Reiner 1992) and 15,374 by 2004 (Fox 2013). By 2012, 68% of recruits had A level education or above; 30% were graduates. Since 2003 the majority of

Table 6.1 Deaths in or following police custody: Ethnicity by financial year, 2004/05 to 2013/14

Ethnic group	Financial year										Total fatalities
	2004/05	2005/06	2006/07	2007/08	2008/09	2009/10	2010/11	2011/12	2012/13	2013/14	
White	34	23	22	19	10	16	20	13	14	10	**181**
Asian	0	2	2	0	2	0	0	0	0	0	**6**
Black	2	1	3	1	3	0	1	1	0	0	**12**
Mixed	0	2	0	1	0	1	0	1	1	1	**7**
Chinese/ Other	0	0	0	1	0	0	0	0	0	0	**1**
Total fatalities	**36**	**28**	**27**	**22**	**15**	**17**	**21**	**15**	**15**	**11**	**207**

Source: IPCC 2014 Deaths during or following police contact: Statistics for England and Wales Time Series 2004/05 to 2013/14.

recruits have been over twenty-six (Fox 2013). In 2009, 6.2% were under twenty-six but by 2012 it was only 3.5%. Withdrawal of cadet schemes has made for a higher average age at recruitment, bringing experience of other work or tertiary education, and thus of other workplace cultures. The Met, employing about a quarter of British police, adopted a policy where most recruits have been Special Constables, boosting age and experience.

Class composition has also been changing (Reiner 1992). With more graduates and broader occupational experience, more officers have middle class work histories and/or families of origin. Policing customarily offered advancement to people from low or intermediate social class positions (Caless 2011). However, the pre-entry qualification and the special constabulary route (whose psychometric test has cultural biases; Bryant et al 2014) deter not only the less well-off but ethnic minorities (Holdaway 2011; Harron 2010; Reed 2010).

Black and Minority Ethnic (BME) applications are consistently fewer than might be expected from their share of workforce (Fielding 1999). Historically they are less likely than whites to be offered interviews, receive a formal offer of employment, or be appointed after probation (Bland et al 1999). While London and the Met are becoming more ethnically diverse, police still lag behind (Table 6.2). BME people were 4.15% of the Met in 2001 but 11.07% in 2014, and 36% of PCSOs and 30% of Specials. Females were 15.75% in 2001 but 25.10% in 2014, and 36% of PCSOs and 32% of Specials (MOPAC 2014). Progress, but BME and Mixed Race people were 40.22% of Londoners in the 2011 Census, and 51.70% were females. Of Commander rank, 6.5% are BME and 22.6% female but the BME and female share of intermediate ranks, Specialist Operations, and Specialist Crime, is smaller. Thus the Met was more diverse in 2014 than 2001 but had a lower rate of increase than the overall population, and, nationally, female and BME presence decreases with rank (Home Office 2014c).

Female recruitment and advancement

Policing opened to women just before the First World War. Women Police Volunteers (WPVs) performed general duties while men were at war, while 'Voluntary Women Patrols' (VWPs) concentrated on policing working class urban females. After the

Table 6.2 Metropolitan police diversity

	Mar-01		Mar-06		Mar-11		May-14 (Current)	
Workforce	Number	%age	Number	%age	Number	%age	Number	%age
Police Officer Total Strength	25,430.48	100%	30,870.67	100%	32,370.29	100%	30,945.08	100%
BME Officers	1,055.25	4.15%	2,285.65	7.40%	3,090.81	9.55%	3,426.49	11.07%
Female Officers	4,004.51	15.75%	6,131.66	19.86%	7,595.73	23.47%	7,768.58	25.10%
Police Staff	10,196.59	100%	13,769.43	100%	14,330.28	100%	11,894.47	100%
BME Police Staff	1,585.75	15.55%	3,032.08	22.02%	3,223.74	22.50%	2,882.02	24.23%
Female Police Staff	5,995.81	58.80%	8,116.89	58.95%	7,975.44	55.65%	6,619.39	55.65%

Source: MOPAC 2014 'MPS Workforce Diversity', London: Mayor's Office for Policing & Crime.

Women Police Service was set up to prosecute STD-infected women accused of having sex with soldiers, the WPV, which had a feminist orientation, was sidelined. Police authorities supported only the VWP and the sex police. By 1935 seventeen forces mustered only 105 WPCs between them, but 804 police matrons. The few women in forces up to the 1960s testified to pride in their minority status but also to male paternalism, dealing with women and children in a separate branch until the 1970s.

The female share of police strength across England and Wales has grown by about 1%/year during the twenty-first century. Across the US, Canada, Australia, New Zealand, several African countries, India, Pakistan, and several Asian countries, female officer proportions range between 5.1% and 28.8%, recruits ranging 26.6% to 37% (Prenzler and Sinclair 2013). Growth in female numbers is levelling out, with tangible but limited promotion gains. Male and female police career experiences differ in perceived need for mentoring interventions, job satisfaction, stress, and thoughts of resignation (Hassell et al 2011).

While formal curricula and policy documents may be gender-neutral, US police training is rife with gender lessons (Prokos and Padacic 2002). Women may be absent from classroom examples, excluded from recruit bonding experiences, and find physical differences between the genders exaggerated in self-defence classes. While 'men learnt masculinity by seeing it contrasted with a caricature of femininity' women 'learned that (their) ... expected role in the criminal justice system is as objects of male workers' fantasies and ridicule' (Prokos and Padacic 2002: 450–2). In the UK, recruit training fitness tests that produced grossly gendered pass/fail rates have been revised. Formerly they were 'normed' solely to men, with 40% of women failing, against 10% of men. Failure means termination of training, conveying a blunt message about what counts in policing. Women had trouble with an upper-body strength 'push pull' test, a grip test, and a 'shuttle run', in which recruits run between two fixed points against an accelerating metronome (Brown 2007). In 2003 the Home Office discontinued the grip strength test and reduced the endurance element of the shuttle runs. Consequently, 99% of men, and 76% of women, passed. Trainers commented that the public would be surprised to know that one could pass if able to carry bags of groceries. This gendered example concluded with snide reference to passmarks being 'obviously ... designed to encourage a more inclusive … workforce' (quoted in Martis 2006: 18). In reality, physical demands change over the first three years' service such that strength training becomes less relevant (Lagestad and van den Tillaar 2014).

Citing a male PC embroiled in a slanging match with youths, a female inspector commented, 'women police will always want to resolve a situation with the least possible upset. Their question is always, can we do this without confrontation? Is it possible without conflict? There just isn't that … macho aggressiveness you get from the men. We're better communicators' (*The Guardian* 29 August 2009). Following the 2009 G20 protests in which Ian Tomlinson died, the Met announced that both senior officers handling the Climate Camp protest would be female due to communication skills. Female senior officers are 'more flexible, emotionally independent, self-assertive, self-confident, proactive and creative' while male peers are 'more authoritarian and prejudiced' (Anderson 2003).

This does not mean females shun force. Women are just as likely to be involved in arrests associated with violence or resistance but much less likely to arrest for 'non-crime' misdemeanours like drunkenness (Westmarland 2001). Lonsway et al (2002) analysed US civil liability cases involving complaints against police use of force. While 13% of officers in urban forces were women, so should account for 13% of upheld excessive force incidents, the actual proportion was far lower. Allegations against males were nine times more likely to be upheld, and males were three times more likely to be named in public complaints over use of excessive force. The average male cost from two and a half to five times more than the average female in compensation payments for excessive force. There was no significant gender difference in use of *legitimate* force in routine patrol duties, including arrests. Women are not reluctant about, or shielded from, using force, but are averse to using excessive force.

Physical strength and aggression are not factors either in general effectiveness or handling dangerous situations. Little police work requires brute strength, even in potentially violent encounters (Fielding and Fielding 1992). Overall competence, effectiveness, and productivity on patrol do not differ by gender (Lonsway et al 2003). Females are aware the public may see them as less authoritative so develop 'psychological techniques and tricks' to compensate 'lack of physique' (Heidensohn 1994). Talk-based skills are decisive in conflict reduction. Women's talk is cooperative, mutually reinforcing, and turn-taking, while men's is declamatory, abrupt, assertive, and features exertions of dominance (Bernstein 1971). Females are better at deploying 'de-escalation' techniques with suspects and more readily display empathy with victims and witnesses (Langworthy and Travis 2003), despite there being no statistically-significant differences in emotional response to stressful tasks (Brown and Grover 1998). Male colleagues value women for gender-based qualities, for instance because they attract less suspicion in plainclothes work, enabling them 'to penetrate criminal environments' (Mac Giollabhui et al 2016).

Women display collateral skills in relating to the public. They display more respect, appear less cynical, and are more inclined to listen, qualities that cohere with procedural justice and also influence male colleagues' approach. Ironically, PCCs and chiefs have made a red-blooded stand against crime the hallmark of their 'traditional' approach, when that tradition is actually founded on exactly the emphasis on public cooperation that female officers display.

Females feel obliged to respond to daily tests of their abilities by male colleagues (Haarr and Morash 2013). Women with family responsibilities initially reconcile conflicts by working harder (Tena 2013). In early service most prioritize their work but with parental responsibilities comes increasing acceptance of traditional sexual divisions of labour and less orientation to promotion, a pattern absent amongst the childless or those with grown children (Chan et al 2010; Table 6.3 shows female share by rank).

When Westmarland (2001) researched one force's departments, gender ratios were Mounted Branch 10:1, Traffic Department 60:1, Marine Unit 14:1, Firearms 12:1 and Territorial Support Group 27:1. Specialist squads 'where there's a toy involved' have changed little (Brown and Heidensohn 2012). Westmarland's male officers doubted women's physical ability (e.g. saying body armour might slow female firearms officers aiding injured colleagues), but were protective and proud of the occasional exceptions. The sole female firearms officer was asked if this status caused her any problems. Her male sergeant answered: ' "Jill fits in with everyone else—she's just like one of the lads" '. With a meaningful look, the WPC added ' "it tells you something that he

Table 6.3 Police officers by rank and gender

Rank	Male	Female	**Total**	% Male	% Female
Chief officers	158	43	**201**	78.6	21.4
Chief superintendent	265	72	**337**	78.7	21.3
Superintendent	663	157	**820**	80.8	19.2
Chief inspector	1,283	374	**1,657**	77.4	22.6
Inspector	4,550	1,152	**5,701**	79.8	20.2
Sergeant	15,123	4,024	**19,148**	79.0	21.0
Constable	69,039	29,915	**98,954**	69.8	30.2
All Ranks	91,081	35,738	**126,818**	71.8	28.2

Source: Home Office (2015) *Police Workforce England and Wales 2015*, London: Home Office.

thinks *that's* a compliment"'. Firearms officers of both genders testify to wanting to fit in (Cain 2011).

Gendered deployment works against promotion by restricting experience, but Westmarland argued deployments were not from being typecast. Women predominated in Child and Family Protection but asserted agency and choice. Indeed, male officers were troubled by dealing with children and had problems with their own emotions in upsetting incidents. Their impassive exterior concealed alcoholism, sudden explosive outbursts, and failed relationships. Four dimensions marked their construction of male officer identity. The first was 'professionalism'—maintaining a 'macho cop' image in public. Second came 'competence'—claiming status as a valid shift member. The third was sexuality—displaying appropriate heterosexual desire while managing credible sympathy with sex crime victims. Last was heroism—protecting women and the vulnerable while remaining emotionally strong in disturbing situations. Neither accepting neo-domestic roles nor acting as pseudo-men challenges the male ethos of the organization (Fielding and Fielding 1992). Enculturated traditional values leave male officers confined by attitudes they themselves find constricting. Whether the gendered nature of different specialisms results from free choice or something less voluntary, it has consequences for service delivery. Moreover the public continues to profess preference for males in work perceived as requiring forceful response like brawls, and for females in handling sexual or domestic abuse victims (Brown et al 2009).

The first woman chief constable, Pauline Clare, a psychology graduate who spent much of her career policing Merseyside, was appointed to lead Lancashire in 1995, becoming responsible for a budget of £155 million, and 3,200 officers. Cressida Dick became the first female Met Commissioner in 2017. Media statements by newly-appointed female chiefs emphasize conventional postures of toughness. Thus, the Surrey chief appointed in 2012 declared she would 'relentlessly pursue the criminal society' (*Surrey Advertiser* 17 February 2012). Policing should not be 'over-complicated' and more people should be charged and tried. The only hint of a slightly different perspective was Chief Owens' comment that she most enjoyed investigating murders: 'there's no worse situation than a family having lost a loved one, and I had to be the level-headed one. The one thing you can do for the family is find the offender and that was a privilege'. Leaving aside that many murders involve one family member killing another, perhaps adopting a 'family' frame differs slightly from male perspectives. If one looks in vain here for the triumph of gender over police culture, Owens' biography does provide a coda to women's promotion. It cannot be said that she served in sections relating to the domestic sphere. After CID, she led territorial divisions, professional standards, and public order. One seldom makes chief without moving forces. Owens served in the Met, Kent, and Surrey, then headed NCA. Wide experience, and moving forces despite family responsibilities, is the archetypal male route to the top.

Ethnic minority recruitment and advancement

Racial discrimination in recruitment persists in all occupations, with a 13.8% difference between BME and overall employment (Department for Work and Pensions 2009). BME people are attracted by policing's pay and intrinsic satisfactions, factors outweighed by concerns over racism, sexism, and denying cultural identities to fit in (Home Office 2001a). Experience of stop-and-search and/or as crime victims (direct or indirect), influences application decisions. Nationally 5% of police are BME compared to a 14% share of general population (Police Foundation 2013). Some 7.5% of *civilian* staff and 10% of PCSOs are BME. Police exceed the fire service (3.3%) and compare to teachers (6.4%), but are behind probation officers (14%) and prosecutors (15%). Only 2.8% of ACPO/NPCC officers and 3.9% of superintendents are ethnic minority, but in 2003 it was only 1.4% of ACPO officers and 1.7% of superintendents. Ethnic minority recruitment co-varies with proportion of minorities in senior ranks (Gustafson 2013), but in large British cities recruitment is impeded by clumsy counter-terrorism efforts (Awan et al 2013).

In the Met, race accounts for most discrimination allegations, 194 (82%) of 238 between 2011 and 2014. Homophobic matters accounted for twenty-four cases, gender nine, religion four, and disability two. There were thirty-four employment tribunal claims alleging racial discrimination, most settled financially after hearings or, expensively, out of court. A BME counter-terrorist detective was treated 'like an enemy of the state' after alerting senior officers to racism and homophobia (*The Guardian* 18 May 2013). He was required by white officers to act as a 'buffer barrier' in stops of BME people, because 'blacks don't complain about blacks'. An employment tribunal found he suffered degrading/humiliating treatment, including homophobic banter (e.g. gay men 'taking it up the arse'). After his win the Met sacked him for gross misconduct for taking sick leave following harassment. A Met policy of deleting records of internal sex and race discrimination was exposed after an employment tribunal found in favour of PC Carol Howard, who was 'directly discriminated against' while one of only two black female firearms officers in the 700 strong Diplomatic Protection Group. Howard's supervisor believed her untrustworthy and dishonest, challenged her commitment in front of colleagues, and treated illness absences as false. When she filed a formal complaint he threatened her in a rage. A sergeant investigating her complaint was told to delete all references to sexual or racial harassment and discrimination in his report. Before the case the Met had asked Ms Howard to do a photo shoot illustrating its diversity.

An Equality and Human Rights Commission investigation into the Met's handling of discrimination cases found that ethnic or sexual minority officers anticipated being victimized and suffering career disadvantage if they complained (EHRC 2016). The Equality and Human Rights Commission (EHRC) could not confirm these fears because of the poor quality of the Met's complaint data. Trumpeting that 'the EHRC has confirmed that they have found no evidence of any unlawful acts in how the Met responds to staff grievances', a deputy commissioner 'utterly rejected' EHRC concerns. What is undeniable is that the large proportion of cases settled by compensation and gagging clauses both makes it hard to confirm the fears and indicates they are not groundless.

When the Home Affairs Committee expressed 'shock' in 2014 that not one force matched its residents' demographics and declared that positive discrimination might be necessary, Commissioner Hogan-Howe proposed legal changes to enable the Met to take half its recruits from ethnic minorities (for five years), but Mayor Johnson demurred. The Met then announced a policy to increase BME numbers by recruiting only candidates who had lived three of the past six years in London. In 2015 four forces had no BME officer, eleven had none above inspector, and only two of 201 chief officers were BME (ONS 2015). The Home Office claim that EU rules prevented positive discrimination fell with Brexit but it still saw 'no need' for quotas, which undermined recruitment and progression 'based on merit alone' (Weinfass 2016).

Diversity and police culture

Police have a general equality duty under the Equality Act 2010. They must have due regard to the need to 'eliminate unlawful discrimination, harassment and victimisation, ... advance equality of opportunity between people who share a protected characteristic and those who do not, and foster good relations' between them. Staff associations promoting diversity lost government funding the same year the law came into force (Clemence 2011).

Whether changes in class composition, graduate status, or minority recruitment change policing is moot. Fox (2013) argues that they make recruits less receptive to 'canteen culture' and more likely to challenge unethical practices. However, discrimination problems in US policing endure despite federally-mandated minority recruitment. Female recruitment helps gauge whether individuals change organizations or organizations change individuals. Women police were granted equal status in 1944 but only performed duties involving women and children. Women were, formally, fully integrated into policing after the Sex Discrimination Act 1975. At an event commemorating this a retired WPC described extensive male prejudice and scepticism despite the new law. However, 'we all knew we were doing something different but it was for us—it wasn't for the greater good of mankind' (*Surrey Advertiser* 23 May 2014). Female joiners knew what they were getting into and accepted it on its own grounds, despite practical obstacles. Truncheons were carried in police-issue handbags, and participants reminisced about preferring to wield the whole handbag rather than extract the truncheon. Such pragmatism helps us understand contemporary female officers' testimony that they are well aware of occupational sexism but if they work in sections associated with female roles it is because they have chosen to do so.

There remains evidence of a hardy 'canteen culture'. Loftus' (2009) ethnography found an exaggerated sense of mission and license (Manning 1977), prioritizing crime-related tasks over all others, and celebrating masculinity. Reforms were neutralized or resisted. Loftus (2010) argues that 'police culture endures because the basic pressures associated with the police role have not been removed'. Loftus heard talk advocating delinquent boot camps and capital punishment. However, such talk is sometimes a pressure release, pursuing an 'in' with peers or even gulling researchers by playing to stereotype (Fielding 1989). What matters is what officers actually do. Loftus' officers seem to have interacted with citizens as bored street bureaucrats (Lipsky 1980) rather than brutes. One arrest involving excessive force occurred in 600 hours fieldwork, plus three attempts to provoke uncooperative people into assault so they could be arrested.

As a concept, culture obscures neat cause and effect relations. 'Cultures are complex ensembles of values, attitudes, symbols, rules, recipes and practices, emerging as people react to the exigencies and situations they confront, interpreted through the cognitive frames and orientations they carry with them from prior experiences' (Reiner 2010: 116). Amongst the 'reactions' and 'cognitive frames' are the knowing exploitation of cultural signifiers by officers negotiating their path through the career and organization, be it pursuing promotion, avoiding discipline charges, or other motives that colour how they enact 'culture' from one set of 'exigencies and situations' to another (Fielding 1989). The issue is whether researchers can 'equate "culture" with thought and talk' and then assume this reflects practices (Waddington 2011a: 91). The idea of levels of occupational culture helps distinguish offensive but inconsequential speech acts exchanged privately between culture members versus beliefs that result in offensive actions (Cockcroft 2014) but beliefs/values that prove useful as guidelines to action become underlying assumptions (Schein 2004).

Waddington (1999) rightly criticizes the elision of negative values expressed in occupational culture with harsh, biased policing. Police culture is an easy target. Through its awfulness, police can be 'blame(d) for the injustices perpetrated (by) the criminal justice system' (Waddington 1999: 107), but the lack of empirical accounts of how negative enculturated values may cause unjust policing is a serious problem. While lambasting poor design in psychometric studies of police authoritarianism and attributing researchers' critiques of 'canteen culture' to liberal reformism, Waddington's most telling point is the lack of an empirically-supported logic model of how harsh occupational values translate into indifference to due process.

Even when examples come by direct observation, knowing research subjects can put on a performance for researchers; Van Maanen (1982) bases an entire analysis of fieldwork relations on just such an occurrence. The despicable assertions about Liverpool fans after Hillsborough, repeated at the new inquest in 2014, were tactical 'justifications' to excuse failures on the ground; linkage to culture is moot. We get closer to a fit between culture and lack of due process in the child sexual exploitation scandals that emerged in 2014, where girls living in 'secure accommodation' were systematically abused because officers considered them 'slags'. But clear evidence of an officer expressing negative enculturated views and demonstrably applying them in an independently witnessed encounter with the subject of prejudice is rare. Waddington is right that we should not visit the shames of criminal justice entirely on the police, but we do not need 'canteen culture' as a scapegoat to recognize malpractice and denial of due process. Culture may be as elusive as reliable authoritarianism tests, but we can identify controls that discourage malpractice without having to get inside officers' heads.

Many argue that police culture is not homogenous, but less often heard is the idea that, accordingly, police reflect the values that are distributed in society (Waddington 2011a). The opposing idea, that policing attracts people of a particularly conservative disposition, is more common. If instead police reflect values found in society, and these are obnoxious, then perhaps society's views are also obnoxious, at least to liberal sensibilities. Law and order would not be a reliable vote winner if it lacked popular appeal. Waddington goes that far, but not far enough. Within mainstream, populist values, the public also has a profound sense of fairness, as witness work on legitimacy. This opens the subtle possibility that perhaps what the public does not like in its police is what it sees of itself. For example, recent years have seen an increasingly open debate about whether immigration is a good thing. If police seem to crack down on minority communities especially hard, the public's better self sees this as wrong, while its backstage self believes this is where crime mostly originates. Bearing contradictory attitudes is human.

While behaviour cannot be read off directly from culture, we should not dismiss culture purely as an 'effect' rather than a 'cause'. We might consider the much-remarked erosion of discretion due to increasing frontline reluctance to stray beyond official guidance in case it causes 'in-the-job trouble', with experienced officers noting rookies' declining confidence (Cockcroft 2013). Professional practice is marked by discretion. Rigid adherence to rules is the exception amongst experienced professionals, with accountants conducting not a single case according to exact prescribed procedure (Suchman 1987). Aspects of occupational culture do change (Bradford et al 2013), and discretion may be inhibited for reasons having little to do with professionalism, but mainstream policework has not been transformed. Since occupational culture is an adaptation that people make to occupational demands, where the job remains essentially the same so will the culture. Despite greater diversity in recruitment, recruits are more likely to be made over by the occupation than to make the occupation over.

Diversity is something that educated people tend to take as a good in itself. We may want to believe that a diverse force will be more effective because it reaches out to more of the community, but when seeking evidence that a more diverse police workforce raises effectiveness the picture is doubtful. Departments with more minority officers have more assaults on police (Barrick et al 2014). Cultural competence is a factor in the effectiveness of Domestic Violence Fatality Review Teams (Bent-Goodley 2013), but BME officers are disproportionally implicated in corruption (Johnson et al 2013). BME officers themselves dismiss cultural diversity training as window-dressing having little impact on practice and insinuate that BME recruitment campaigns attract people who owe their job to ethnicity and are 'coathangers' marking time until collecting a pension whereas BME officers recruited normally are ambitious achievers (Cashmore 2002). Many insist that 'the job comes first'—in uniform, ethnic identity is secondary. However, Black Police Association (BPA) officials view recruitment drives and diversity training positively, due to BPA involvement (O'Neill and Holdaway 2007). This may seem self-serving but the officials freely criticize failed drives and spurn accelerated BME promotion. O'Neill and Holdaway argue that the BPA is changing police culture because minority officers find it less necessary to play down their ethnicity.

The real question is whether minority police impact on service delivery. While systematic review finds no overall evidence that minority recruitment benefits crime rates or public satisfaction, it does not make them worse, and the balance includes some successes. Bullock, Fielding, and Fielding's systematic review (2017) examined the evidence on the impact of BME recruitment on arrest rates, crime rates, and public satisfaction, and the mechanisms through which BME recruitment was expected to benefit policing. They identified just eleven studies satisfying standard inclusion criteria for systematic reviews. Seven related to crime rates and arrests, and four to public satisfaction. All were conducted in the USA. The evidence of these studies is equivocal about the effectiveness of BME recruitment on crime or public satisfaction but does suggest that it does not worsen arrest or crime rates or negatively influence public satisfaction. Minority officers perform fewer searches but have better hit rates, the gain being greatest in squads where minority members exceed a third (Mason 2007), suggesting that majority officers emulate effective practices where BME numbers exceed tokenism. Female officers obtain more reports of sexual assaults from women and secure higher rates of arrest and conviction (Meier and Nicholson-Crotty 2006).

However, large sample US studies find that with diversity, turnover increases, negatively affecting crime clearance (Hur 2012). Hur implicated within-force conflict due to cultural differences, leading to less solidarity and cooperation. Research on diversity's effects finds effective selection, training and ongoing support critical. Diversity on its own is insufficient. Careful management is needed to reduce conflict with other personnel, nurture minority employees' motivation, and manage their career pathways (Andrews et al 2005).

Sickness and Stress

The fact that injuries have a significance wider than their effects on individual officers or staff members is reflected in the longstanding use in HMIC inspections of injury/sickness rates to index occupational problems. Changes between inspections are monitored and the trend is examined, for example, Gwent's officer and staff sickness levels rose 50% from 1996–2001 (HMIC 2001). Across all police employee groups, absences of up to twenty days for common maladies (colds, flu, stomach bugs) occur at rates similar to the general population. For police, longer-term absences relate to stress, anxiety and depression, musculoskeletal disorders, fractures, head injuries, and lacerations. Under-resourcing, bureaucratic demands, organizational change, and perceived lack of support contribute to absence (IES 2007). Policies may have unanticipated effects on sickness and stress. Removal of police gyms to inhibit litigation if injury is sustained, and canteen closures due to pressure on space, can affect fitness and sickness absence.

Retirement on medical grounds is an occupational health indicator. In 2000 this accounted for 31% of officer retirements (Home Office 2001b). The mid–2000s move from central government to local police authority responsibility for financing ill-health retirement impacted on levels of retirement, with levels reflecting the proportion of force budgets met from local taxation (Crawford and Disney 2013). Retirements are also used to manage out problematic staff. Patterns reflect force culture and managers' inclination to grant restricted duties and planned leaving schemes (IES 2007).

Police have high occupational stress (Bonifacio 1991), with 46% regarding their work as very/extremely stressful (Houdmont et al 2012). Risk of assault is the highest of all occupations and five times above average (Health and Safety Executive 2014). In 2013 health professionals' risk of assault at work was 3.9% and social workers was 3.5% but the police figure was 7.6% (HSE 2014). A survey of German police found that violence against officers by citizens decreased commitment (Ellrich 2016). Police typically work shifts rotating on a weekly basis. Sleep deprivation induces dangerous fatigue and can cause serious accidents (Senjo 2011). Even compared to other emergency services, police stand out, with higher fatigue, exhaustion, and disengagement than firefighters (Basinska and Wiciak 2012).

Senior and frontline officers rate the same duties as most stressful—suspect pursuit, witnessing traumatic events, physical violence (Korre et al 2014). Stress also arises from routine activities, including appearing in court, and public order duties (Brown and Campbell 1993). Dealing with violence is linked to increased alcohol consumption amongst those who lack training to handle such situations or who are not debriefed afterwards (Leino et al 2011). There is higher incidence of binge drinking than other occupations (Weir et al 2012). Stress indicators—alcoholism, relationships dissolved, violence, self-harm—are high relative to other occupations.

Policing has a high array of suicide risk factors, with five prominent features associated with suicidal ideation: organizational stress, critical incident trauma, shift work, relationship problems, alcohol abuse (Chae and Boyle 2013). Two elements of traditional police culture, burnout and authoritarianism, are significantly related to intimate partner violence (Blumenstein et al 2012). Burnout amongst civilian staff is driven by similar factors (McCarty and Skogan 2013).

Stress-related problem behaviours generally increase nearing retirement (Harris 2011). Age, service length, and rank correlate with lower stress resilience (Balmer et al 2014). PTSD and depression rise with career length (Regher et al 2013). Officers may misuse powers under stress; those primed by, for example, family arguments, are more likely to arrest for minor offences (Johnson 2013). There are gender differences in exposure to, and effects of, occupational stress (see Brown 2011). Females are less likely to be exposed to potential violence, with more severe adverse reactions if exposed (Brown and Fielding 1993). In males, potential violence induces excitement and gratification, less common among females (Jermier et al 1989). Organizational stressors affect the sexes similarly but females report more sex discrimination, prejudice, and harassment (Brown and Campbell 1990). Female sergeants show higher emotional exhaustion than males but the burn-out process features the same drivers—work/life conflict, relations with peers and supervisors (McCarty 2013). Stress varies by demand (Backteman-Erlanson et al 2013), roles that isolate incumbents from contact with fellow officers (Brown and Fielding 1993), and by function; thus, stressors for homicide work include time pressure, case complexity, differential caseload, and ownership of case files (Dabney et al 2013).

Suppressed response to stressful events can cause cynicism, burnout, and aggressiveness. Police culture inhibits disclosure of psychological injury and mental ill-health to colleagues and managers, aggravated by budget cuts reducing awareness training (Bell and Eski 2016). Officers are customarily reluctant to seek help. After the Piper Alpha oil rig explosion officers retrieved rotting corpses from the submerged accommodation module; none sought counselling (Alexander and Wells 1991). 'Psychological first aid' like Critical Incident Stress Debriefing is declined. Heavy drinking with other officers involved, moodiness and domestic abuse show that first recourse is to intimates and immediate workgroup; a survey of Canadian officers found that help with post-traumatic effects of incidents was most often sought from family and friends (Heffren and Hausdort 2016). Involving significant others, and immediate supervisors, shows promise (Can et al 2013), but forces customarily keep families at a distance, and supervisors are reserved about providing such support.

Role and gender shape the experience of injury. A large-scale survey (N = 10,897) triangulated with sub-sample interviews (N = 59) found that psychological injury was the most commonly-reported injury (anxiety being most common, then depression and PTSD) (Fielding et al 2017). While all respondents ranked support for mental health needs as high priority, a statistically-significantly higher percentage of females did so. Females assigned higher priority to: psychological support following major incidents; better access to mental health services; support from welfare personnel who can liaise with supervisors; and better line manager training. Special Constables also stood out in seeing a need for psychological support following major incidents. Specials, PCSOs and civilian staff felt they were treated less favourably than regular officers.

A high profile case involving police stress was the suspected suicide of the Greater Manchester Police chief in 2008. An experienced mountaineer and fitness fanatic, Todd was found dead on a notoriously dangerous Welsh mountain he had climbed many times. He set off in a violent storm with three hours daylight remaining, which anyone who knew the mountain would know was insufficient for a return trip. Beside his body was a half-emptied gin bottle and he had taken sleeping tablets. The inquest ruled that he died of exposure 'while his mind was in turmoil'. The force's PCC subsequently appealed for evidence relating to suspected financial malpractice by Todd, involving 'golden handshake' redundancy payoffs for senior staff. However, media coverage revolved around Todd's sex life, reportedly having had thirty-eight mistresses with whom he made sexually explicit video recordings. The press suggested Todd thought his affair with the head of the Chamber of Commerce was about to be exposed. Such relationships breach safeguards against blackmail. While this links with the relationship turbulence factor in occupational stress, perhaps more telling was Todd's nickname 'Tigger', reflecting his boundless energy. He took a close interest in his officers' concerns, constantly monitoring demand, reviewing performance and making arrests from his chauffuered car. Before his death, colleagues noted exhaustion. He expressed disappointment at working too hard to exercise and spoke of suicide. Whether driven to his end by alleged corruption or relationship problems, the stresses of leading police in one of Britain's toughest cities would have contributed.

The term 'police family' is widely used to represent policing functions performed by others in addition to sworn officers but also has another sense. While occupational culture is often treated as problematic it does function as a support for officers and their families. When officers are seriously injured or die in the line of duty that meaning of the police family is important. PC Stan Jones was a motorcycle officer who died after a collision in 2004. A police charity supported his family during his hospitalization and after his death. The family lived in police housing—'we live it and breath it 24 hours a day ... I have got constant reminders', his wife said (*Surrey Advertiser* 20 June 2014). Living together as a workgroup is declining as police housing is sold off, and as Mrs Jones hinted, has its downside, but policing provided a supportive network of survivors.

Public Confidence and Trust

Confidence in police has been declining in most Western countries since the early 1980s (Van de Walle and Raine 2008). UK attitudes are close to the European average. Trust in criminal justice is positively associated with trusting other people and satisfaction with one's life, both relating to social class, and, in the UK, to education. Some 65% of people trust police to be truthful but 29% do not, putting police below judges (82%) but above civil servants (50%) (Ipsos-MORI 2013). Over thirty years, those trusting police vary only between 58% and 65%. In 2014 exactly the same percentage trusted police as in 1983, while slightly more did not (31%). Thus, over three decades a third consistently distrust police.

Relative to other countries, Britons generally believe police are doing a good job—more so than other justice institutions—unless they have been in contact with police (Home Office 2000b). Contact's impact is 'asymmetrical'; positively-rated contact only maintains existing confidence but negatively-rated contact lowers it (Miller et al 2004). Those who found contact unsatisfactory were least confident, regardless whether they or police initiated contact (Myhill and Beak 2008). Only 37% of victims felt very or fairly well informed about their investigation's progress, and 34% felt not well-informed or not at all informed (Ministry of Justice 2010).

Minorities are generally less confident about police. Gypsies/Travellers, sex workers, young black men, people with mental ill-health, learning disabilities or physical disabilities, and recent migrants, are sensitive to perceived fairness (APA 2011). Most feel their circumstances, culture or needs are misunderstood. Anticipating this, many expect unfair treatment. When confounded they form particularly positive impressions, indicating the value of fair conduct (Murphy and Cherney 2012). Relations with police play a significant part in the formation of social identity. Perceived police fairness is associated both with young BME males' social identity and their cooperativeness, particularly those having multiple national identities and thus affinities for another country (Bradford 2014). For them, perceived unfair policing triggers broader conclusions about British society.

Most people claim above average respect for police, with around three-quarters saying they view police with respect but only a quarter thinking others do (Home Office 2004, Statistical Bulletin 2/2004). In 2008, when only 44% of adults were confident in the criminal justice system's effectiveness, police were its highest rated element, and generally place highly (Smith 2010). The public broadly favours police decisions even when deviating from correct procedure (Waddington 2011a: 96) and appraise the rightness or otherwise of their actions similarly to officers (Waddington 2011b). The principal reservation is unprofessional language, especially attempts at ingratiation by false 'matey-ness'.

High satisfaction ratings in surveys require not only effective performance but the public perception that performance is effective. The headline measure is whether the public think police are effective in bringing offenders to justice, but views on the national and local picture diverge and confidence can remain low despite increases in offences brought to justice (Singer and Cooper 2008). Public satisfaction is highly geo-local. In relatively compact York, factors most influencing resident views of police vary wildly depending on perceptions of their locale (Perkins 2016). Personal experience plays most part in perceptions of common crimes while serious crime perceptions are influenced by media reporting. There is a clear linear relationship between actual and perceived crime levels in one's locale; 29% of residents in high crime areas perceive their crime as above average, against 1% in the lowest crime areas (Home Office 2009). While local perceptions are realistic, people are much more inclined to believe national crime levels are increasing, so the perception gap is widest for those in the lowest crime areas. Professional policing involves reassuring those whose actual risk is low while responding to those most at risk.

Legitimacy

Public confidence thus condenses several inter-related judgements concerning police that apply across population groups and levels of experience of crime. Victims want their case solved, but their satisfaction also requires that police provide reassurance, support, and information (Rinkevics and Landmane 2013/2014). Even recent victims and those anxious about crime place police fairness and community involvement above effectiveness (Bradford and Jackson 2010). Police legitimacy is the perceived right to hold authority, which underpins public acceptance and cooperation (Tyler et al 2010). This is granted when 'authorities are concerned with the well-being of people in the community and are honest and respectful when dealing with them' (Tyler et al 2010: 370), enabling 'the transformation of power into legitimate authority in a way that generates normative compliance'

(Hough and Maffei 2013). Public confidence matters because it engenders the trust that facilitates the cooperation with police from which legitimacy grows. Perceived legitimacy and trust increase police effectiveness (Myhill and Quinton 2011) and also predicts cooperation with police against terrorism (Cherney and Murphy 2013; Kundnani 2013). Where Muslims' trust and confidence is low they are less likely to report crimes, provide information or cooperate with police (Huq et al 2011). Legitimacy involves not only proper legal authority but public acceptance, witness societies like Russia where most distrust the police and cooperation is minimal (Semukhina and Reynolds 2014).

Well-received contact depends on police conduct (Myhill and Bradford 2012). Fair treatment even predominates over the outcome of interventions, and influences whether defendants' and convicted offenders' believe their trial was just (Baker et al 2014). Procedural justice strongly co-varies with perceived police legitimacy even amongst offenders (White et al 2016). Procedural fairness involves officers explaining their motives, granting opportunities for citizen input, and not stereotyping, operationalized as: citizen participation prior to police reaching decisions; perceived neutrality in decision-making; treating citizens respectfully throughout; and conveying trustworthy motives. Lack of procedural fairness inhibits crime reporting, deters cooperation (Van Craen 2013) and reduces arrests (Kirk and Matsuda 2011). An intervention's substantive form (law enforcement, advice etc.) is secondary in its effects on legitimacy to a procedurally-just dialogue underpinning interventions (Mazerolle et al 2013b: 10). Even a brief, police-initiated, but procedurally-just traffic stop can boost public confidence (Mazerolle et al 2013a).

Evidence for legitimacy's role in public cooperation was originally inferred from survey measures showing its association with perceived effectiveness, but displayed low reliability. However, Sunshine and Tyler's (2003) 'Perceptions of Police Trustworthiness' sub-scale proved reliable (Tankebe 2008). Effectiveness directly affected perceived trustworthiness but procedural fairness strengthened the relationship. Effective detection certainly affects public perceptions in serious crime, where Community Impact Assessments show impact across many more than those directly involved (Innes 2010). Effectiveness is a necessary, but not sufficient, condition of legitimacy: 'perceived procedural fairness was significantly predicted by judgements about outcome fairness, outcome favourability and police effectiveness' (Tankebe 2008: 196). We are unlikely to be confident about police who are incompetent, but neither does effectiveness excuse procedural unfairness.

The view that police can raise confidence by their conduct is not universally accepted. Rosenbaum et al (2005) and Skogan (2006a, 2006b) argue that, at best, police conduct can maintain existing satisfaction levels. This position can be reconciled with the legitimacy thesis if we note that even when people believe specific decisions are wrong they can continue to support the police institution if they believe it to be impartial, just, and competent (Tyler 2006). Inept interventions leave people dissatisfied with their treatment regardless of outcome.

The picture includes how police understand public confidence. The strongest predictor of officers' confidence in their own authority is identification with their force, which strongly associates with perceived managerial and policy fairness (Bradford et al 2013). Perceived unfairness strengthens identification with 'canteen culture' (Bradford and Quinton 2014). Public cooperativeness also contributes but Bottoms and Tankebe's (2013) dialogic notion of legitimacy suggests general esteem is less influential than officers' experience in actual encounters. Officers who identify with 'canteen culture' believe public attitudes do not matter provided interventions are lawful. Those whose sense of legitimacy relies on formal legal authority may police aggressively because they *lack* confidence in their individual authority, not have too much.

For its part, the public's confidence relates to police visibility as well as manner. Cuts meant that fewer people saw an officer on patrol at least once a week, coinciding with perception that policing had deteriorated under austerity (BBC 2013). Growth in restorative justice (Rix et al 2009) confronted suspicion that it was adopted simply to save money (HMIC 2012a). 'Power-holder legitimacy' (Bottoms and Tankebe 2013) is an important index of professionalism but measures of confidence that remain obstinately fixed at a third of us not trusting the police suggest that training requires a closer understanding of police/public interaction than is afforded by opinion surveys and the somewhat abstract legitimacy heuristic.

Professional Competence and Training

A professional force prepares entrants to negotiate tough times and earn public confidence. Competent policing requires the development of situational awareness, attuned to the context of the community policed, mediated by the resources available. A role theory approach asks us to understand the 'definition of the situation' (Thomas 1923) or 'frame of reference' (Mead 1934) that officers bring to public encounters, to which Merton added the latent consequences of decisions (Lee 2010). This involves a refined understanding of 'matter out of place', features that do not look right. For centuries the term for police was 'the Watch'; a document of 1312 describes men of the Watch 'well and fittingly armed' surveying from the city walls all who came 'to enter the City' (quoted in Ackroyd 2001). US officers refer to 'JDLR', the 'Just Doesn't Look Right' concept, and keeping a 'BOLO', or Be On the Look Out book. The beat books of Victorian London endured into the 1990s, with remarkably similar annotations about people and illicit activities (Fielding 1995).

Observing car engine tuners, Sandberg distinguished three forms of competence: '(i) competence as accurately optimising separate qualities of the engine; (ii) competence as accurately optimising interacting qualities of the engine in the right order; and (iii) competence as optimising interacting qualities of the engine through a practical sense of the engine' (Sandberg 1994: abstract). The analogous policing competencies are: delivering given interventions such as to satisfy specific situated requirements; drawing on qualities underlying appropriate, staged practice across cognate intervention types; and respecting qualities underlying appropriate practice across all police interventions.

Frontline police acquire practical knowledge of what works and why, contextualized against granular knowledge of locales (Bayley 2008), a form of 'craft knowledge' which understands that 'to do good work means to be curious about, to investigate, and to learn from ambiguity' (Sennett 2008: 48). Craft skills demand resources of time and temperament that infuriate modern management. Wizened officers talk of requiring a decade to know a beat well enough to play it. Such tenure is now so exceptional that it is reported in the local press. Contemporary organizations are about 'closing down the ambiguities of the world in the name of ever tighter efficiency (which nevertheless fails precisely because of the inescapability of ambiguity)' (Tester 2008: 45). An average force generates over 4,500 intelligence reports a month (Bullock 2013) including source reliability assessments, classification of information type, and a 'handing code' for dissemination. This did not ensure officers planning a drug arrest in another force's area received crucial information. The suspect was a suicide risk who fatally plunged a knife into his chest during the search (IPCC 2014b).

Meanwhile police trainers deride emphasis on competency because 'officers make decisions based on minimum information' and 'only have to know about evidence-gathering' (quoted in Murrell-Abery 2003: 56). Professional policing requires information to inform judgement. In studied understatement, experienced officers simply say 'we play it by ear', but trainees lack experience through which to attune the ear. Experience is accumulated knowledge on which anticipatory understandings of contingent possibilities are based. The striking difference between chess masters and novices is the 'large database of chess scenarios [masters] have stored in their memories' (Thacher 2008: 53). Both select moves by considering what is open to them and its possibilities. Both consider similar numbers of possible moves and look ahead as far. But masters perform against more previously-encountered scenarios. Police reasoning is case-based, not deduced from abstract logic or set guidance. Standards cannot cover every contingency (Suva 2012).

Some commend Cognitive Load Theory (CLT) (Swellert 1988) for learning complex policing skills. The heuristic differentiates working memory (which temporarily stores information for immediate use) and long-term memory. Working memory is transient and holds up to nine items simultaneously. Long-term memory is unlimited but requires assignment of items to 'schema'. Schema hold extensive information (e.g. evidence procedures) and reduce cognitive load by absorbing items from working memory. Schema-directed action becomes 'automated' with experience. Mugford et al (2013) thus declare that training should instil schema and encourage 'automation'. Rigidity and ethical dilemmas are obvious drawbacks. CLT's pedagogy minimizes 'element interactivity' amongst dimensions of an issue, for example, diversity syllabi would teach population change separately to ethnic cultural history. It is unsurprising that a pedagogy directed to lowering cognitive load is based on the model of applying handcuffs because each step 'can be learned in isolation' (ibid: 317). CLT's schema are reservoirs without pipelines.

'Local knowledge' is often highlighted amongst police competencies. Rubinstein's (1971) classic treatment emphasized a fine-grained understanding of problem locations. Officers learn that bars, transport hubs, and schools are positively associated with violent, property, and disorder crime, while a narrower range of crime is associated with halfway houses and drug treatment centres and is confined within a shorter distance (Groff and Lockwood 2014). The 'scripts' officers develop around frontline competencies draw on granular decision schema or knowledge structures. 'The script is an event schema [that] organises our knowledge about how to understand and enact commonplace behavioural processes or routines' (Cornish 1994: 158). Scripts help negotiate recurrent situations. Officers experience verbally disrespectful behaviour more often than physical assaults (Pizio 2014) and courts take account of swearing directed at officers (Martis 2012). Accordingly officers develop scripts for citizens who are shouting drunk.

Role theory can be combined with the 'scripts' approach to develop 'control scripts' for frontline police roles. 'Control scripts' seek to develop systematic frames on what it takes to 'do' control in common policing situations by exhaustively describing actions from an officer's perspective at the unfolding temporal stages of an intervention. However, unlike CLT's 'schema', the scripts approach acknowledges that scripts alone do not generate competence. Competencies are best seen as 'incomplete instructions for behaviour' (Ekblom and Gill 2016). Generating professional performance from them is conditioned by information from the situation, as it presents itself both *ex ante* and *in situ*. It demands a degree of improvization when available competencies fall short of what is needed (Cornish 1994). The quality of improvized performance relates to 'reflexes, instincts and habits', 'perceptual motor skills', and 'voluntary planned behaviour' (Ekblom and Gill 2016). Training can credibly influence only the last of these, but it is the element with most effect on performance quality.

While psychological elements are only transferable by imitation, the voluntary planned element can be the subject of reflective practice, and can also be transferred to others. Transferring competency knowledge can inspire refinement and development, by making neglected features explicit and through learners volunteering points from their own experience. Professional training encourages dialogue over what constitutes the competencies needed to resolve given types of intervention, one consideration being accommodating situational contingencies, others being risk to officer(s), effort required, and reward (Cornish and Clark 1986). Like offenders, officers learn role-specific signifiers and cues. Compared to others, both are distinctively predisposed to mundane situational prompts (Wikstrom 2014). A ladder negligently left near a corner shop will signal 'means of entry' to both. Competence also involves knowing when to ignore or doubt predispositions.

The point about 'situational contingency' as a factor complicating prediction of the process and outcome of interventions is generally made by example rather than a logic model. A logic model would work from one overarching feature of crime and disorder: their conflictual nature. Conflict in real time makes competencies and their accompanying performance scripts vulnerable to counter-moves by offenders. Scripts must be revised *in situ*. Professional training's message is not the script but deft improvization in the spirit of the script.

Competence requires a measure of empathy with recipients, even where conflict is the relationship's main feature. The idea of 'emotional labour' (Hochschild 1983) skates the line between empathy (an aid to effective intervention) and sympathy (risking favouritism; Clark 1987). In role-taking the empathizer thinks themselves into the other's situation so as to grasp the other's perspective, enabling a suitable physical display of demeanour and expression (Clark 1997). In 'identification' the empathizer experiences the other's emotions through the empathizer's own feelings. Such interactional work is conditioned by the officer's wider brief, perception of the situation (and thus their relation to the recipient), and the officer's expected role, the specific values attaching to it, and the reference group for their performance (e.g. supervisors, peers; Morton 2013). Since framing emotions derive from the context of the intervention, experience in similar situations is a guide to current action but not a blueprint.

To act as their role requires professionals must draw a line between taking on board the others' perspective and adopting the others' perspective as their own. They must guard against over-identification from shared traits. Both a sense of fellowship and sharp difference pose tests. One can think oneself into another's perspective without liking them (else there would be few biographies of Hitler), but wanting to be liked can be as much a threat to professionalism as bearing a cold and suspicious estimation of human nature.

A 2014 incident encapsulates the inconsiderate approach that often ensnares police. A noted artist was arrested and held. Concerned about noise and pollution, Jock McFadyen had repeatedly complained about police vehicles from a nearby station parking outside his home with their engines running at length. On the Sunday in question he asked officers to turn off their engine. They refused. As he walked away he slapped the bonnet of an unattended police car and was arrested for criminal damage (*Evening Standard* 29 July 2014). Police later released McFadyen without charge but the practice continued. 'Runlock' keeps car computers booted up, telling despatchers where vehicles are; rebooting takes seven minutes after switching off. Professional policing involves the kind of empathy that informs simple courtesy. If despatchers' need to know where unassigned vehicles are, stop the vehicles leaving the station yard until they need to, either booting up the computer en route to its first call, or polluting the station rather than neighbours. Slapping a car bonnet is no more likely to cause criminal damage than brushing against it. Petty spite is unprofessional. The officers' inability to control themselves alienated someone with a hotline to the media and neighbours sharing the same grievance. It tied police up in a pointless piece of theatre and wasted custody resources.

Barriers to empathic skills abound in policing, starting with failure to acknowledge them in recruitment decisions and training. On the job, they are inhibited by demand and time pressure. However, those with good interactional competence can moderate those challenges. The problem lies more in such competence not being seen as equivalent in importance to technical skills like handcuffing. Officers lacking in communicative repertoire and strongly drawn to professional detachment deny themselves an important resource for making others' actions comprehensible when negotiating everyday interventions (Karp and Stenmark 2011). If we approach interventions simply as a matter of establishing 'the facts' we blind ourselves to the role emotion plays in perceiving that something is a fact.

Traditional assessments of police performance target misconduct—eliminating the bad rather than documenting the good. Measuring *good* performance customarily assesses investigative outcomes rather than the peacekeeping work that dominates frontline officers' time (Reiner 1998), particularly that of probationers. Assessing peacekeeping necessitates focus on process and quality of service rather than outcome, because many factors affect outcomes and it is often unknown what happens once police leave. In customary assessments of training and of policing more generally a relatively polished and intricate suite of administrative indicators suggests a closely monitored and managed system but the indicators measure the countable rather than the necessarily meaningful. Although the performance measurement vocabulary comprises 'three Es'—efficiency, effectiveness and economy (Table 6.4)—effectiveness measures that demonstrate impact are difficult to devise and collect, so efficiency construed as cost ('economy') predominates. The pursuit of training's impact hinges on implementation. Unless it is clear that training was implemented as designed it cannot be credited with specific impacts, and the diffuse system of multiple entry qualifications and multiple training-providers obstructs such an evaluation. Meanwhile, misconduct and sub-optimal performance reflect serious training deficits.

The existence of codes of ethics tells us that training alone cannot secure effective, humane, and fair policing, but training remains a principal means of intervention in those terms, and when combined with apt in-service training and genuine supervisory mentoring and appraisal it can be the *prime* means of intervention. We earlier sought to use the demands that policing faces and the legal, material, and social resources it is given to meet those

Table 6.4 The Three Es

A system is <u>effective</u> if it achieves the desired results
A system is <u>efficient</u> if it uses resources to maximum effect
A system is <u>economic</u> if its services are procured at the optimal ratio of cost and quality
The <u>efficiency relationship</u> is that between inputs (resources) and outputs (services)
The <u>effectiveness relationship</u> is that between outputs and impact (what is achieved by the services produced)

Source: P. Drucker (1993) *The Effective Executive*, NY: Harper.

demands, to provide a context for training as it has been and as it is now. In this chapter we have, on similar lines, used pressure points, scandals, and outright disasters to highlight both at individual officer level and organizational level the consequences that flow when policing is ineffective, inhumane, and unfair. Personal and systemic corruption, misconduct and complaints, problems achieving diversity, officer sickness and stress, and failure to secure public confidence, each offer nuances of what it means to be professional (and unprofessional), and differing implications for training. Addressing them is the definitive tall order. We now consider whether officialdom's 'new policing landscape' is competent to satisfy that order and, if not, the lessons to learn.

7

The New Policing Landscape

We may have a 'new policing landscape' but the ground is unstable. Recent times have seen much experiment in delivery of policing functions, from the 1990s onwards. The 'New Public Management' policies of the 1990s imposed market-based practices on public services. To control 'gaming', regulators were introduced, including the Independent Police Complaints Commission (IPCC) and the Home Office Police Standards Unit (Patrick 2012). New Labour's Workforce Modernisation programme sought efficiencies through civilianization and recruiting auxiliaries to relieve officers' administrative burden, from custody and prisoner-handling to response policing and criminal investigation (HMIC 2004). Pronounced resistance was attributed to occupational culture (Loveday 2007) but the initiative cherry-picked functions, with inconsistent application and continual realignment of content, structures, and processes (Pellegrinelli et al 2007). New Labour was keen on Key Performance Indicators (KPIs), setting annual targets under the Best Value regime. In 2009 this gave way to the 'Analysis of Police and Community Safety' performance assessment framework, with thirty-six indicators monitoring service delivery, but instead of a suite of KPIs there was a single target—to increase public confidence by 15%. The single KPI was welcomed half-heartedly, with much debate over focusing measurement on a single figure.

New Labour's later years saw substantial initiatives. It moved against bureaucracy and 'over-regulation', via the Flanagan Report (2008), which also raised accountability reform. Labour introduced the National Policing Pledge in 2009 with ten national commitments from service standards like response times to broad principles ('being treated with dignity and respect') (Cabinet Office 2008). As noted earlier, after implementation no force was assessed as 'excellent' across the board (HMIC 2009c).

Professionalizing the Police: The Unfulfilled Promise of Police Training. Nigel G. Fielding © Nigel G. Fielding 2018. Published 2018 by Oxford University Press

Regarding public confidence, the satisfaction pledge was crucial. Four forces were 'good', thirty-five 'fair', and four were 'poor', the worst performance of any pledge. The Policing Pledge was abandoned after a year. The Coalition declared this would free police from 'central control'.

The twenty-first century has seen a move from 'bureaucratic professionalism' (routinized administration) to managerialism (emphasizing productivity and performance). First wave managerialism had conflicting currents: organizational restructuring versus taking a consumerist approach to quality of the police 'product'. While the Association of Chief Police Officers (ACPO) favoured the consumerist option, restructuring won out. After Northamptonshire replaced the customary territorial division and subdivision structure with Basic Command Units (BCUs), eliminating a whole tier, Audit Commission praise was followed by Her Majesty's Inspectorate of Constabulatory (HMIC) adopting BCUs nationally. When home secretaries gained authority to set national targets and performance indicators over the heads of police authorities the Home Office effectively offloaded responsibility for performance, and accountability, to BCUs.

However, the logical extension, granting BCU commanders financial control, was too much for ACPO and the police authorities. Latterly BCUs have faded, with many forces moving from territorial to functional structures, and chiefs' consumerist preference re-emerging. Consumerism focuses on cultural rather than structural change. 'Citizen-focused policing' emphasizes localism and a consumerist approach via Neighbourhood Policing (NP), and is less threatening to chiefs than are BCUs (Gilling 2014: 92). In Loader and Sparks' terms, consumerism and localism offer democratic openings.

If police managerialism premiered with New Labour, it played to mixed reviews during the Coalition. The dance between the customary principals—home secretary and chiefs—suddenly changed when the wallflowers representing the public interest—police authorities—turned into that new class of politician, the Police and Crime Commissioner (PCC). Future PM Cameron's 2006 vision for a 'policing revolution' included PCCs, 'modern' pay and conditions, and force amalgamations (Brain 2013). In government, Cameron claimed PCCs would 'reconnect police and people', 'increasing democratic accountability' while 'removing bureaucratic accountability' (Home Office 2010). The

Coalition also abolished the National Policing Improvement Agency (NPIA), which had 13% of the policing budget. A jaded rendering might thus be that government's agenda boiled down to: cut budgets, impose US-style elected PCCs, leave forces to cope. Home Secretary May said simply 'value for money will have to drive everything the police do'. Police offered no counter-narrative, unlike their 1989 Operational Policing Review when confronting Sheehy's reforms. Preoccupation with Brexit left the 2015 Conservative government little capacity for policing initiatives. May's transit from home secretary to prime minister reinforced policing's austerity woes.

Two decades of UK police reform thus saw interventions in standards-setting, performance management, marketization, and governance. They bespeak a historically unfamiliar willingness of politicians to take on police (Manning 2014). Politicians have increasingly construed policing purely as crime control, tellingly by the police minister at the College of Policing launch (Loader 2014a). Officers themselves value their multifaceted role and do not want simply to be crime fighters (Hoggett et al 2013). We earlier noted Loader and Sparks' (2011) argument that, despite the polity's retreat from social democracy, there have been positive developments, like greater sensitivity to human rights. Officers have welcomed new procedures under Human Rights legislation for more frontline accountability because they offer protections against potential complaint (Bullock and Johnson 2012).

Nevertheless, making policing a site for reworking social democracy has limits (Loader and Sparks 2011: 34). 'Just ordering' can advance ameliorative interventions and enlist the public, as where restorative justice engages citizens in the justice done in their name, but is not an agent of redistributive transformation. Inequality's ultimate causes are beyond police influence. What is in their grasp is to foster a democratic element in professionalism (Dzur 2008).

Topography of the Police Landscape

The structure of the new policing landscape was unveiled at the 2012 ACPO conference by the Home Office. HMIC survived but with 'lighter touch', more accessible inspections; the National Crime Agency (NCA) replaced the Serious Organised Crime Agency (SOCA); the College of Policing replaced NPIA; PCCs arrived, later described as 'monsters' by Home Secretary May; the IPCC was little disturbed bar powers to investigate PCC misconduct; and ACPO was to dismantle, then reassemble, itself.

A large question mark in the new landscape was ACPO's status, branded a 'boys club' obstructing reform by the *Daily Mail*, organ of newfound Conservative hostility to police. This is important because, with NPIA, ACPO formed a principal institutional locus of professional knowledge. Its 300 committees dealt with areas of science, social science, and technology on which policing draws. However, the committees sowed complexity and overlap, and ACPO was an anomalous limited company without public accountability. The Association of PCCs gave ACPO a year to decide how it would deliver in an environment whose key players—PCCs, the College of Police (CoP), and NCA—were all new. General Parker's review found an unelected 'inner core' of experienced chiefs wielding power, with other members 'dormant', but Parker agreed chiefs needed a body for operational and managerial coordination, informing policy, and implementing practice, functions requiring more transparent committee briefs. The National Police Chiefs' Council (NPCC) was established in 2015 on those lines. Its brief included operational implementation of standards and policy set by CoP and government, and developing, with CoP, national approaches to efficiency, service transformation, performance management, misconduct, and discipline.

HMIC has increasingly filled the void around what professionalism means, both through force inspections and thematic reviews. However, making informing the public a principal driver of force inspections has narrowed the issues pursued (HMIC 2014c). Lessening scope, increasing frequency, and pre-digesting information for public consumption inhibits professional relevance.

The NCA was announced in 2010 as 'a fresh start' (Home Office 2011c). Unlike SOCA, NCA directors can require chief constables to do as s/he requests. NCA is responsible to the home secretary, and exempt from Freedom of Information requests. It became operational in 2013, with 4,500 officers and a £464 million budget. Since the organizations it subsumed had a combined budget of £812 million, savings clearly featured. NCA absorbed the Child Exploitation and Online Protection Centre despite protests by its director and victims' groups. ACPO/

NPCC, government, and the Home Affairs Committee (HAC) continually bickered over assigning counter-terrorism responsibility to NCA rather than the Met (HAC 2011a); about 2,000 officer posts accompany the brief. NCA acquired a reputation for secrecy after refusing to acknowledge arresting Prime Minister Cameron's policy advisor. Its early period was marked by borrowing officers from forces to cover investigations referred by an over-eager home secretary. Ignoring chiefs' protestations, May insisted that the newly appointed NCA head lead an inquiry into historic abuse in children's homes, without officers, budget, or agreed structure. Prompted by an abuse allegation against a senior Conservative—a charge that disintegrated shortly afterwards—May's interference took investigators off live cases.

The IPCC (now the 'Independent Office for Police Conduct') has a considerable role in the drive for professionalism but, like NCA, its principal problem is under-resourcing, leaving forces still having the major role in investigating complaints. When government announced in 2013 it would finance IPCC expansion by reducing force budgets PCCs claimed it was 'unaccountable'. One blared 'the IPCC is going through various police officers, linked with journalists. They have the power to break down your door, seizing property, seizing your house, and you have got no way of complaining about it' (*Surrey Advertiser* 27 December 2013), a bizarre account of IPCC's role. PCCs proposed a governing panel of PCCs, hardly a guarantor of independence.

Fashioning a new landscape under Coalition and ensuing Conservative administrations coincided with increasing antagonism between police and government. 'Plebgate', in which officers lied about Chief Whip Andrew Mitchell's language after blocking him cycling through a Parliamentary access point, undermined Conservative regard for police. Following the incident, in which Mitchell did not deny swearing at police, the Police Federation abandoned a reconciliation meeting after he denied calling police 'plebs'. Mitchell eventually resigned but Plebgate proved to have been fabricated by officers with Federation interests. Informed comment suggested that Cameron's reluctance to force Mitchell's resignation reflected desire to break the Federation.

Cameron's perspective was reflected in his home secretary's belligerence. The relatively anodyne preamble of May's speech to the 2014 Police Federation conference made her sudden change in tone the more menacing. Malevolently uttering the words 'make no mistake', she threatened that if they did not reform themselves she would change the law and force reform. She then withdrew government funding from the Federation. At previous Federation conferences May had been heckled and booed, and in 2012 organizers manoeuvred her into delivering her address in front of a banner saying 'Criminal'. Revenge may have been a collateral benefit of her carefully planned ploy.

The Conservative press confirmed the impression of a political agenda at work, declaring May's 'one of the most incredible speeches delivered by a British politician in peacetime' (*Daily Telegraph* 22 May 2014) and May 'the hammer of the cops'. The *Daily Mail* (23 May 2014) said she was 'gimmick-free' and 'a formidable politician who actually makes things happen' while *The Spectator* (24 May 2014) announced 'she is the tiger woman who rips her enemies to shreds' and 'the great reformer of this parliament'. Beyond these considered assessments was the betraying fact that the Federation had already accepted May's reform agenda. The real insight into the new policing landscape this offered was that May would not have proceeded thus without calculating that the balance had shifted between the public's instinctive support for the police and its growing anger over successive policing disasters. Negating ingrained Conservative support for police amplified the signs that public confidence was in serious jeopardy. For the British police that is as close to a sea change as it gets.

The Police Professional Body

Neyroud's (2010) proposals for a police professional body came in the midst of damaging policing scandals but were coloured by accommodating NPIA abolition and ACPO reform as much as by promoting professionalization (HAC 2011a). Parliament wanted the Police Professional Body (PPB) to be subordinate to the Home Office, it being directly answerable to Parliament, and for ACPO's successor to be operationally focused and not make policy. However, Parliament's aspirations confronted enduring ambiguities. Both the PPB and NPCC were burdened from birth with policing's 'old landscape' of indistinct boundaries between operational and policy matters, and the overlapping responsibilities and lack of accountability flowing from them (HAC 2011 Oral Evidence, 26 April, p. 4).

Government's response to Parliament emphasized PPB independence but did not hazard what constituted professional policing (Home Office 2011a). As close as official pronouncements got to addressing professionalism as a concept were assertions that falling crime and (supposedly) rising public confidence were 'to a large extent a result of increased professionalism' (Home Office 2012a). Policing had 'come to see itself as a profession ... a specialist and expert group of crime fighters', a particularly narrow stab at defining professionalism. This foundational document declared that the CoP would develop professionalism without saying what professionalism was. It referred to the CoP giving 'all those working in policing a stronger say in charting the future of the police profession driven by evidence-based practice' but the word 'profession' could be replaced with 'occupation' without making any difference. The idea that every employee would have an interest in Evidence-based Practice (EBP) ignores the daunting challenge of knowledge transfer in policing; Hunter et al (2017) found EBP had no significant currency with operational officers. The Home Office document hurried on to say that professional status would lead to recognition and rewards. A PR briefing (CoP 2012) implied a mechanical definition of professionalism based simply on the CoP's assigned role. 'As a professional body [CoP] will set the framework and "own" on behalf of the profession the tools to ensure professionalism, including: operational and training standards; knowledge base of "what works"; the professional development framework' (Table 7.1). The CoP would be 'independent of government', but its independent chair and four lay members sit alongside PCCs, three chief constables, and a representative each for the Police Federation, Superintendents Association, and Unison. The home secretary told Parliament in 2012 that she would 'establish a company with the intention of replacing it with a statutory body'. Independence is hardly satisfied by formal status as a private company whose sole shareholder is the home secretary. HM Treasury insists CoP must generate half its own budget before receiving a charter and statutory status; in late 2016 it was generating 33% (HAC 2016). Police resistance over paying for membership is an obstacle, a greater one being the autonomy associated with established professions.

The CoP's stated brief is to 'support the fight against crime and safeguard the public by ensuring professionalism in policing'. The College would not issue licences to practice, duplicate HMIC or

Table 7.1 Professionalism in Practice

Protect the Public Interest	Set and enhance first-class national standards of professionalism to ensure excellence in operational policing	Identify evidence of what works in policing and share best practice	Support the education and professional development of police officers and staff	Enable and motivate staff and partners to work together to achieve a shared purpose
Promote the values of effective policing	Develop a set of nationally agreed standards for officers and staff to attain	Share best practice nationally and internationally	Develop and maintain the national policing curriculum and supporting assessment and accreditation frameworks	Work with partners to make the best use of specialist knowledge
Learn from and support improvement in policing service and efficiency	Provide the frameworks for these standards to be tested and for achievement to be rewarded	Provide access to a body of knowledge informed by evidence based research to allow the service to keep up to date with the latest thinking on policing	Deliver leadership and specialist training	Support desired behaviour and actions that embody the service's values
Ensure that this work continues to evolve	Support a national business area infrastructure	Be at the forefront of understanding the evolving threats to public safety and enable the service to retain the capabilities needed	Accredit and quality assure training providers	Work with partners to enhance interoperability with other sectors
Maintain ethics and values			Develop the future leaders and future expertise through effective talent management	

Source: College of Policing (2012), 'Welcome to the College of Policing', Bramshill: College of Policing.

IPCC, 'be a re-branded NPIA', or create 'a raft of bureaucratic guidance'. The CoP was to engage in 'market making' for training (setting standards) and quality-assure all training. The CoP's *effective* brief is to farm out training, retaining only specialist and/or confidential training. In mid-2014 there were forty-five authorized providers, and even small forces commission external consultants who compete with the CoP's Quality Assurance brief. For example, Surrey Police spent £1,463,002 on consultants in 2011, £608,581 of it on 'advice and services for human resources' (BBC 2012). CoP has no way to quality-assure such work. NPCC committee leads are core of CoP's professional committee. Thus, the standards and licensing functions associated with independent professional bodies remain firmly in police hands. A Home Affairs Committee inquiry (2012) compared CoP's brief to police professional bodies elsewhere. It raised doubts whether one institution could balance representing the police service, setting and upholding standards, delivering training, and protecting the public interest.

HMIC saw reforming the frontline officer role as prime in professionalization (HMIC 2012c). HAC successfully recommended a new Code of Ethics and Integrity, registers of chief constables' and PCCs' financial interests, and of dismissed officers, to prevent them joining another force (Home Secretary's Statement to House of Commons 12 February 2013) but CoP cites preventing re-employment only as an aspiration. HMIC (2013c) found that frontline personnel and supervisors largely had a clear ethical sense but one guided by their own 'moral compass', not policy and procedure. Longer service, and supervisory status, increase reporting of malpractice, and training must raise awareness of codes of conduct and whistle-blowing procedures (Westmarland 2011).

Force Discipline Codes customarily regulate policing. One sergeant observed that the Met's General Orders contained '"140 years of fuck-ups. Every time something goes wrong, they make a rule about it"' (Manning and Van Maanen 1977: 79). There are 'presentational rules', like exacting custody procedures, and 'working rules', what actually happens. Officers develop a hierarchy: 'dead wrong, wrong but not bad, wrong but everybody does it' (Baker 1985). For Waddington (1999) the fact that, literally applied, law would impede just outcomes, is an 'invitational edge to corruption'. Strict rulebook approaches prompt resistance, feeding loyalty to peers which inhibits whistle-blowing (Westmarland 2014). Active ethical support by relevant peers and supervisors encourages integrity (Brown and Quinton 2014). Discipline Codes do not require acceptance of values, instead majoring on punishment. Personal integrity is stronger because it represents beliefs that are independent of institutions (Irving 1986: 148; Fielding 2003). 'Code(s) of ethics regulate the behaviour of autonomous individuals, while individuals whose working practices allow no autonomy have need only of a discipline code' (Edwards 1999: 150). A Discipline Code will prohibit accepting a gift while a Code of Ethics will allow that a soft drink after bringing home a lost child is different to a gift for tearing up a traffic ticket. Discipline Code performance can be perverse; parents may be offended by refusing the soda. To form an effective alternative to Discipline Codes, Codes of Ethics must secure buy-in. A classic failure was the Met's 1985 book *The Principles of Policing and Guidance for Professional Behaviour*, issued without discussion, requests for feedback or linked training. It went unread, with no traceable effects (Edwards 1999: 162–3).

Mirroring the Council of Europe Code of Police Ethics (Table 7.2), the College of Policing Code of Ethics defines exemplary police behaviour, with principles (Table 7.3), standards of professional behaviour (Table 7.4), and practical everyday examples.

Table 7.2 Council of Europe Code of Ethics: Training of Police Personnel

Police training, which shall be based on the fundamental values of democracy, the rule of law and the protection of human rights, shall be developed in accordance with the objectives of the police.
General police training shall be as open as possible towards society.
General initial training should preferably be followed by in-service training at regular intervals, and specialist, management and leadership training, when it is required.
Practical training on the use of force and limits with regard to established human rights principles, notably the European Convention on Human Rights and its case-law, shall be included in police training at all levels.
Police training shall take full account of the need to challenge and combat racism and xenophobia.

Source: European Code of Police Ethics, 2001, Council of Europe.

Table 7.3 Code of Ethics for Policing: Nine Principles

Accountability: you are answerable for your decisions, actions and omissions
Fairness: you treat people fairly
Honesty: you are truthful and trustworthy
Integrity: you always do the right thing
Leadership: you lead by good example
Objectivity: you make choices on evidence and your best professional judgement
Openness: you are open and transparent in your actions and decisions
Respect: you treat everyone with respect
Selflessness: you act in the public interest

Source: College of Policing (2014) *Code of Ethics*, Ryton-on-Dunsmore: College of Policing.

Table 7.4 Ten Standards of Professional Behaviour

1. Honesty and integrity: I will be honest and act with integrity at all times, and will not compromise or abuse my position.
2. Authority, respect and courtesy: I will act with self-control and tolerance, treating members of the public and colleagues with respect and courtesy. I will use my powers and authority lawfully and proportionately, and I will respect the rights of all individuals.
3. Equality and diversity: I will act with fairness and impartiality. I will not discriminate unlawfully or unfairly.
4. Use of force: I will only use force as part of my role and responsibilities, and only to the extent that it is necessary, proportionate and reasonable in all the circumstances.
5. Orders and instructions: I will, as a police officer, give and carry out lawful orders only, and will abide by Police Regulations. I will give reasonable instructions only, and will follow all reasonable instructions.
6. Duties and responsibilities: I will be diligent in the exercise of my duties and responsibilities.
7. Confidentiality: I will treat information with respect, and access or disclose it only in the proper course of my duties.
8. Fitness for work: I will ensure, when on duty or at work, that I am fit to carry out my responsibilities.
9. Conduct: I will behave in a manner, whether on or off duty, which does not bring discredit on the police service or undermine public confidence in policing.
10. Challenging and reporting improper behaviour: I will report, challenge or take action against the conduct of colleagues which has fallen below the standards of professional behaviour.

Source: College of Policing (2014) *Code of Ethics*, Ryton-on-Dunsmore: College of Policing.

However, forces vary in adopting it (HAC 2016). They absorb extracts of the Code into existing values statements or do nothing. HAC wanted each officer to pledge an oath based on the Code and formally sign a copy, with the Code being integrated with Police (Conduct) Regulations, but CoP said it lacked resources to check compliance.

CoP's pursuit of evidence-based professional practice was to involve universities and joint research between practitioners and academics. This would provide knowledge 'informed by evidence-based research and best practice' (CoP 2012; note the reference to experiential knowledge). An idea of what achieving more evidence-based practice confronts comes from Australia. An academic with a UK policing background was appointed head of New South Wales Police (NSW) training. Finding no research base for NSW firearms training, he tested officers' firearms skills. When serious deficits emerged the work was stopped by senior officers fearing bad publicity (Bradley 2005). Bradley's critique of there being no curriculum underpinning Special Operations Group training was later redacted by the Police Education Advisory Council, fearing it would undermine public confidence. In UK, after a university inaugurated a police research centre former Chief John Alderson was made visiting professor. Revealing another EBP challenge, police boycotted all activities involving him. The local chief explained that 'he spat upon the cloth', an ugly reference to Alderson's evidence to the Scarman Inquiry about the Met's role in the Brixton riots.

An *intellectual* problem with EBP in the professionalization of policing is the baggage it brings from clinical medicine, which elevates Random Control Trial studies above others. This rules out important fine-grained work and often identifies as robust only US studies whose context is not transferable. Policing likes certainty and direct explanations. A profession understands that research evidence can be extensive but uncertain (Holdaway 2017b). Moreover, 'evidence doesn't speak for itself, it always requires interpretation' (Kelly 2017), a point that usefully connects with the police emphasis on experience, which allows practitioners to gauge whether evidence applies to the problem at issue. Officers emphasize that training must acknowledge the importance of experience; that EBP makes resource demands that need weighing against others; that applying EBP requires tailoring to local contexts; and that EBP confronts managerial aversion to frontline innovation (Fyfe 2017). Rather than polarized 'evidence versus experience', this calls for synthesis. Chiefs want a mechanism for experience of implementing EBP at force level to form a national evidence base. Rather than researchers providing evidence and practitioners applying it, practitioners may interpret evidence in their own way and disseminate their interpretation via practitioner channels, encouraged by innovations like forces commissioning officers and postgraduates to write research reviews for force intranets. There is even testimony that police unions and civilian staff increasingly question what evidence base informs policy and managerial assumptions (Hunter et al 2017). In-force short courses in EBP, its niche application in masterclasses on, for example, EBP for NP, and 'research cafes' for frontline officers may thus prove lively occasions.

While only half of those responding to the CoP Survey 2016 saw EBP as a fad and 53% thought it was relevant to their role, only 23% saw evidence as more important than experience (Wheller 2017). CoP delivered EBP Masterclasses tailored to participants' skills/interests to 400 officers/staff in 2016/2017 and runs Evidence Base Camps where participants conduct a Rapid Evidence Assessment (REA) and present their findings to the NPCC lead for that topic. Middle-ranking and senior officer use of research evidence showed statistically significant increases between 2014 and 2017 (Hunter et al 2017). Those reporting collaboration with universities rose from 25% to 73%. But HMIC's overview of force inspections (HMIC 2017a) revealed that inspectors found little evidence of EBP being used in forces. Budgets, and public opinion, can trump evidence (Hunter et al 2017: 22), and some see CoP as both controlling and cautious about anything seen as politically sensitive.

Nevertheless, EBP is moving to occupy the space that was formerly held by professional discretion. The exercise of judicious discretion marks the traditional professions and allows for experience and judgement in a way that EBP fixated on RCTs and the experimental research design does not. Officers' emphasis on experience as key resource in interpreting evidence reflects both the lack of good, granular evidence and the failure of the EBP enterprise to connect evidence with police work in a direct way. Training cannot rest with distillations of EBP but must extend to how evidence applies to specific circumstances.

Narrow EBP cannot cope with profound, system-level change whose effects are uncertain or that raise fundamental dilemmas. For instance, a notable agent changing the contours of the landscape is the proliferation of institutions loosely coordinated around risk: 'insurance companies, regulatory agencies, financial institutions, health and welfare agencies and motor vehicle agencies' (Ericson and Haggerty 1997: 17). Satisfying another organization's informational requirements is a major drain. A drunk-driving accident with personal injury can require two reports for police use but fourteen for other bodies. Risk management exerts a pull towards expansive technological and regulatory systems. This is a major problem for professionalism's imperative to demonstrate competence over the domain comprising its jurisdiction. Keeping a place in a dynamic network of rent-seeking institutions means that the professional police jurisdiction is constantly shifting. The diffusion of information federated across the risk network threatens policing's authority to define the specialized knowledge it uniquely holds. Such authority is central to professions and is benign insofar as it maintains the standards against which members and governance can evaluate professional competence. An officer developed a profound knowledge of fraudulently-altered vehicle registration numbers, interviewing manufacturers, examining thousands of stolen renumbered cars, studying heat and acid restoration, and developing a formal investigative concept and procedure. Having established a standard whereby his expertise could not be challenged in court, he held a monopoly. A police profession must decide where it stands on such initiative. Professions grant licensed practitioners autonomy on the reasonable basis that what matters is excellent quality of service. The practical meaning of professionalism is daily tested in ways that narrow conventional renderings of EBP cannot capture.

An austere landscape

Transition to policing's new landscape was set against 'policing under austerity'. HMIC (2017a, 2017b) exposed effects including downgrading 999 calls, erosion of Neighbourhood Policing, detective shortfalls, and avoiding classifying violent gangs as organized crime. Rather than explicit policies there was 'an unconscious form of rationing'. One force was 'inadequate', thirteen 'required improvement', including the Met. Detective shortages—800 in London—caused excessive workloads, stress, and resignations, leaving 'unqualified' officers to cope. In 2017 the Met appealed to retired detectives to return. NP, 'the bedrock of British policing', was being 'chipped away by stealth', with 20% of NP officers on other duties three times a week. Even Winsor (2017) declared the cuts 'unacceptable'. In response, the policing minister claimed budgets had been 'protected'; they fell 22%, with 32,000 posts lost.

Austerity revived efficiency arguments over the number of forces. It remains a principal unconquered mountain in the landscape. Amalgamations came close under New Labour but hit an election. New Labour's impetus was towards mergers. The Coalition years differed. The Liberal Democrat and Conservative localism agenda favoured small forces. Home Secretary May lambasted 'the traditional ACPO solution of continually merging forces and taking accountability further and further away from local communities' (May 2013). Loader (2014b) saw a case for greater collaboration, particularly against cross-border and organized crime. PCCs, chiefs, the Federation, and Treasury agreed structural reform was needed but could not agree its form (Police Foundation 2014). One model involved bottom-up collaboration—partnerships or full amalgamation; another was amalgamations down to ten forces; the third, a national police service. The first model's drawback was leaving it to forces. The second is costly to enact and requires new accountability structures. The third's drawback is centralizing power over local policing.

The same options preceded creation of Scotland's single force (Fyfe 2014b). 'Police Scotland' was formed in just eighteen months, without significant public consultation. What swung the cause was advocacy by the chief of Strathclyde, the largest force. Local authorities lost control over budgets, resourcing, and oversight of complaints, leaving little more than input to local policing plans. A claimed £130 million saving was not independently verified, and drew largely on station closures, done in England without reorganizations. Worse, it is ambiguous whether the Scottish Police Authority (SPA) or Chief Constable is in charge, or where accountability lies—the SPA is an unelected scrutiny-only body. The majority of citizens did not favour a national force, but got top-down, compliance-based, target-driven policing. The Scottish government's failure to evaluate the new force was condemned after the chief was forced to retire early by public outcry over his officers ignoring reports of a car accident for three days, leaving a young couple slowly dying in a ditch.

The bottom line? '[F]orce amalgamations ... [are] off the agenda given government's localism agenda and the introduction of PCCs' (Police Foundation 2014: 6). When the Desborough Commission first mooted amalgamations—in 1919—the Home Office was a keen backer, but public scepticism then was as now. What differs is the prevailing 'small government' ideology. Forces like Sussex and Surrey, which planned merger, have increasingly collaborated not only in back-office functions and equipment procurement but operationally. Forces increasingly operate 'policing hubs' collaboratively investigating homicide, organized crime, terrorism, and cybercrime. But hubs and shared operations pose governance problems. Structure cannot be reformed democratically without attention to accountability and governance.

The new landscape does not promise enhanced accountability. Morgan's (1985) models of accountability endure: the stewardship model with autonomous chiefs and *post hoc* accountability; the directive model, where government sets objectives and chiefs operationalize them; and the partnership model, where policy objectives involve negotiation. Only the last offers democratic openings. Whereas the period 1980–2012 saw chiefs unconvincingly bound by local policing plans 'owned' by police authorities, the baton of democratic accountability has passed to PCCs 'accountable' via the ballot box. What has not been addressed is the 'under-specification of statutory responsibilities' that, in Walker's magisterial judgement, was the defining characteristic of the defective system of governance that the new landscape has replaced (Walker 2000: 72).

Trimming ACPO, trading SOCA for NCA, and the immolation of NPIA, are a short-run sideshow set against government's enduring inability to resolve policing's constitutional status. The sideshow diverts attention from the main event—perhaps because that has played for centuries without the curtain coming conclusively down. None of the elements of what less resembles a landscape than a scrapyard show real promise of advancing police professionalism. Moreover, professionalization is to be delivered while officers scurry to 'do more with less'.

Training to Negotiate the New Terrain

It is natural to ask how training will prepare recruits and officers to negotiate the new environment. Official inspections, reviews, and reports necessarily have concerns determined by policy interests, not the interplay between training, experience, socialization, and culture. Although training evaluation is an established practice, it focuses on the least rigorous indicators: identifying aims and objectives for training sessions and collecting evaluation questionnaires afterwards. This is incapable of identifying training effects and cannot predict future practice. Direct observation of post-session practice is expensive, conducting it often exceeds the competence of staff responsible, and wizened managers dismiss observational findings as anecdotal because questionnaire data display more 'face validity' (a methodologist's way to say they look more factual than they are).

Policymakers can undermine training that strives for professionalism. Following scandals ranging across undue force, sexual misdemeanours, gambling, and drugs, a Royal Commission into New South Wales Police found systemic, entrenched corruption. Reforms included overhauling recruit training. From 1998, recruits took a university Diploma of Policing Practice and were no longer police employees but students, an explicit step towards professionalization. Curriculum, environment, and staff all changed (Chan and Dixon 2007: 455). Training's context was no longer the force—renamed 'service'—but its community. Recruitment saw an unprecedented increase. Formerly struggling to get enough recruits to form a class, the new approach saw a waiting list of 2,000. Recruit demographics, skills and experience changed. Corruption fell and markers of professionalism, like willingness to report peer misconduct, grew. Yet structural and cultural changes to control police chiefs' fads and politicians' interference were not implemented. A new chief proclaimed a crime-busting agenda. Politicians replaced police reform themes with fighting crime. Amidst media foment NSW Police's name reverted to 'force'.

Given media and political influence over reforms, the disputed relevance of higher education, and training's declining salience as experience grows, one cannot expect training alone to deliver professionalism. In 2006 Trinidad's homicide rate was 78 *per month*; extrapolated to the UK that would be 4,019 a month or roughly six times the *annual* UK rate. Trinidad embarked on police reform. Mastroski's 'transformation programme' involved divisional training, data analysis training, and new equipment. The security minister declared that officers must see the job as a calling—police 'came second only to God'—but the justice minister acknowledged that importing US police reforms was a gamble. A year after the training homicide reached a record high. Training is an important lever but reform also demands organizational change and secular rather than divine accountability.

In UK, recruits need skills for work in a more variegated organization. Out-sourced custody suites and call-handling run alongside more auxiliaries, volunteers, and partners. HMIC (2016) found frontline civilian staff lacked even basic crime prevention training, and PCSOs increasingly dealing with demands beyond their training, with half of cases lacking supervisory input or investigation plans. Austerity-driven managers target Neighbourhood Policing, cutting PCSOs and civilians whilst 're-purposing' officers' role. Yet the case of teaching assistants shows that while auxiliaries are ineffective when replacing trained practitioners they are highly cost-effective in ancillary tasks (Hunter et al 2017). After the 2011 riots London's mayor demanded cuts be reversed because they endangered NP information-gathering that could anticipate unrest. The public wants steady, visible NP but by 2016 'NP officers' were spending only half their time on NP (HMIC 2016). NP and partnership work requires training and attentive supervision that imparts analytical and lateral thinking, and project management skills. For some, these needs imply higher education.

Police and Higher Education

While the new landscape declares a greater role for education institutions some argue that a police service granted professional status would exert greater control over the training curriculum (Heslop and White 2011a). In reality, that already obtains. A cadre of 'practitioner-lecturers' rivals CoP curriculum designers and academics (White and Heslop 2011). When Canterbury Christ Church University (CCCU) sought to design a curriculum 'from' policing practice, they found that the Initial Police Learning and Development Programme (IPLDP) was heavily scripted, with little room for 'imaginative and creative contributions towards ... learning experiences'. Moreover, NPIA had assiduously laid down what officers should know but assessment packages did not match it (Bryant et al 2014). Vital formative assessment is compromised because connecting knowledge acquisition with knowledge application relies on workplace supervision forces cannot deliver. Requiring all Kent Police recruits to spend their first year taking CCCU's Certificate of Higher Education in Policing 'did little more than transfer the location of ... police training from a traditional police training centre to a university campus'.

Higher Education (HE) is a non-essential element in police training, an 'accessorising of the practitioner', without social capital in the job (Heslop and White 2011b). University programmes must include the Certificate in Knowledge of Policing to satisfy IPLDP's Diploma in Policing knowledge requirement. The 'Approved Providers' include colleges and education businesses, not just universities. Private providers offer shorter, cheaper programmes, and this sends signals about the dispensable nature of university learning. University programmes' marginalization is aggravated by timetables misaligned with other students, buildings on campus fringes and temporary staff. Participants leave feeling dissatisfied (Heslop 2011c).

Apart from polarizing the debate about HE's role in police training there is little else to recommend present arrangements. If professionalism requires an element of 'intellectual space' (Bryant et al 2014) the present system is unpromising ground. HE can facilitate professionalism by enabling learners to assess things from different angles and take account of different perspectives (Dominey and Hill 2010). Professionals exercise 'epistemic authority' (evidence-based) not '*de facto* authority' (mandated by office). Yet full police powers are acquired within a week of police employment.

Meanwhile, evidence for HE's benign effects is neither firm nor extensive. Foundation degree graduates display 'more critical and culturally aware and sensitive police professionalism' (Crisp and Ward 2008: 65) but recruits have problems with extended writing and lectures (Heslop 2010). In Northern Europe police training is relatively academic and lengthy (two years of a two and a half year overall training period in Sweden, two years of a three year overall programme in Norway and Denmark) whereas in Canada recruits to federal police agencies receive only twenty-four weeks academy training and the US average is nineteen weeks (Stanislas 2014). US police departments encouraging graduate entry do not have lower levels of malpractice although in 'diverse' cities graduate status mildly predicts less use of force (Chapman 2012). In the 1970s German police education moved from forces to technical colleges, and academic components were extended. Some foresaw an integrative 'police science' but it is debatable whether it would satisfy either educators or police. 'Are lawyers legal scholars? Are doctors medical scientists? Hardly ... [T]hese professional groups would consider themselves to be "practitioners" rather than "scholars" or "scientists" ' (Jaschke and Neidhardt 2007: 305). Moreover, 'officers' scepticism still goes very deep and ... even amounts to open rejection' (ibid: 313).

In other occupations seeking professionalization and an evidence base the professional doctorate features. Professional doctorates involve assessed postgraduate modules and an extended study of an occupational issue. Some argue that expectations of independent critical thinking obstruct professional doctorates in policing (Creaton and Clements 2010) but officers seldom show inhibition expressing criticism. The real problem for the professional doctorate as a means of professionalizing the police is preference for the MBA. It involves similar effort but is seen as less narrow and more portable to other careers.

If we believe that professionalizing police requires professionalizing training we must ask whether training arrangements satisfy Muir's (1977: 256) epitome: 'training ... provides the motives, the tools, the stimulation, and the sanctuary which busy [people] need to get perspective on their lives, redefine purposes, challenge old assumptions, and become morally creative'. Muir's (1977: 3–4) 'good cop' develops two virtues: 'Intellectually, he has to grasp the nature of human suffering. Morally, he has to resolve the contradiction of achieving just ends with coercive means'. These are not the terms of the policy world, but speak to the qualities that make good policing a preoccupation of every human civilization. The intellectual question behind debates over training and professionalism is simply 'what is good policing?'

A Professional Practice?

In Plato's *Republic*, Socrates argued that professionalism was doing a single thing well. In an ideal polity 'one man does one job and does not play ... a multiplicity of roles'. This secured social cohesion, because 'then every man would do his own business, and be one and not many; and so the whole city would be one and not many' (Jowett 1942: 311). Professionalism construed as specialization contradicts policing's long emphasis on the generic ('omnicompetent') constable. Socrates' flaw is that a situation where 'everything becomes divorced from everything else' obstructs professional coherence.

Sklansky (2014) offers four meanings of police professionalism. First, '*high expectations*' represented by codes of practice and discipline. Second, that police should be '*self-regulating*', like doctors, a kind of elegant closed shop. Self-regulation's honourable core is freedom from political interference; its dishonourable twin is freedom from public accountability. Third is occupation-specific '*expertise*', distinctive knowledge representing an evidence-base beyond common sense. The fourth is policing being guided by '*internalized norms*' rather than orders. The four are not mutually exclusive. They can, and should, coexist, but often do not. Thus, mid-twentieth century US professionalism emphasized standards, organizational autonomy, and expertise, but not internalized norms, consequently inhibiting officer discretion and creating a rigid, self-regarding system disconnected from the public.

Sklansky's meanings of professionalism help identify what needs emphasis in a particular society at a particular time. In the US, following the 'political era' (1900–1930s) of unhealthily close relations between police and politicians there was the 'reform era' (1930s–1960s) of Vollmer's 'scientific police management', in which technologies had profound effect (Kelling and Moore 1988), enabling the 'legalistic' style emphasizing aggressive preventive patrol that minorities experienced as harassment. A 'constitutional era' (1960s–1980s) was followed by the 'community policing era' (1980s–present), but at different times community policing has accented problem-solving, restorative justice, social capital, intelligence, or reassurance (Wood and Shearing 2007).

In the UK the 'unit beat system', reliant on police radio and patrol cars, altered patrol from being place-based to being incident-based (Innes 2014a). Cars stretched 'beats' beyond local knowledge. With cars and radio despatch came 'command and control'—central direction and tasking—enabling calls to be prioritized (and de-prioritized). This strengthened supervisors' power, eroded discretion, and sufficiently alienated the public that beat policing had to be reinvented as community policing. Computerized databases extended centralization (Sparrow et al 1997). Yet technologies do not have to centralize. They can form a virtuous circle in which information flows between both hub and locale, delivering the community responsiveness of democratic criminal justice (Loader and Sparks 2011). However, while information environments can be used progressively, they cannot in themselves professionalize (Innes and Roberts 2011).

Professionalism can be understood as the competencies relating to good policing, and governance as the conduct associated with being a good officer (Brown 2014). In such individualized conceptions, professionalism results from being college-educated, orientated to public service, respecting codes of ethics, and exercising appropriate autonomy (Fleming 2014). The competency approach to professionalism emphasizes techniques, like problem-solving (Laycock and Tilley 2014), having little to say about governance. Policing involves guilty knowledge about means of lawbreaking that the unscrupulous can exploit (Dingwall 2008). Self-regulation must mean more than adhering to national standards. Beyond individualized approaches are bureaucratic policing—accountability by adherence to regulations—and democratic policing—accountability through public involvement and legislative scrutiny. The bureaucratic model as agent of professionalism is inadequate when applied to a practice largely conducted beyond active supervision (Waddington 1999). The low visibility of routine policing means we cannot achieve professionalism simply by law and codes of practice (Black 1980). When Scottish forces merged, bureaucratic policing prevailed over democratic policing (Fyfe 2014a). The headstrong chief constable introduced side-arms without consultation. The ensuing furore obliged reversal. Professionalism does not choose between lawfulness and democratic responsiveness. It chooses both (Manning 2014).

Professionalism's meaning changes. In mid-twentieth century it meant using radio and patrol cars which, fifty years later, were the antithesis of professionalism. In contemporary South Africa it means curbing police violence and corruption. In Germany it means in-service higher education. In contemporary Britain it often means reviving Peelian principles, whilst amongst managers and policymakers it means harnessing technologies to 'transform' service delivery along lines entirely unlike Peel's. Democratic openings enable police to grasp what needs to change, and how practice on the ground can deliver it. Professionalization implies devolution of discretionary decisions. For that to work, frontline staff need knowledge and skills for decision-making without close supervision, under relationships akin to doctors with the General Medical Council.

Constitutionally, professionalism is a police imperative because reconciling police powers with the interests of the public is a democratic necessity. External oversight cannot protect us against malpractice, as witness the IPCC caseload. An internalized ethical sense, using appropriate evidence to inform practice, and a sense of service, are more compelling. Life is simply survival without such moral emblems. Thinking whether they can be embedded in policing without training playing a role is perhaps the best case for training. Professionalism depends on qualities that would have marked good policing in 1829 or, indeed, in the *Vigiles Urbani* of Augustus's Rome. Emblems like legitimacy, fairness, and accountability are foundational, but we also need to impart an understanding of professionalism that does not just recite the marks of a civilized society but knows how to get there.

The professional organization

Since the profession concept is socially constructed and historically contingent (Johnson 1972; Watson 2002) it cannot be defined around invariant practices, but it can be treated as a 'yardstick' for distinguishing groups of occupations (Burrage et al 1990; Crompton 1990). Professionalization involves 'the delineation of specialized skills and systematic knowledge, institutionalized training and continuous development, defined standards of professional behaviour and a strong service orientation' (Bond 2016). To understand professions as a special case of employment status, social science has been preoccupied with how professions seek to achieve 'social closure' for instrumental ends (Macdonald 1995), that is, to maximize their autonomy and remuneration by controlling entry, fees and rates, and the discipline of members by setting standards internally so as to maintain self-regulation. This approach certainly accounts for a proportion of organizational behaviour by professional bodies, but tells us little about the sense of service and dedication that many professionals bring to their vocation, nor does it help us to understand how they go about 'the actual work' (Kritzer 1990: 5). For the individual officer the point of professionalism is to provide intellectual resources for resilience against the unexpected.

Critics see the claim to professional status as a rhetorical device cynically deployed by government to tap into the aura of established professions. 'Unlike traditional professions […] policing has no abstract theory, no control of its market or clientele (it serves all), few internal modes of assuring quality, a very short training period … and no requirements for sustained higher education' (Manning 2008: 16). The professionalization agenda is regarded as an attempt to impose workplace discipline on practitioners and break occupational culture rather than empower them with professional discretion (Cockcroft 2015; Cockcroft 2013; Evetts 2013; Fournier 1999).

Claiming professional status is certainly a recurrent rhetorical move that should be read against the policy context, being refashioned to address the specifics of scandal or crisis (Holdaway 2017a: 1). Thus, the claim was central to Commissioner Sir Robert Mark's 1970s efforts to reform the Met Police CID following the exposure of massive corruption. Mark emphasized the professionalism of the uniformed ranks, engineering the eventual subordination of CID to uniformed command. For Holdaway contemporary professionalization represents a 'loosely-coupled' (Weick 1976) framework of police regulation contrasting the tightly-coupled twentieth-century framework of force annual plans, HMIC inspections, standards set by ACPO, and NPIA 'guidance'. That apparatus is to be replaced by a single source of guidance—evidence-based policing—and a single agent—the College of Policing. An early test of this approach was a string of cases raising questions about senior officer integrity, crystallized around chiefs who manipulated appointments of relatives and friends as police staff. The response was the Code of Ethics combining principles with practical scenarios, a DIY guide to professionalism. The loosely-coupled approach is also represented by the localism agenda which imposed Police and Crime Commissioners.

If the police claim to professionalism is rhetorical something else must drive its espousal by policymakers. That something is an attempt to have it both ways by diluting the accountability of central government bodies responsible for police while seeking to responsibilize officers for their own professional conduct such that lapses are read as individual misdemeanours rather than organizational failures. Responsibility is lodged in the individual rather than the individual-in-organization. This maximizes wriggle room for home secretaries and chiefs but denies the public clear lines of accountability, with regulation of police actions not only varying from the domain of one PCC to another but from one officer to the next. Rather than performance management, plural, decentred regulation becomes a form of impression management.

Perhaps this approach suits the times, in which we 'understand' more about the world from illuminated screens than our own daily experience. Ephemeral understandings implant malleable criteria for judging action as 'professional', undermining accountable and transferable standards. Loosely-coupled regulation produces uncertainty and makes every policing episode a 'moment' in which claims are made as to what is professional, repeatedly but unpredictably remaking regulation according to local *causes celébrè*. This may not trouble policymakers who do not wish to hold responsibility but cannot provide sufficient accountability to satisfy the third of the population that has serious reservations about police legitimacy. Their concerns are best met through openings into police governance. If good policing's twin poles are professionalism and accountability through democratic, participatory governance, the present governance arrangements are as troublesome as professionalism. Accountability of home secretary and PCCs lies as far from democratic responsiveness as the occasional ballot. It leaves professionalism carrying the full burden of delivering good policing.

From Peel's time to the present the police have struggled with the concept of professionalism. In Britain the Victorians veered from regarding police as members of the servant class to sanctifying policing as a special calling, while the supposed Golden Age of Policing was riven by divisions of social class as sharp as those of the social diversity that poses one of contemporary policing's harshest tests. Police training has reflected these ambiguities and uncertainties. While it has grown from the risibly cursory to the ostensibly comprehensive, the ground its curriculum covers, the pedagogy it employs, and the structures through which training operates have been contested, troublesome to manage, and blamed for policing's failures. Behind these frictions lie large issues of governance, and even larger issues of policing's place in society. The twenty-first century has seen major changes in training stagger along more or less in step with an increasing sense that professionalization is the way ahead. The challenge of professionalism is to encourage pro-social discretion while maintaining officers' personal accountability and forces' ultimate responsibility.

Policing's contemporary rhetoric of managerialism, consumer focus, and technological fixes is an expression of unreconstructed modernism. Its vision of professionalism is as mechanistic as laying down 'national occupational standards' and providing checklists to show they have been met. Even those suited by a narrow formulaic take on what will bring about a professional practice of policing have been unable to tame the unruly semi-marketized, semi-managed reality of police training. Forces competing with each other and with the central training authorities are now joined by for-profit education businesses and academics bemused by the task of bringing educational breadth to a constricting and unimaginative curriculum and CPD requirement.

Late modernity is a time of uncertainty and scepticism. In 'post-truth' times, professionalism must accommodate ambiguities of class, faith, ethnicity, and sexuality. Rather than 'community policing' there is 'policing communities of risk', in which a shared fear of crime does not imply shared community spirit. We now understand that the public assess risk not by the reality of crime but by imagined realities. Even sustained and substantial impact on crime rates does not improve public confidence. The police languish as last believers in a monochrome vision of society while the norms that make for contemporary sociality have moved on to a multiplex of diversities that harbour new extremes both of tolerance and hate.

True contemporary professionalism alerts practitioners to other ways of delivering social control and just societies: empowering citizens and encouraging autonomy; acting through new modes of family structure, social relationships, lifestyle, and media; fitting provision to cases; pluralizing services. This context colours the problem of police professionalism. It challenges the recruit curriculum and that of in-service career development but also reveals the options around which professionalism can be configured and embedded such that it comes to play its part in a humane, coherent, and accountable framework of police governance.

References

Ackroyd P. (2001). *London: the Biography*, London: Vintage

Association of Chief Police Officers (2005). *Guidance on PCSOs*. London: ACPO

Association of Chief Police Officers (2012a). *Abuse of Police Powers to Perpetrate Sexual Violence*. London: ACPO

Association of Chief Police Officers (2012b). *Benchmarking Police Integrity Programmes*. London: Transparency International

Adler, Z. (1999). *Standards in Police Training*. Bramshill: National Police Training

Adult Learning Inspectorate (2005). *Evaluation of the New IPLDP*. London: Adult Learning Inspectorate

Akarsu, H. (2014). 'Recalibrations of State-Society Encounters in Turkey', Turkish Police Academy Conference on 'Securing Liberty, Civilizing Security', Ankara, 19 October

Akhtur, Z. (2014). 'Child sex grooming', *European Journal of Crime, Criminal Law and Criminal Justice*, 22 (2), 167–96

Alain, M. and C. Baril (2005). 'Crime prevention, crime repression and policing', *International Journal of Comparative and Applied Criminal Justice*, 29 (2), 1–26

Alain, M. and M. Gregoire (2008). 'Can ethics survive the shock of the job?', *Policing & Society*, 18 (2), 169–89

Alarid, L. Fiftal and C. Montemayor (2012). 'Implementing restorative justice in police departments', *Police Practice and Research*, 13 (5), 450–63

Alcott, C. (2012). 'Reforming the force', *British Journal of Community Justice*, 10 (1), 5–14

Alexander, D. and A. Wells (1991). 'Reactions of police officers to body handling after a major disaster', *British Journal of Psychiatry*, 159, 547–55

Anderson, L. (2003). *Women in Law Enforcement*, Ann Arbor MI: Ann Arbor Police Department

Andrews, R., G. Boyne, J. Law, and R. Walker (2005). 'External constraints on local service standards', *Public Administration*, 83 (3), 639–56

Anonymous (2017). 'Degree level police must not forget basic bobbying', *Times Higher Education*, 5 January, 28–9

Ariel, B. and H. Partridge (2016). 'Predictable policing', *Journal of Quantitative Criminology*, 32 (1), 1–25

Ariel, B., A. Sutherland, and D. Henstock (2016). 'Wearing body cameras increases assaults against officers and does not reduce police use of force', *European Journal of Criminology*, 13 (6), 744–55

Ariel., B, W. Farrar, and A. Sutherland (2017). 'Contagious accountability', *Criminal Justice and Behaviour*, 44 (2), 293–316

Ariza, J. (2014). 'Police initiated contacts: young people, ethnicity and the usual suspects', *Policing & Society*, 24 (2), 208–23

Association of Police Authorities (2011). *Confidence in Policing Among 'Seldom Heard' Audiences*, London: APA

Atak, K. (2014). 'Spatial Permit: urban privatization and protest control in the USA', Turkish Police Academy Conference on 'Securing Liberty, Civilizing Security', Ankara, 19 October

Atkinson, P. (1983). 'The reproduction of the professional community', in R. Dingwall and P. Lewis (eds.), *The Sociology of the Professions*, Basingstoke: Macmillan, 224–41

Audit Commission (1998). *Examination of police establishment management*, London: Audit Commission

Audit Commission (2008). *Police Data Quality*, London: Audit Commission

Awan, I., B. Blakemore, and K. Simpson (2013). 'Muslim communities attitudes towards and recruitment into the British police service', *International Journal of Law Crime and Justice*, 41 (4), 421–37

Backteman-Erlanson, S., M. Padyab, and C. Brulin (2013). 'Prevalence of burnout and associations with psychosocial work environment', *Police Practice and Research*, 14 (6), 491–505

Bailey, R. (2015). 'Policing the Police and Crime Commissioners', *Policing*, 9 (4), 305–13

Baker, M. (1985). *Cops*, NY: Simon & Schuster

Baker, T., W. Pelfrey, L. Bedard, K. Dhungana, M. Gerz, and K. Golden (2014). 'Female inmates' procedural justice perceptions of the police and courts', *Criminal Justice and Behaviour*, 41 (2), 144–62

Balmer, G., J. Pooley, and L. Cohen (2014). 'Psychological resilience of Western Australian police officers', *Police Practice and Research*, 15 (4), 270–82

Bandy, C. et al (1986). 'Police performance in resolving family disputes', *Psychological Reports*, 58 (3), 743–56

Banton, M. (1964). *The Policeman in the Community*, London: Tavistock

Barrett, G. et al (2014). 'BME communities and levels of satisfaction with policing', *Criminology and Criminal Justice*, 14 (2), 196–215

Barrick, K., M. Hickman, and K. Storm (2014). 'Representative policing and violence towards the police', *Policing: A Journal of Policy and Practice*, 8 (2), 193–204

Basic Skills Agency (2002). *Basic Skills and Crime*, London: BSA

Basinska, B. and I. Wiciak (2012). 'Fatigue and professional burnout', *Internal Security*, 4 (2), 265–73

Bayley, D. (2008). 'Police reform: who done it?', *Policing & Society*, 18 (1), 7–16

Bear, D. and J. Rieken (2014). 'Those cheering for police body worn cameras must think a little deeper', *The Guardian*, 15 August

Becker, H. et al (1961). *Boys in White*, Piscataway NJ: Transaction

Bell, S. and Y. Eski (2016). '"Break a leg- it's all in the mind"', *Policing: A Journal of Policy and Practice*, 10 (2), 95–101

Bent-Goodley, T. (2013). 'Domestic violence fatality reviews and the African American community', *Homicide Studies*, 17 (4), 375–90

Bernstein, B. (1971). *Class, Codes and Control*, London: Routledge

Berry, G., P. Briggs, R. Erol, and L. Van Staden (2011). *Effectiveness of Partnership Working in a Crime and Disorder Context*, London: Home Office

Berry, J. (2009). *Reducing Bureaucracy in Policing*, London: Home Office

Berry, J. (2010). *Reducing Bureaucracy Final Report*, London: Home Office

Besemer, S. (2014). 'Impact of timing and frequency of parental criminal behaviour and risk factors on offspring offending', *Psychology, Crime and Law*, 20 (1–2), 78–99

Bhaskar, R. (1998). 'Philosophy and scientific realism', in M. Archer et al (eds.), *Critical Realism*, London: Routledge, pp. 16–47

Bittner, E. (1970). *The Functions of the Police in Modern Society*, Cambridge MA: Oelgeschlager, Gunn and Hain

Black, D. (1980). *The Manners and Customs of the Police*, NY: Academic

Bland, N. et al (1999). *Career Progression of Ethnic Minority Police*, London: Home Office

Blumenstein, L., L. Fridell, and S. Jones (2012). 'Link between traditional police subculture and police intimate partner violence', *Policing: An International Journal*, 35 (1), 147–64

Body-Gendrot, S. (2013). 'Urban violence in France and England', *Policing & Society*, 23 (1), 6–25

Bohm, R. et al (2000). 'Perceptions of neighbourhood problems and their solutions', *Policing: An International Journal*, 23 (4), 439–65

Bond, R. (2016). 'From ARMA to avatars', *Research Fortnight*, 8 June, p. 22

Bonifacio, P. (1991). *The Psychological Effects of Police Work*, NY: Springer

Bossler, A. and T. Holt (2013). 'Assessing officer perceptions and support for online community policing', *Security Journal* 26 (4), 349–66

Bottoms, A. (2012). 'Developing socio-spatial criminology', in M. Maguire et al (eds.), *Oxford Handbook of Criminology*, Oxford: Oxford University Press, 450–88

Bottoms, A. and J. Tankebe (2013). 'Beyond procedural justice', *Journal of Criminal Law and Criminology*, 102 (1), 119–70

Bourdieu, P. (1992). *The Logic of Practice*, Cambridge: Polity

Bowers, K. et al (2011). 'Spatial displacement and diffusion of benefits among geographically-focused policing initiatives', *Journal of Experimental Criminology* 7 (4), 347–74

Bowling, B. and J. Foster (2002). 'Policing and the Police', in M. Maguire et al (eds.), *Oxford Handbook of Criminology*, Oxford: Oxford University Press, pp. 980–1033

Bowling, B., C. Phillips, A. Campbell, and M. Docking (2004). 'Policing and Human Rights', Geneva: UN

Bradford, B. (2011). *Police Numbers and Crime Rates*, London: HMIC

Bradford, B. (2014). 'Policing and social identity', *Policing & Society*, 24 (1), 22–43

Bradford, B. and J. Jackson (2010). 'What is trust and confidence in the police?', *Policing: A Journal of Policy and Practice*, 4 (3), 241–48

Bradford, B. and P. Quinton (2014). 'Self-legitimacy, police culture and support for democratic policing', *British Journal of Criminology*, 54 (6), 1023–46

Bradford, B., P. Quinton, A. Myhill, and G. Porter (2013). 'Why do "the law" comply? Procedural Justice, group identification and officer motivation in police organizations', *European Journal of Criminology*, 11 (1), 110–31

Bradford, D. and J. Pynes (1999). 'Police academy training', *Police Quarterly*, 2 (3), 283–301

Bradley, D. (2005). 'Evidence informed policy and practice in policing', Conference on Delivering Crime Prevention, Sydney, 21–22 November 2005

Braga, A. (2007). *Effects of Hot Spots Policing on Crime*, NY: Campbell Systematic Reviews

Braga, A., D. Kennedy, E. Waring, and A. Piehl (2001). 'Problem-oriented policing, deterrence and youth violence', *Journal of Research in Crime and Delinquency*, 38 (3), 195–225

Braga, A., D. Kennedy, E. Waring, and A. Piehl (2012). 'The effects of focused deterrence strategies on crime', *Journal of Research in Crime and Delinquency*, 49 (3), 195–225

Braga, A. and D. Weisburd (2012). *The effects of 'Pulling Levers' Deterrence Strategies*, NY: Campbell Systematic Reviews

Brain, T. (2009). Address to Police Foundation/ESRC Citizen Focus and Community Engagement seminar, House of Lords, 12 February

Brain, T. (2013). *A Future for Policing in England and Wales*, Oxford: Oxford University Press

Brain, T. (2014). 'PCCs: the first twelve months', *Safer Communities*, 13 (1), 40–50

Brandl, S. et al (2001). 'Who are the complaint-prone officers?', *Journal of Criminal Justice*, 29, 521–29

Bray, A. et al (1996). *Probationer Training Review*, London: Home Office

British Broadcasting Corporation (2012). 'Surrey Police spent £2.9M on consultants'. The Sunday Politics, 13 May.

British Broadcasting Corporation (2013). *Public Services Poll*. London: BBC

Brodeur, J-P. (2005). 'Cops and spooks', in T. Newburn et al (eds.), *Policing*, Cullompton: Willan, pp. 797–812

Brogden, M. and P. Nijhar (2005). *Community Policing: National and International Models*, Cullompton: Willan

Brown, D. and P. Quinton (2014). *Impact of Codes of Ethics on Behaviour*, Bramshill: College of Policing

Brown, G. (2016). 'Blue Line on Thin Ice', *British Journal of Criminology*, 56 (2), 293–312

Brown, J. (1996). 'Police Research: some critical issues', in F. Leishman et al (eds.), *Core issues in policing*, London: Longman, pp. 179–90

Brown, J. (2007). 'From cult of masculinity to smart macho', in M. O'Neill et al (eds.), *Sociology of Crime, Law and Deviance*, volume 9, NY: JAI Press, pp. 205–28

Brown, J. (2011). 'Stress and Policing', in T. Davenport (ed.), *Managing Stress*, NY: NOVA, pp. 127–60

Brown, J. (2014). 'Supporting policing', in J Brown (ed.), *The Future of Policing*, Abingdon: Routledge, pp. 333–40

Brown, J. and E. Campbell (1990). 'Sources of occupational stress in the police' *Work & Stress*, 4, 305–18

Brown, J. (1993). *Stress and Policing*, Chichester: Wiley

Brown, J. and Jane Fielding (1993). 'Qualitative differences in men and women police officers' experience of occupational stress', *Work & Stress*, 7 (4), 327–40

Brown, J., J. Fielding, and S. Wolfenden (2009). *Added Value? The implications of increasing the proportion of women in the police service*, London, British Association for Women in Policing

Brown, J. and J. Grover (1998). 'Stress and the Woman Sergeant', *The Police Journal*, 71 (1), 47–54

Brown, J. and F. Heidensohn (2012). 'From Juliet to Jane: Women Police in TV Cop Shows, Reality, Rank and Careers', in T. Newburn and J. Peay (eds.), *Policing: Politics, Culture and Control*, Oxford: Hart, pp. 111–34

Brunetto, Y. et al (2012). 'Emotional intelligence, job satisfaction, well-being and engagement', *Human Resource Management Journal*, 22 (4), 428–41

Brunger, M. (2013). 'Policing in the Blues', *Howard Journal*, 52 (3), 336–41

Bryan, K. (2004). 'Preliminary study of the prevalence of speech and language difficulties in young offenders', *International Journal of Language and Communication Disorders*, 39, 391–400

Bryan, K., J. Freer, and C. Furlong (2007). 'Language and communication difficulties in juvenile offenders', *International Journal of Language and Communication Disorders*, 42, 505–20

Bryant, R. et al (2014). 'Police Training and Education', in J. Brown (ed.), *The Future of Policing*, Abingdon: Routledge, pp. 383–97

Bull, R. and P. Horncastle (1986). *Metropolitan Police Recruit Training*, London: Police Foundation

Bullock, K. (2013). 'Community, intelligence-led policing and crime control', *Policing & Society*, 23 (2), 125–44

Bullock, K., R. Chowdhury, and P. Hollings (2009). *Public Concerns about Organised Crime*, London: Home Office

Bullock, K., J. Fielding, N. Fielding, and A. Lloyd (2017). *The Police Service, Diversity and Organisational Outcomes: A Systematic Review*, College of Policing: Ryton.

Bullock, K. and P. Johnson (2012). 'The Impact of the Human Rights Act 1998 on Policing in England and Wales', *British Journal of Criminology*, 52 (3), 630–50

Bullock, K. and D. Leeney (2013). 'Participation, "responsivity" and accountability in neighbourhood policing', *Criminology and Criminal Justice*, 13 (2), 199–214

Bullock, K. and N. Tilley (2003). *Shootings, Gangs and Violence Incidents in Manchester*, London: Home Office

Burns, S. (2012). 'Kettling is only lawful in exceptional circumstances', *Solicitors' Journal*, 156 (19), 14–15

Burnasco, W. (2008). 'Them again: same offender involvement in repeat and near-repeat burglaries', *European Journal of Criminology*, 5 (4), 411–31

Burrage, M. et al (1990). 'An actor-based framework for the study of professionalism', in M. Burrage and R. Torstendahl (eds.), *The professions in theory and history*, London: Sage, pp. 203–25

Burruss, G. and M. Giblin (2014). 'Modeling isomorphism on policing innovation', *Crime and Delinquency*, 60 (3), 331–55

Cabinet Office (2008). *Crime and Communities Review*, London: Cabinet Office

Cabinet Office (2011). *The August riots in England*, London: SO

Cain, D. (2011). *Gender Within a Specialist Police Department.* Unpublished PhD, University of Portsmouth

Caless, B. (2011). *Policing at the Top*, Bristol: Policy Press

Cameron, David (2011). *Speech, 15 August 2011*; full text at http:www.newstatesman.com/politics/2011/08/society-fight-work-rights, accessed 5/4/12

Camp, D., J. Auten, F. Fuller, K. Locklear, and H. Locklear (2013). 'Developing competence, confidence and cooperation in law enforcement supervisors', *Policing: A Journal of Police and Practice*, 7 (2), 158–66

Can, H., H. Hendy, and M. Imbody (2013). 'Models for aggression by police officers towards romantic partners and police partners', *International Journal of Police Science and Management*, 15 (4), 273–80

Carr, P. (2005). *Clean Streets*, NY: New York University Press

Carter, E. (2011). *Analysing Police Interviews*, London: Continuum

Casey, L. (2008). *Engaging Communities in Fighting Crime*, London: Cabinet Office

Cashmore, E. (2002). 'Behind the window dressing', *Journal of Ethnic and Migration Studies* 28 (2), 327–41

Cassan, D. (2010). 'Police socialisation in France and in England', *Journal of Police Studies*, 3 (16), 243–60

Cederborg, A-C., D. Da Silva Nises, and M. Lamb (2013). 'Investigative interviewing of alleged child abuse victims', *Police Practice and Research*, 14 (3), 242–54

Centrex (2003). 'Modernising probationer training', *Horizons*, October

Chae, M. and D. Boyle (2013). 'Police suicide', *Policing: An International Journal*, 36 (1), 91–118

Chambers, S. (2014). 'Who is policing the PCCs?' *Safer Communities*, 13 (1), 32–9

Chan, J. (2001). 'Negotiating the field: new observations on the making of police officers', *Australian and New Zealand Journal of Criminology*, 34, 114–33

Chan, J., C. Devery, and S. Doran (2003). *Fair Cop: learning the art of policing*, Toronto: University of Toronto Press

Chan, J. and D. Dixon (2007). 'The politics of police reform', *Criminology and Criminal Justice*, 7 (4), 443–68

Chan, J., S. Doran, and C. Marel (2010). 'Doing and undoing gender in policing', *Theoretical Criminology*, 14 (4), 425–46

Chapman, C. (2012). 'Use of force in minority communities is related to police education', *Police Practice and Research* 13 (5), 421–36

Chappell, A. (2007). 'CP: is field training the missing link?', *Policing: An International Journal*, 30 (3), 498–517

Chappell, A. (2008). 'Police academy training: comparing across curricula', *Policing: An International Journal*, 31 (1), 36–56

Chatterton, M. et al (2009). *How it measures up*, London: Police Federation

Cherney, A. and K. Murphy (2013). 'Policing terrorism with procedural justice', *Australian and New Zealand Journal of Criminology*, 46 (3), 403–21

Child Exploitation and Online Protection Agency (2007a). *A Scoping Project on Child Trafficking in the UK*, London: CEOPA

Child Exploitation and Online Protection Agency (2007b). First Annual Report, London: CEOPA

Choi, K. and J-l. Lee (2016). 'Citizen participation in community safety', *Policing & Society*, 26 (2), 165–84

Clark, C. (1987). 'Sympathy Biography and Sympathy Margin' *American Journal of Sociology*, 93, 290–321

Clark, C. (1997). *Misery and Company: sympathy in everyday life*, Chicago: University of Chicago Press

Clarke, C. and R. Milne (2001). *National Evaluation of the PEACE investigative interviewing course*, London: Home Office

Clarke, J. (2002). 'Re-inventing community?', Spacing for Social Work conference, Bielefeld, 14–16 November

Clarke, K. (2011). 'Punish the feral rioters but address our social deficit too', *The Guardian*, 5 September

Clarke, R. and M. Hough (1984). *Crime and Police Effectiveness*, London: Home Office

Clemence, H. (2011). 'Minority retort', *Police Review*, 25 March, pp. 18–19

Cloke, P. (2004). 'Rurality and racialised others', in N. Chakraborti and J. Garland (eds.), *Rural Racism*, Cullompton: Willan, pp. 17–35

Cockcroft, T. (2013). *Police Culture: Themes and Concepts*, Abingdon: Routledge

Cockcroft, T. (2014). 'Police culture and transformational leadership', *Policing*, 8 (1), 5–13

Cockcroft, T. (2015). 'Golden Ages, Red Herrings and Post-Keynesian Policing', *Nordisk Politiforskning*, 2 (2), 183–96

Colquitt, J. (2008). 'Two decades of organizational justice', in C. Cooper and J. Barling (eds.), *The Sage Handbook of Organizational Behaviour*, London: Sage, 73–88

College of Policing (2012). *Welcome to the College of Policing*, Bramshill: CoP

College of Policing (2014). *Body Worn Cameras*, Bramshill: CoP

College of Policing (2015). *Leadership Review*, Ryton: College of Policing

College of Policing (2016). *Developing and delivering an education qualification framework for policing*, Ryton: College of Policing

Commission for Racial Equality (2004). *A Formal Investigation of The Police Service*, London: CRE

Committee of Local Police Authorities (1996). *Strategic Review of National Police Training*, London: COLPAS

Community Security Trust (2014). 'Anti-Semitic Incidents Reach Record Level', www.thecst.org.uk, accessed 4/9/14

Conti, N. (2006). 'Role Call: pre-professional socialization into police culture', *Policing & Society*, 16 (3), 221–42

Cooper, C. (2006). *A National Evaluation of Community Support Officers*, London: Home Office

Cooper, C. and S. Ingram (2004). *Retention of Police Officers*, London: HMSO
Cooper, J. (2012). 'Noble cause corruption as a consequence of role conflict', *Policing & Society*, 22 (2), 169–84
Corcoran, H. and K. Smith (2016). *Hate Crime, England and Wales*, London: Home Office
Cornish, D. (1994). 'The procedural analysis of offending and its relevance for situational crime prevention', in R.V. Clarke (ed.), *Crime Prevention Studies volume 3*, Monsey NY: Criminal Justice Press, 151–96
Cornish, D. and R. Clarke (1986). *The Reasoning Criminal*, NY: Springer
Craig, C. et al (2010). 'Shared leadership with minority ethnic communities', *Policing & Society*, 20 (3), 336–57
Crane, L. et al (2016). 'Experiences of ASD and policing in England and Wales', *Journal of Autism and Developmental Disorders*, 46 (6), 2028–41
Crank, J. and M. Caldero (2000). *Police Ethics*, Cincinnati OH: Anderson
Crawford, A. and S. Lister (2004). 'The patchwork shape of reassurance policing', *Policing: An International Journal*, 27 (3), 413–30
Crawford, A., S. Lister, S. Blackburn, and J. Burnett (2005). *Plural Policing*, Bristol: Policy Press
Crawford, R. and R. Disney (2013). *Reform of Ill Health Retirement of Police*, London: Institute for Fiscal Studies
Creaton, J. and P. Clements (2010). 'Trust me, I'm a doctor', *British Journal of Community Justice*, 18 (2), 69–78
Creedon, M. (2014). *Operation Herne*. London: Metropolitan Police Service
Crisp, A. and D. Ward (2008). 'Policing the community in the 21st century', in B. Stout et al *Applied Criminology*, London: Sage, pp. 50–67
Critchley, T. (1978). *A History of Police in England and Wales*, London: Constable
Crompton, R. (1990). 'Professions in the Current Context', *Work, Employment and Society*, 4 (5), 147–66
Crown Prosecution Service (2005). *Racist and Religious Crime*, London: Stationery Office
Crown Prosecution Service (2012). *Hate Crime and Crimes Against Older People*, London: Stationery Office
Dabney, D., H. Copes, R. Tewsbury, and S. Hawk-Tourtelot (2013). 'Qualitative assessment of stress perceptions', *Justice Quarterly*, 30 (5), 811–36
Dando, C. et al (2009). 'Cognitive interview: novice police officers', *Psychology, Crime and Law*, 15 (8), 679–96

Davies, M. (2014). 'The path to PCCs', *Safer Communities*, 13 (1), 3–12
Denicolo, P. and M. Pope (2009). *Transformative Professional Practice*, London: Whurr
Department for Work and Pensions (2009). *A Test for Racial Discrimination*, London: NatCen
Department of Justice (US) (2017). Investigation of the Chicago Police Department, Wash., DC: Department of Justice
Desborough Committee (1920). *Final Report*, London: HMSO
Deukmedjian, J. and W. de Lint (2007). 'Community into Intelligence', *Policing & Society*, 17 (3), 239–56
Dick, P. et al (2014). 'Women police', in J. Brown (ed.), *The Future of Policing*, Abingdon, Routledge, pp. 134–48
Dingwall, R. (2008). *Essays on Professions*, Aldershot: Ashgate
Doleac, J. (2016). *The Effects of DNA Databases on Crime*, Charlottesville VA: Batten School Working Papers
Dominey, J. and A. Hill (2010). 'Higher education contribution to police and probation training', *British Journal of Community Justice*, 18 (2), 5–16
Durlauf, S. and D. Nagin (2011). 'Imprisonment and crime', *Criminology and Public Policy*, 10 (1), 13–54
Dzur, A. (2008). *Democratic Professionalism*, Philadelphia: Penn State University Press
Eck, J. and W. Spelman (1987). *Problem Solving: Problem Oriented Policing in Newport News*, Washington, DC: Police Executive Research Forum
Ekblom, P. and M. Gill (2016). 'Re-writing the script', *European Journal on Criminal Policy and Research*, 22 (2), 319–39
ECPAT UK (2014). www.ecpat.uk.org, accessed 12/9/14
Edwards, C. (1999). *Changing Policing Theories for 21st Century Societies*, Melbourne: Federation Press
Eitle, D., S. D'Alessio, and L. Stolzenberg (2014). 'Effect of organisational and environmental factors on police misconduct', *Police Quarterly*, 17 (2), 103–26
Elliott, J. and S. Kushner (2003). *Review of the Learning Requirement for Police Probationers Training*, Norwich: University of East Anglia
Ellison, G. et al (2012). 'Responsible participation, community engagement and policing in transitional societies', *Howard Journal*, 51 (5), 488–502
Ellrich, K. (2016). 'Influence of violent victimisation on police officers' organizational commitment', *Journal of Police and Criminal Psychology*, 31 (2), 96–107
Emsley, C. (1996). *The English Police*, London: Longman
Engel, R. et al (2012). 'From the officer's perspective', *Justice Quarterly*, 29 (5), 650–83

Engel, R. and S Peterson (2014). 'Leading by example', in J. Brown (ed.), *The Future of Policing*, Abingdon: Routledge, pp. 398–413

Equality and Human Rights Commission (2009). *Promoting the Safety and Security of Disabled People*, London: EHRC

Equality and Human Rights Commission (2012a). *Out in the Open: Tackling Disability-Related Harassment*, London: Department for Work and Pensions

Equality and Human Rights Commission (2012b). *Race Disproportionate in Stops and Searches*, London: EHRC

Equality and Human Rights Commission (2013). *Stop and Think Again*, London: EHRC

Equality and Human Rights Commission (2014). *Hidden in Plain Sight*, London: EHRC

Equality and Human Rights Commission (2016). *Section 20 Investigation into the MPS*, London: EHRC

Ericson, R. and K. Haggerty (1997). *Policing the Risk Society*, Oxford: Clarendon

Evetts, J. (2013). 'Professionalism: Value and Ideology', *Current Sociology*, 61 (5–6), 778–96

Fahsing, I. and K. Ask (2016). 'Making of an expert detective', *Psychology Crime and Law*, 22 (3–4), 203–33

Farrington, D.P. et al (2007). *Criminal Careers*, London: Home Office

Farrell, G. et al (2005). 'Repeat victimization in the International Crime Victimization Survey', *Crime Prevention and Community Safety*, 7 (3), 7–18

Fekjaer, S. Brinsrud, and S. Halrynjo (2012). 'Promotion aspirations among male and female police', *International Journal of Police Science and Management*, 14 (1), 71–82

Fenn, L. (2016). 'The Copper and the Customer', Research Seminar, University of Surrey, 12 December

Fielding, N. (ed.) (1988a). *Actions and Structure*, London: Sage

Fielding, N. (1988b). *Joining Forces: Police Training, Socialisation and Occupational Competence*, London: Routledge

Fielding, N. (1989). 'Police culture and police practice', in M. Weatheritt, ed., *Police Research: Some Future Prospects*, London, Avebury, pp. 77–88

Fielding, N. (1995). *Community Policing*, Oxford: Oxford University Press

Fielding, N. (1999). 'Policing's dark secret: the career paths of ethnic minority officers', *Sociological Research Online*, 4 (1), http://www.socresonline.org.uk/socresonline/4/lawrence/fielding/html, accessed 21/11/14

Fielding, N. (2002). 'Theorizing Community Policing', *British Journal of Criminology*, 42 (1), 147–63

Fielding, N. (2003). '"Integrity is non-negotiable": cultural, legal and organisational responses to police corruption in the UK', in S. Einstein and M. Amir (eds.), *Police Corruption: Paradigms, Models and Concepts*, Huntsville, Texas: Office of International Criminal Justice, 53–74

Fielding, N. (2005). *The Police and Social Conflict*, London: Routledge

Fielding, N. (2009a). 'Going out on a limb: postmodernism and multiple method research', *Current Sociology*, 57 (3), 427–47

Fielding, N. (2009b). *Neighbourhood/Community Policing*, London: Police Foundation

Fielding, N., K. Bullock, and J. Fielding (2017). 'Patterns of Injury on Duty amongst Serving Police Personnel in England and Wales', *Policing & Society*, DOI:10.1080/10439463.2017.1374386

Fielding, N. and N. Caddick (2017). *Police Communications and Social Media*, Cardiff: Universities' Police Science Institute

Fielding, N. and J. Fielding (1992). 'A comparative minority: female recruits to a British constabulary force', *Policing & Society*, 2 (4), 205–18

Fielding, N. and A. Fowles (2000a). 'Penal Policy File', *Howard Journal of Criminal Justice*, 39 (3), p. 308

Fielding, N. and A. Fowles (2000b). 'Penal Policy File', *Howard Journal of Criminal Justice*, 39 (2), pp. 199–200

Fielding, N. and M. Innes (2006). 'Reassurance Policing, Community Policing and Measuring Police Performance', *Policing & Society*, 16 (2), 127–45

Fielding, N., C. Norris, C. Kemp, and J. Fielding (1992). 'Black and blue: an analysis of the influence of race on being stopped by the police', *British Journal of Sociology*, 43 (2), 207–24

FitzGerald, Marian (2000). *Final Report into Stop and Search*, London: Metropolitan Police

Flanagan, Sir Ronnie (2008). *The Review of Policing*, London: Home Office

Fletcher, A. (2017). 'Applying critical realism in qualitative research', *International Journal of Social Research Methodology*, 20 (2), 181–94

Fleming, J. (2014). 'The pursuit of professionalism', in J. Brown (ed.), *The Future of Policing*, Abingdon: Routledge, pp. 355–368

Foster, J. (2002). '"People pieces": the neglected but essential elements of community crime prevention', in G Hughes and A Edwards, (eds.), *Crime Control and Community*, Cullompton: Willan, pp. 167–96

Foster, J. and C Jones (2009). Address to Police Foundation/ESRC Citizen Focus and Community Engagement seminar, House of Lords, 12 February

Foster, J. et al (2005). *Impact of the Stephen Lawrence Inquiry*, London: Home Office

Fournier, V. (1999). 'The appeal to "professionalism" as a disciplinary mechanism', *The Sociological Review*, 47 (2), 280–307

Fox, J. (2013). Doctoral thesis, Guildford: University of Surrey

Fruhling, H. (2012). 'A realistic look at Latin American Community Policing', *Policing & Society*, 22 (1), 76–88

Fyfe, N. (2014a). 'A different and divergent trajectory', in J. Brown (ed.), *The Future of Policing*, Abingdon: Routledge, pp. 493–506

Fyfe, N. (2014b). Presentation, Fifteenth Oxford Policing Policy Forum, All Souls, Oxford, 13 May

Fyfe, N. (2017). 'Doing what works: implementation and training', What Works conference, British Library, 21 January

Gallo, G. (2001). *Armed and Dangerous*, NY: Macmillan

Garland, Jessica and C. Terry (2012). 'How not to Run an Election', London: Electoral Reform Society

Garland, Jon et al (2014). *Leicester Hate Crime Project*, Leicester: University of Leicester

Garland, J. and N. Chakraborti (2007). 'Protean times: exploring the relationships between policing, community and "race" in rural England', *Criminology and Criminal Justice*, 347–65

Garland, J. and P Hodkinson (2014). '"F**king freak! What the hell do you think you look like?": Experiences of Targeted Victimisation Among Goths', *British Journal of Criminology* 54 (4), 613–31

Garland, J. and J. Treadwell (2012). 'The new politics of hate', *Journal of Hate Studies*, 10 (1), 99–122

Giblin, J. (2011). *HMIC Review Promised so Much but Delivered so Little*, London: Police Federation

Gibson, V. (2009). *Training Evaluation: The Case of the Police Service*, Manchester: Manchester Metropolitan University

Gill, M. and A. Spriggs (2005). *Assessing the Impact of CCTV*, London: Home Office

Gilling, D. (2014). 'Reforming police governance', *Policing & Society*, 24 (1), 81–101

Gilmore, M. (2012). 'Poll reflects public concerns about PCCs', *RUSI Journal*, 157 (5), 12–15

Glenn, R. W., B. R. Panitch, D. Barnes-Proby, E. Williams, J. Christian, M. W. Lewis, S. Lerwehr, and D. W. Brannen (2003). *Training the 21st Century Police Officer: Redefining Police Professionalism for the LAPD*, LA: RAND

Goldstein, H. (1979). 'Improving policing: a problem-oriented approach', *Crime and Delinquency*, 25, 236–43

Goldstein, H. (1990). *Problem-Oriented Policing*, NY: McGraw Hill

Gottschalk, P. (2011). 'Police misconduct behaviour', *Policing: A Journal of Policy and Practice*, 5 (2), 172–79

Gould, L. (1997). 'Can an old dog be taught new tricks?', *Policing: An International Journal*, 20 (2), 339–56

Grace, K. and T. Bucke (2010). *Public Annoyance and Complaints About the Police*, London: IPCC

Grace, S. (2014). 'Swift, simple and effective justice?' *Howard Journal*, 53 (1), 69–82

Graham, J. with J. Karn (2013). *Policing young adults*, London: Police Foundation

Graziano, L., D. Rosenbaum, and A. Schuck (2014). 'Building group capacity for problem solving and police community partnerships through feedback and training', *Journal of Experimental Criminology*, 10 (1), 79–103

Grint, K. and C. Holt (2011). *HPDS evaluation report*, London: NPIA

Groff, E. and B. Lockwood (2014). 'Criminogenic facilities and crime', *Journal of Research in Crime and Delinquency*, 51 (3), 277–314

Grove, L. et al (2012). *Preventing repeat victimisation*, Stockholm: Swedish National Crime Prevention Council

Guadagno, B., C. Hughes-Scholes, and M. Powell (2013). 'What themes trigger investigative interviewers to ask specific questions when interviewing children?' *International Journal of Police Science & Management*, 15 (1), 51–60

Gustafson, J. (2013). 'Diversity in municipal police agencies', *Police Strategies and Management*, 36 (4), 719–36

Haarr, R. and J. Hultsman (1997). 'A textual interpretation of police organization', *Policing & Society*, 8, 93–115

Haarr, R. and M. Morash (2013). 'Effect of rank on police women coping with discrimination and harassment', *Police Quarterly* 16 (4), 395–419

Haas, N. and J. de Keijser (2014). 'Public support for vigilantism, confidence in police and police responsiveness', *Policing & Society* 24 (2), 224–41

Haggerty, K. (2008). 'Surveillance, Identity, and the Future of Privacy in the 21st Century', Seminar, James Martin Institute, Oxford

Hales, J. et al (2010). *Longitudinal Analysis of the Offending, Crime and Justice Survey*, London: Home Office

Hallingan-Davis, G. and K. Spicer (2005). *Piloting On-the-Spot Penalties*, London: Home Office

Hamilton-Smith, N., S. Mackenzie, A. Henry, and C. Davidones (2014). 'Community policing and reassurance', *Criminology and Criminal Justice*, 14 (1), 160–78

Hannan, M., I. Hearnden, K. Grace, and T. Bucke (2011). *Deaths In or Following Police Custody*, London: IPCC

Harcourt, B. (2005). *Illusion of Order*, Cambridge MA: Harvard University Press

Harfield, C. and K. Harfield (2005). *Covert Investigation*, Oxford: Oxford University Press

Harron, M. (2010). 'White police, social apartheid', *Constabulary*, August-September issue, pp. 8–9

Harris, C. (2010). 'Longitudinal patterns of internally generated complaints', *Policing & Society*, 20 (4), 401–15

Harris, C (2011). 'Problem behaviours in later portions of officers' careers', *Policing: An International Journal*, 34 (1), 135–52

Hassell, K., C. Archbold, and A. Stichman (2011). 'Comparing the workplace experiences of male and female police officers', *International Journal of Police Science and Management* 13 (1), 37–53

Hawkins, K. (2003). 'Order, Rationality and Silence', in L. Gelsthorpe and M. Padfield (eds.), *Exercising Discretion*, Cullompton: Willan, pp. 186–219

Hayes, C. (2002). 'A consideration of the need for ethics training for police', *Police Journal*, 75, 322–29

Health and Safety Executive (2014). *Violence at Work*, London: HSE

Health and Social Care Information Centre (2013). *Annual Report*, London: HSCIC

Heaton, R. (2010). 'We could be criticized! Policing and risk aversion', *Policing*, 5 (1), 75–86

Heffren, C. and P. Hausdort (2016). 'Post-traumatic effects in policing', *Police Practice and Research*, 17 (5), 420–33

Henry, V. (1996). 'Realigning police discretion and accountability structures', Queensland Criminal Justice Centre Conference, Brisbane: University of Queensland

Henstock, D. and B. Ariel (2017). 'Testing the effects of police body-worn cameras on use of force during arrests', *European Journal of Criminology*, 14 (6), 1–31

HM Inspectorate of Constabulary (1999). *Managing Learning: A Study of Police Training*, London: HMIC

HM Inspectorate of Constabulary (2000). *Essex Police Inspection*, London: HMIC

HM Inspectorate of Constabulary (2001). *Gwent Police Inspection*, London: HMIC

HM Inspectorate of Constabulary (2002). *Training Matters*, London: HMIC

HM Inspectorate of Constabulary (2004). *Modernising the Police Service*, London: HMIC

HM Inspectorate of Constabulary (2006). *Closing the Gap*, London: HMIC

HM Inspectorate of Constabulary (2008a). *Frontline Officers Supervision*, London: HMIC

HM Inspectorate of Constabulary (2008b). *Leading from the Frontline*, London: HMIC

HM Inspectorate of Constabulary (2009a). *Adapting to Protest*, London: HMIC

HM Inspectorate of Constabulary (2009b). *Get Smart: Planning to Protect*, London: HMIC

HM Inspectorate of Constabulary (2009c). *Policing Pledge*, London: HMIC

HM Inspectorate of Constabulary (2009d). *Serving Neighbourhoods and Individuals*, London: HMIC

HM Inspectorate of Constabulary (2010a). *Major Challenge: a thematic inspection of major crime*, London: HMIC

HM Inspectorate of Constabulary (2010b). *Management of gang issues among children and young people*, London: HMIC

HM Inspectorate of Constabulary (2010c). *Police Governance in Austerity*, London: HMIC

HM Inspectorate of Constabulary (2010d). *Valuing the Police: Policing in an Age of Austerity*, London: HMIC

HM Inspectorate of Constabulary (2011a). *Demanding Times: the front line and police visibility*', London: HMIC

HM Inspectorate of Constabulary (2011b). *Policing ASB*, London: HMIC

HM Inspectorate of Constabulary (2011c). *Policing Public Order*, London: HMIC

HM Inspectorate of Constabulary (2011d). *Without Fear or Favour*, London: HMIC

HM Inspectorate of Constabulary (2012a). *Facing up to Offending*, London: HMIC

HM Inspectorate of Constabulary (2012b). *Policing in Austerity: One Year On*, London: HMIC

HM Inspectorate of Constabulary (2012c). *Taking Time for Crime*, London: HMIC

HM Inspectorate of Constabulary (2013a). *Everyone's Business: Improving the Police Response to Domestic Abuse*', London: HMIC

HM Inspectorate of Constabulary (2013b). *Revisiting Police Relationships*, London: HMIC

HM Inspectorate of Constabulary (2013c). *Stop and Search Powers*, London: HMIC

HM Inspectorate of Constabulary (2014a). *Core Business*, London: HMIC

HM Inspectorate of Constabulary (2014b). *Crime Recording*, London: HMIC

HM Inspectorate of Constabulary (2014c). *Inspection Programme 2014/15*, London: HMIC

HM Inspectorate of Constabulary (2016). *Police Effectiveness 2015*, London: HMIC
HM Inspectorate of Constabulary (2017a). *Police Effectiveness: a National Overview*, London: HMIC
HM Inspectorate of Constabulary (2017b). *State of Policing 2016*, London: HMIC
Heidensohn, F. (1994). 'We can handle it out here: women officers in Britain and the USA', *Policing & Society*, 4, 293–303
Heslop, R. (2010). 'They didn't treat us like professionals', Critical Perspectives on Learning conference, University of Leeds, 11 January
Heslop, R. (2011a). 'British police service: professionalization or McDonaldization', *International Journal of Police Science and Management*, 13 (4), 312–21
Heslop, R. (2011b). 'Community engagement and learning as "becoming"', *Policing & Society*, 21 (3), 327–42
Heslop, R. (2011c). 'Reproducing police culture in a British university', *Police Practice and Research*, 12 (4), 298–312
Heslop, R. and D. White (2011a). 'A "New Police studies" for a "new professional police service', Police Learning Conference, University of Northampton
Heslop, R. and D. White (2011b). 'Ready to serve: can universities instil professionalism in budding police officers', *Police Review*, 4 February, 20–21
Hipp, J. (2013). 'Assessing crime as a problem', *Crime and Delinquency*, 59 (4), 616–48
Hirst, P. (1994). *Associative Democracy*, Cambridge: Polity
Hobbs, D. (1988). *Doing the Business*, Oxford: Oxford University Press
Hobbs, D. (2013). *Lush Life*, Oxford: Clarendon
Hochschild, A. R. (1983). *The Managed Heart*, LA: University of California Press
Hodgson, J. (2001). 'Police violence in Canada and the USA', *Policing: An International Journal*, 24 (4), 520–549
Hogan-Howe, B. (2011). *Undercover Tactics in Public Order and Extremism*, London: HMIC
Hoggett, J. et al (2013). *Police Identity in a Time of Rapid Change*, Plymouth: University of West of England
Holdaway, S. (2011). 'Through what mechanisms should policing be delivered?', Conference on Policing in a Time of Contraction and Constraint, 27 September, British Academy, London
Holdaway, S. (2017a). 'The re-professionalisation of the police in England and Wales', *Criminology and Criminal Justice*, 29 (1), 1–17
Holdaway, S. (2017b). 'What we thought we knew about What Works and what we learned', What Works conference, January 21, British Library

Holdaway, S. and S. Parker (1998). 'Policing Women Police', *British Journal of Criminology*, 38 (1), 40–60
Holgersson S. and J. Knutsson (2011). 'Dialogue Policing', in T. Madensen and J. Knutsson (eds.), *Preventing Crowd Violence*, London: Lynne Rienner, 191–215
Home Affairs Committee (2002). *Second Report on Police Reform Bill, HC 612*, London: Stationery Office
Home Affairs Committee (2008). *Domestic Violence, Forced Marriage and Honour-Based Violence, HC 263-I*, London: SO
Home Affairs Committee (2009a). *Knife Crime, HC 112-1*, London: SO
Home Affairs Committee (2009b). *Macpherson Report: Ten Years On, HC 427*, London: SO
Home Affairs Committee (2009c). *Policing of the G20 Protests, HC 418*, London: SO
Home Affairs Committee (2010). *The Work of the IPCC, HC 366*, London: SO
Home Affairs Committee (2011a). *New Landscape of Policing*, London: Stationery Office
Home Affairs Committee (2011b). *Police Finances, HC 695*, London: SO
Home Affairs Committee (2011c). *Policing: PCCs*, London: SO
Home Affairs Committee (2012). *New Landscape of Policing, 14th Report of Session 2010-2012*, London: SO
Home Affairs Committee (2013). *Leadership and Standards in the Police Part 1, HC 67-1*, London: SO
Home Affairs Committee (2014a). *Leadership and Standards in the Police Part 2, HC 67-2*, London: SO
Home Affairs Committee (2014b). *PCCs 16th Report*, London: SO
Home Affairs Committee (2016). *College of Policing: Three Years On, HC 23*, London: SO
Home Office (1995). *Review of Police Core and Ancillary Tasks*, London: Home Office
Home Office (1998a). *Planning Police Trainee Throughput*, London: Home Office
Home Office (1998b). *Review of National Police Training*, London: Home Office
Home Office (2000a). *Complaints Against the Police*, London: Home Office
Home Office (2000b). *Policing and the Public*, London: Home Office
Home Office (2001a). *Attitudes of People from Minority Ethnic Communities toward a Career in the Police*, London: Home Office
Home Office (2001b). *Managing Medical Retirements in the Police Service*, London: Home Office
Home Office (2001c). *Widening Access: Improving Police Relations With Hard-to-Reach Groups*, London: Home Office

Home Office (2002). *Policing a New Century: a Blueprint for Reform*, London: Home Office
Home Office (2003a). *An Evaluation of the New Police Misconduct Procedures*, London: Home Office
Home Office (2003b). *Policing: Building Safer Communities Together, Consultation Document*, London: Home Office
Home Office (2004a). *IPLDP: Guidance for Chief Officers*, London: Home Office
Home Office (2004b). *Building Communities, Beating Crime*, London: Home Office
Home Office (2004c). *National Policing Plan 2005-08*, London: Home Office
Home Office (2008). *From the Neighbourhood to the National: Policing our Communities Together*, London: Home Office
Home Office (2009). *Protecting the Public*, London: Home Office
Home Office (2010). *Policing in the 21st Century: Reconnecting Police and the People*, London: Home Office
Home Office (2011a). *Government Response to the 14th Report of the HAC Session 2010-12*, London: Home Office
Home Office (2011b). *Tackling Organised Crime*, London: Home Office
Home Office (2011c). *The National Crime Agency: a plan*, London: Home Office
Home Office (2012a). *College of Policing: an Introduction*, London: Home Office
Home Office (2012b). *Detentions in the 12 Months to March 2011*, London: Home Office
Home Office (2012c). *Statutory Guidance for Police Collaboration*, London: Home Office
Home Office (2013a). *Ending Violence Against Women and Girls*', London: Home Office
Home Office (2013b). *Evaluation of the Pilot of Domestic Violence Protection Orders*, London: Home Office
Home Office (2013c). *Police Powers and Procedures 2011/12*, London: Home Office
Home Office (2014a). *Best Use of Stop-and-Search Scheme*, London: Home Office
Home Office (2014b). *Police Powers and Procedures*, London: Home Office
Home Office (2014c). *Police Workforce*, London: Home Office
Hopkins, A. (2010). *The Police Service*, London: Consumer Focus
Hopkins, M. and N. Tilley (2011). *Exploring the Links Between Homicide and Organised Crime*, London: Home Office
Hornqvist, M. (2014). 'The fluid legitimacy of the Husby riots', *Criminology in Europe*, 13 (1), 4–7

Houdmont, J., R. Kerr, and R. Randall (2012). 'Organisational psycho-social hazard exposures in UK policing', *Policing: An International Journal*, 35 (1), 182–97

Hough, M., J. Jackson, and B. Bradford (2013). 'The drivers of police legitimacy', *Journal of Policing, Intelligence and Counter-Terrorism*, 8 (2), 144–65

Hough, M. and S. Maffei (2013). 'Trust in Justice', *Criminology in Europe*, 2, 4–10

House of Lords (2009). *Surveillance: Citizens and the State*, London: HMSO

Howard League (2014). *Child Arrests in England and Wales 2013*, London: Howard League

Howell, K. (2009). 'Broken lives from Broken Windows', *Social Change*, 33 (3), 271–330

Hoyle, C. and A. Sanders (2000). 'Police response to domestic violence', *British Journal of Criminology*, 40 (1), 14–36

Huberts, L. et al (2007). 'A study of the impact of three leadership styles on integrity violations', *Policing: An International Journal*, 30, 586–607

Hughes G. and M. Rowe (2007). 'Neighbourhood policing and community safety', *Criminology and Criminal Justice*, 7 (4), 317–46

Huntington S. (1957). *The Soldier and the State*, NY: Vintage

Huq, A., T. Tyler, and S. Schulhjofer (2011). 'Mechanisms for eliciting cooperation in counterterrorism policing', *Journal of Empirical Legal Studies*, 8 (4), 728–61

Hunter, G., T. May, and M. Hough (2017). *An Evaluation of the What Works Centre for Crime Reduction*. London: Birkbeck ICPR

Hur, Yongbeom (2012). 'Turnover, Voluntary Turnover and Organizational Performance: Evidence from Municipal Police Departments, *Public Administration Quarterly*, 37 (1)

Independent Police Complaints Commission (2005). *Making the New Police Complaints System Work*, London: IPCC

Independent Police Complaints Commission (2006). *Confidence in the Police Complaints System*, London: IPCC

Independent Police Complaints Commission (2010). *Police Complaint Statistics*, London: IPCC

Independent Police Complaints Commission (2011a). *Corruption in the Police Service, Part 1,* London: IPCC

Independent Police Complaints Commission (2011b). *Learning From Appeals Bulletin 13* London: IPCC

Independent Police Complaints Commission (2012a). *Corruption in the Police Service Part 2,* London: IPCC

Independent Police Complaints Commission (2012b). *Deaths During or Following Police Contact*, London: IPCC

Independent Police Complaints Commission (2012c). *Police Complaints*, London: IPCC

Independent Police Complaints Commission (2013). *Learning the Lessons Bulletin 19*, London: IPCC

Independent Police Complaints Commission (2014a). *Police Handling of Allegations of Discrimination*, London: IPCC

Independent Police Complaints Commission (2014b). *Learning the Lessons Bulletin 20*, London: IPCC

Independent Police Complaints Commission (2014c). *Review of IPCC's Work in Investigating Deaths*, London: IPCC

Information Commissioner (2007). *A Surveillance Society*, London: SO

Institute for Employment Studies (IES) (2007). *Managing Sickness Absence in the Police Service*, London: Home Office

Institute for Public Policy Research (IPPR) (2009) *Arrested Development*, London: IPPR

Ipsos-MORI (2007). *Public Perceptions of the Police Complaints System*, London: MORI

Ipsos-MORI (2013). *Trust in Professions*, London: MORI

Innes, M. (2010). 'Criminal legacies: community impact assessments and defining success and harm in police homicide investigations', *Journal of Contemporary Criminal Justice*, 26 (4), 367–81

Innes, M. (2014a). 'Reinventing the office of constable', in J. Brown (ed.), *The Future of Policing*, Abingdon: Routledge, pp. 64–78

Innes, M. (2014b). *Signal Crimes*, Oxford: Oxford University Press

Innes, M., N. Fielding, and N. Cope (2004). 'The appliance of science: the theory and practice of crime intelligence analysis', *British Journal of Criminology*, 45 (1), 2004, 39–57

Innes, M. and C. Roberts (2011). *Policing, situational intelligence and the information environment*, London: HMIC

Irving, B. (1986). 'The interrogation process', in J. Benyon and C. Bourn (eds.), *The Police: Powers, Procedures and Proprieties*, Oxford: Pergamon, pp. 136–49

Jackson, J., B. Bradford, B. Stanko, and K. Hohl (2012a). *Just Authority?: Trust in the Police in England and Wales*, Abingdon: Routledge

Jackson, J., B. Bradford, M. Hough, A. Myhill, and P. Quinton (2012b). 'Why do people comply with the law?', *British Journal of Criminology*, 52 (6), 1051–71

James, Z. (2007). 'Policing marginal places', *Criminology and Criminal Justice*, 7 (4), 367–89

Jaschke, H-G. (2010). 'Knowledge-led policing and security', *Policing*, 4 (3), 302–9

Jaschke, H-G. (2014). 'Security Management and Human rights', Turkish Police Academy Conference on 'Securing Liberty, Civilizing Security', Ankara, 19 October

Jaschke, H-G. and K. Neidhardt (2007). 'A modern police science as an integrated academic discipline', *Policing & Society*, 17 (4), 303–20

Jennings, C. (2014). '70:20:10 Framework Explained', *Forum*, Victoria: Forum

Jermier, M. et al (1989). 'Reactions to physically dangerous work', *Journal of Organisational Behaviour*, 10, 15–33

Johnson, H., G. Smith and C. Roberts (2013). 'Disproportionality in internal misconduct and counter-corruption proceedings', *Policing: A Journal of Policy and Practice*, 7 (4), 359–69

Johnson, P. and R. Vanderbeck (2011). '"Hit them on the nose": representations of policing in Parliamentary debates', *Policing*, 5 (1), 65–74

Johnson, R. (2013). 'Arrest as displaced aggression', *Criminal Justice and Behaviour*, 40 (10), 1149–62

Johnson, T. (1972). *Professions and Power*, Basingstoke: Macmillan

Johnston, L. (2006). 'Diversifying police recruitment?', *Howard Journal*, 45 (4), 388–402

Johnston, L. (2007). '"Keeping the family together": PCSOs and the "police extended family"', *Policing & Society*, 17 (2), 119–40

Johnston, N. and B. Politowski (2016). *Police Funding*, London: Commons Library

Jones, P. (2011). *'F' Word: Failure Factors in UK Student Police Officers*, Leatherhead, Police Federation

Jones, B. and N. Tilley (2004). *The Impact of High Visibility Patrols on Personal Robbery*, London: Home Office

Jones, T. and T. Newburn (1998). *Private Security and Public Policing*, Oxford: Clarendon Press

Jowett, B. translator (1942). *Plato*, Roslyn NY: Walter J. Black

Kaariainen, J. (2007). 'Trust in the police in 16 European countries', *European Journal of Criminology*, 4, 409–35

Kaminski, R. and J. Martin (2000). 'An analysis of police officer satisfaction with defense and control tactics', *Policing: An International Journal*, 23 (2), 132–53

Kane, R. and M. White (2016). 'Taser exposure and cognitive impairment', *Criminology and Public Policy*, 15 (1), 79–107

Kanter, R. (1983). *The Change Masters*, NY: Simon and Schuster

Karn, J. (2013). *Policing and Crime Reduction*, London: Police Foundation

Karp, S. and H. Stenmark (2011). 'Learning to be a police officer', *Police Practice and Research*, 12 (1), 4–15

Katz, J. (1990). *Seductions of Crime*, NY: Basic Books

Kelling, G. (1981). *The Newark Foot Patrol Experiment*, Washington DC: Police Foundation

Kelling, G. and M. Moore (1988). *The Evolving Strategy of Policing*, Washington DC: NIJ

Kelly, M. (2017). 'The role of experience in determining What Works', What Works conference January 21, British Library

Kemshall, H. and J. Wood (2010). *Child Sex Offender Review*, London: Home Office

Khan, S. (2012). 'Kettling will not always be lawful', *Solicitors Journal* 156 (12), p. 9

Krahenbuhl, S. (2009). 'Interviewing young children' *Childhoods Today*, 2 (1), 1–23

Kim, B., A. Matz, J. Gerber, D. Beto, and E. Lambert (2013). 'Facilitating police-probation/parole partnerships', *Policing: An International Journal*, 36 (4), 752–67

King, M. (2013). 'Birmingham revisited', *Policing & Society*, 23 (1), 26–45

Kirby, P. (2016). *Leading People 2016*, London: Sutton Trust

Kirk, D. and M. Matsuda (2011). 'Legal cynicism, collective efficacy, and the ecology of arrests', *Criminology*, 49 (2), 443–72

Kirkpatrick, D. (1975). 'Techniques for evaluating training programs', in D. Kirkpatrick (ed.), *Evaluating training programs*, Alexandria VA: ASTD, 119

King, R. and G. Sutton (2013). 'High times for hate crimes', *Criminology*, 51 (4), 871–94

Klockars, C. (1988). 'Rhetoric of community policing', in J. Greene and S. Mastrofski (eds.), *Community Policing: Rhetoric or Reality*, NY: Praeger, 239–58

Knowles, M. et al (1973). *Andragogy in Action*, San Francisco: Jossey Bass

Kodz, J. and I. Campbell (2010). *What Works in Leadership Development*, London: NPIA

Koehnken, G. et al (1999). 'The Cognitive Interview: a meta-analysis', *Psychology, Crime and Law*, 5, 101–16

Kolb, D. (1984). *Experiential Learning*, Englewood Cliffs, NJ: Prentice Hall

Kooi, G. Vander and L. Palmer (2013). 'Problem-based learning for police academy students', *Journal of Criminal Justice Education*, 25 (2), 175–95

Koper, C. and E. Mayo-Wilson (2006). 'Police crackdowns on illegal gun carrying', *Journal of Experimental Criminology*, 2 (2), 227–61

Korre, M., A. Farioli, V. Varvarigou, S. Sato, and S. Kales (2014). 'Survey of stress levels and time spent across law enforcement duties', *Policing: A Journal of Policy and Practice*, 8 (2), 109–22

Kritzer, H. (1990). *The Justice Broker: Lawyers and Ordinary Litigation*, New York: Oxford University Press

Kumar, T. (2014). 'Differing services, rising expectations and greater demands', *Policing: An International Journal*, 37 (1), 170–89

Kundnani, A. (2013). *The Muslims are Coming!*, London: Verso

Kurtz, D. (2012). 'Roll call and the second shift', *Police Practice and Research*, 13 (1), 71–86

Lagestad, P. and R van den Tillaar (2014). 'Longitudinal changes in physical activity patterns of police', *International Journal of Police Science and Management*, 16 (1), 76–86

Langworthy, R. and L. Travis (2003). *Policing in America*, Upper Saddle River NJ: Prentice Hall

Lave, J. and E. Wenger (1991). *Situated Learning*, Cambridge: Cambridge University Press

Laycock, G. and N. Tilley (2014). 'The police as professional problem solvers', in J. Brown (ed.), *The Future of Policing*, Abingdon: Routledge, pp. 369–82

Leblanc, L. (2013). *Pretty in Punk: Girls' Gender Resistance in a Boys' Subculture*, Newark: Rutgers University Press

Lee, R.M. (2010). 'The Secret Life of Focus Groups', *American Sociologist*, 41, 115–41

Leino, T., K. Eskelinen, H. Summala, and M. Virtanen (2011). 'Work-related violence, debriefing and increased alcohol consumption among police officers', *International Journal of Police Science and Management*, 13 (2), 149–57

Lentz, S. and R. Chaires (2007). 'The invention of Peel's principles', *Journal of Criminal Justice*, 35 (1), 69–79

Lewis, C. (2013). 'Safer Sutton Partnership Service', *Police Journal*, 86 (1), 15–28

Lewis, P., T. Newburn, M. Taylor, C. McGillivray, A. Greenhill, H. Frayman, and R. Procter (2011). *Reading the Riots*, London: Guardian Books

Lieberman, J., D. Koetzle, and M. Sakiyama (2013). 'Police departments' use of Facebook', *Police Quarterly*, 16 (4), 438–62

Liederbach, J., E. Fritsch, D. Carter, and A. Bannister (2008). 'Exploring the limits of collaboration in community policing', *Policing: An International Journal*, 31 (2), 271–91

Lindstrom, P. (2013). 'More police less crime?', *Police Journal*, 86 (4), 321–39

Lipsky, M. (1980). *Street-Level Bureaucracy*, NY: Russell Sage Foundation

Lister, M. (2011). 'Anti-terrorism measures undermine citizenship', *Society Now*, Autumn, p. 7

Lister, S. (2014). 'Scrutinising the role of the Police and Crime Panel in the New Era of Police Governance', *Safer Communities*, 13 (1), 22–31

Lloyd, K. and J. Foster (2009). *Citizen focus and community engagement*, London: Police Foundation

Loader, I. (2005). 'Policing, recognition and belonging', *British Society of Criminology conference*, Leeds, July

Loader, I. (2014a). 'Why do the police matter?', in J. Brown (ed.), *The Future of Policing*, Abingdon, Routledge, pp. 40–51

Loader, I. (2014b). 'If 43 police forces is the problem, what is the solution', Report of the Fifteenth Oxford Policing Policy Forum, All Souls, Oxford

Loader, I. and R. Sparks (2011). 'Beyond Lamentation: Towards a Democratic Egalitarian Politics of Crime and Justice', in T. Newburn and J. Peay (eds.), *Policing: Politics, Culture and Control*, Oxford: Hart, pp. 11–42

Loftus, B. (2009). *Police Culture in a Changing World*, Oxford: Oxford University Press

Loftus, B. (2010). 'Police occupational culture', *Policing & Society*, 20 (1), 1–20

Lonsway, K. et al (2002). *Men, Women and Police Excessive Force*, Washington DC: The National Centre for Women and Policing

Lonsway, K. (2003). *Hiring and Retaining More Women: the Advantages to Law Enforcement Agencies*, Washington DC: The National Centre for Women and Policing

Loveday, B. (2007). 'Re-engineering the police organization', *The Police Journal*, 80, 3–27

Loveday, B. (2012). 'Commentary: the PCC elections', *The Police Journal*, 2012, 85 (3), 183–89

Loveday, B. (2013). 'Despite the manner of their election, PCCs are bringing about a significant change in the governance of police', *Democratic Audit*; http://www.democraticauudit.com, accessed 2/7/14

Lowe, T. and M. Innes (2012). 'Can we speak in confidence: community intelligence and neighbourhood policing', *Policing & Society*, 22 (3), 295–316

Lumsden, K. (2014). 'Anti-Social Behaviour Legislation and the Policing of Boy Racers', *Policing*, 8 (2), 135–43

Lustgarten, L. (2002). 'The future of stop and search', *Criminal law Review*, August, 601–16

MacDonald, B. (1982). *Policy and Practice: an Informed Educational Critique*, Norwich: CARE

MacDonald, B., M. Argent, J. Elliott, N. May, J. Taylor, and N. Norris (1987). *The Stage Two Review Final Report*, London: HMSO

Macdonald, K.M. (1995). *The Sociology of Professions*, London: Sage

Mac Giollabhui, S., B. Goold, and B. Loftus (2016). 'Watching the Watchers', *Qualitative Research*, 16 (6), 630–45

McCarty, W. (2013). 'Gender differences in burnout', *Policing: An International Journal*, 36 (4), 808–18

McCarty, W. and W. Skogan (2013). 'Job related burnout among civilian and sworn police personnel', *Police Quarterly*, 16 (1), 66–84

McClellan, S. and B. Gustafson (2012). 'Communicating law enforcement professionalization', *Policing: An International Journal*, 35 (1), 104–23
McElroy, J. et al (1993). *Community Policing: the CPOP in New York*, London: Sage
McGarrell, F. et al (2010). 'Project Safe Neighbourhood and violent crime trends', *Journal of Quantitative Criminology*, 26 (2), 165–90
McLaughlin, E. (1994). *Community, Policing, and Accountability*, Aldershot: Avebury
McLean, F. and J. Hillier (2011). *An Observational Study of Response and Neighbourhood officers*, London: NPIA
McNamara, J. (1967). *Complaints Against Police*, Indianapolis: Wiley
McPhail, C., D. Schweingruber, and J. McCarthy (1998). 'Policing protest in the US', in D. della Porta and H. Reiter (eds.), *Policing Protest*, Minneapolis: University of Minnesota Press, 49–69
Maguire, M. (2008). 'Criminal investigation and crime control', in T. Newburn (ed.), *Handbook of Policing*, Cullompton: Willan, pp. 430–64
Maguire, M. and C. Corbett (1991). *A study of the police complaints system*, London: HMSO
Man, Lan-Ho et al (2003). 'Dealing with alcohol-related detainees', London: Home Office
Manning, P. (1977). *Police Work*, Cambridge, MA: MIT Press
Manning, P. (1992). 'Information technologies and the police', in M. Tonry and N. Morris (eds.), *Modern Policing*, Chicago: University of Chicago Press, pp. 349–98
Manning, P. (2008). *The Technology of Policing*, NY: New York University Press
Manning, P. (2010). *Democratic Policing in a Changing World*, London: Paradigm
Manning, P. (2014). 'Policing: privatizing and changes in the policing web', in J. Brown (ed.), *The Future of Policing*, Abingdon, Routledge, pp. 23–39
Manning, P. and J. Van Maanen (1977). 'Rules, colleagues and situationally justified actions', in P. Manning (ed.), *Policing*, NY Random House, pp. 71–89
Martis, R. (2006). 'Let's get physical', *Police Review*, 2 June, pp. 16–18
Martis, R. (2012). 'You must be f@3k!&g joking: on swearing at police officers', *Police*, February, pp. 16–17
Mason, G. (2013). 'Future of community policing', *Police Product Insight*, 4, p. 16
Mason, M. (2009). *Findings from the Second Year of National Neighbourhood Policing*, London: Home Office

Mason, P. (2007). 'Driving while black: do police pass the test', *Swedish Economic Policy Review*, 14, 79–113
Mastrofski, S. (1998). 'Community Policing and Police Organization Structure', in J-P. Brodeur (ed.), *How to recognize good policing*, London: Sage, pp. 161–92
May, Theresa (2013). 'PCC's warts and all', speech to Policy Exchange, London, 7 November
May, T. et al (2007). *Local Resolution: the Views of Complainants and Police*, London: Police Foundation
Mazerolle, L., E. Antrobus, S. Bennett, and T. Tyler (2013a). 'Shaping citizen perceptions of police legitimacy', *Criminology*, 51 (1), 33–63
Mazerolle, L., S. Bennett, J. Davis, E. Sargeant, and M. Manning (2013b). *Legitimacy in Policing: A Systematic Review*, NY: Campbell Systematic Reviews
Mead, G.H. (1934). *Mind, Self and Society*, Chicago IL: University of Chicago Press
Meier, K. and J. Nicholson-Crotty (2006). 'Gender, Representative Bureaucracy and Law Enforcement', *Public Administration Review*, 66 (6), 850–60
Merritt, J. (2007). *Law for Student Police Officers*, Exeter: Learning Matters
Merritt, J. (2009). 'Pluralist models of policing', *Policing: An International Journal*, 32 (2), 377–94
Meyer, P. (1973). *Precision Journalism*, Bloomington IL: Indiana University Press
Millen, F. and M. Stephens (2011). 'Policing and accountability', *Policing & Society*, 21 (3), 265–83
Miller, J., N. Bland, and P. Quinton (2000). *The Impact of Stops and Searches on Crime and the Community*, London: Home Office
Miller, J., R. Davis, N. Henderson, J. Marcovic, and C. Ortiz (2004). *Public Opinions of the Police*, Washington, DC: US Department of Justice
Millie, A. (2014). 'What are the police for?', in J. Brown (ed.), *The Future of Policing*, Abingdon: Routledge, pp. 52–63
Ministry of Justice (2010). *Satisfaction and Willingness to engage with the Criminal Justice System*, London: Ministry of Justice
Ministry of Justice (2012). *Statistical Bulletin*, London: Home Office
Ministry of Justice (2014). *Youth Justice Annual Statistics*, London: Ministry of Justice
Mitchell, D. and L. Staeheli (2005). 'Permitting protest', *International Journal of Urban & Regional Research*, 29 (4), 796–813
Monjardet, D. (2000). 'Policing in France and Britain', Address to Franco-British Council, 7 November
Monjardet, D. and C. Gorgeon (1992). *La socialisation professionnelle*, Paris: IHESI

MOPAC (2014). *MPS Workforce Diversity*, London: Mayor's Office for Policing & Crime

Moran, L. (2007). 'Invisible minorities', *Criminology and Criminal Justice*, 7 (4), 417–41

Morgan, J. (1990). *The Police Function and the Investigation of Crime*, Aldershot: Avebury

Morgan, R. (1985). 'Setting the PACE: police community consultation arrangements', Bath: University of Bath Social Policy Paper 4

Morton, A. (2013). *Emotion and Imagination*, Cambridge: Polity

Mugford, R., S. Corey, and C. Bennell (2013). 'Improving police training from a cognitive load perspective', *Policing: An International Journal*, 36 (2), 312–37

Mulvey, P. and M. White (2014). 'Potential for violence in arrests of persons with mental illness', *Policing: An International Journal*, 37 (2), 404–419

Muir, W. K. (1977). *Police: Streetcorner Politicians*, Chicago, University of Chicago Press

Muir, W. K. (2008). 'Police and social democracy', *Policing & Society*, 18 (1), 18–22

Murphy, K. and A. Cherney (2012). 'Understanding cooperation with the police in a diverse society', *British Journal of Criminology*, 52 (1), 181–201

Murrell-Abery, G. (2003). *Learning from the Learners' Perspective*, doctoral thesis, University of Reading

Murray, J. (2005). 'Policing Terrorism', *Police Practice and Research*, 6, 347–61

Myhill, A. (2006). *Community Engagement in Policing*, London: Home Office

Myhill, A. and K. Beak (2008). *Public Confidence in the Police*, London: NPIA

Myhill, A. and B. Bradford (2012). 'Can police enhance public confidence by improving quality of service?', *Policing & Society* 22 (4), 397–425

Myhill, A. and P. Quinton (2010). 'Confidence, neighbourhood policing and contact', *Policing*, 4 (3), 273–81

Myhill, A. (2011). *It's a Fair Cop*, London: NPIA

Myhill, A., P. Quinton, B. Bradford, A. Poole, and G. Sims (2011). 'It depends what you mean by confident: operationalizing measures of public confidence', *Policing: A Journal of Policy and Practice*, 5 (2), 114–24

National Audit Office (2010). *National Cybersecurity Strategy*, London: NAO

National Policing Improvement Agency (2008). 'Neighbourhood Policing Programme: PCSO review', Bramshill: NPIA

National Policing Improvement Agency (2010). *National Investigator's Curriculum Handbook*, Wyboston: NPIA

Newburn, T. (2012). 'Young people and the August 2011 riots', *Howard Journal*, 51 (3), 331–35

Neyroud, P. (2010). *Review of Police Leadership and Training*, London: Home Office

Norris, C. (2014). 'Big Data and the Democratic Deficit', Justice and Society in the Age of Big Data conference, Selsdon Park, 22 November

Novak, K., J. Frank, B. Smith, and R. Engel (2002). 'Revisiting the decision to arrest', *Crime and Delinquency*, 48 (1), 70–98

Oberwittler, D. and S. Roche (2013). 'Variations of police-adolescents relationships in French and German cities', *Criminology in Europe*, 12 (3), 4–10

Office for National Statistics (2013). *Crime Statistics: Focus on Victimisation and Public Perceptions* 2012/13, London: HMSO

Office for National Statistics (2014a). *Crime in England and Wales 2013*, London: SO

Office for National Statistics (2014b), *Overview of Hate Crime*, London: SO

Office for National Statistics (2014c), *Police Powers and Procedures 2012/13*, London: SO

Office for National Statistics (2015). *Police Workforce*, London: SO

Office of the Surrey Police and Crime Commissioner (2014). *Operation Siren*. Guildford: OPCC Surrey

Oldershaw, M. (2013). *Why Don't Experienced Specialist Police Interviewers Utilise Cognitive Techniques?* MSc dissertation, University of Portsmouth

O'Neill, M. (2014). 'Playing nicely with others', in J. Brown (ed.), *The Future of Policing*, Abingdon: Routledge, pp. 203–16

O'Neill, M. and S. Holdaway (2007). 'Examining Window Dressing: The Views of Black Police Associations', *Journal of Ethnic and Migration Studies*, 33 (3), 483–500

O'Neill, M. and D. McCarthy (2014). '(Re)negotiating police culture through partnership working', *Criminology and Criminal Justice*, 14 (1), 143–59

Otwin, M. (2004). 'Police training for democracy', *Police Practice and Research*, 5, 107–23

Palmiotto, M., M. Birzer, and N. Unnithan (2000). 'Training in community policing', *Policing: An International Journal*, 23 (1), 8–21

Pate, A. (1986). 'Experimenting with foot patrol', in D. Rosenbaum (ed.), *Community Crime Prevention*, Newbury Park CA: Sage, pp. 137–56

Paternoster, R. et al (1997). 'Do fair procedures matter?', *Law and Society Review*, 31(1), 163–204

Paterson, C. and K. Clamp (2012). 'Exploring recent developments in restorative policing', *Criminology and Criminal Justice*, 12 (5), 593–611

Patrick, R. (2012). 'Public champions or protectors of professional interests', *Police Journal*, 84 (4), 344–71

Peace, R.J. (2006). 'Probationer Training for Neighbourhood Policing in England and Wales: fit for purpose?', *Policing: An International Journal*, 29 (2), 335–346

Pearce, J. and J. Snortum (1983). 'Police effectiveness in handling disturbance calls', *Criminal Justice and Behaviour*, 10 (1), 71–92

Pears, E. (2013). 'Black people have become victims of war on drugs', *Voice*, Number 1591, p. 11

Pease, K. (1994). 'Crime Prevention', in M. Maguire et al (eds.), *Oxford Handbook of Criminology*, Oxford: Oxford University Press, pp. 659–703

Pease, K. (1998). *Repeat Victimisation*, London: Home Office

Pellegrinelli, S., D. Partington, C. Hemingway, Z. Mohdzain, and M. Shah (2007). 'The importance of context in programme management', *International Journal of Project Management*, 25(1), 41–55

Perkins, M. (2016). 'Modelling public confidence of the police', *Police Practice and Research*, 17 (2), 113–25

Perpetuity Research International (2011). *Can Private Policing replace the Police*, Tunbridge Wells: Perpetuity Research

Pizio, W. (2014). 'London Metropolitan Police: experiences and perceptions of citizen disrespect', *Police Practice and Research*, 15 (3), 249–60

Plotnikoff, J. and R. Woolfson (2002). *A Fair Balance?*, London: Home Office

Police Complaints Authority (1998). *Custody Officer Training*, London: PCA

Police Complaints Authority (2001). *Annual Report*, London: PCA

Police Federation (2014). *The Consequences of a Target-Driven Culture Within Policing*, London: MPF

Police Foundation (2011). *Policing Policy Forum*, Oxford: Oxford Centre for Criminology

Police Foundation (2013). 'Director's Blog', 8 April

Police Foundation (2014). *Report of the Fifteenth Oxford Policing Policy Forum*, Oxford: Oxford Centre for Criminology

Police Training Council (1983). *Police Probationer Training*, London: Home Office

Porter, L., T. Prenzler, and J. Fleming (2012). 'Complaint reduction in the Tasmania Police', *Policing & Society*, 22 (4), 426–47

Powell, M., C. Hughes-Scholes, R. Smith, and S. Sharman (2014). 'Relationship between investigative interviewing experience and open-ended question usage', *Police Practice and Research*, 15 (4), 283–92

Prenzler, T., A. Beckley, and S. Bronitt (2013). 'Police gifts and benefits scandals', *International Journal of Police Science and Management*, 15 (4), 294–304

Prenzler, T. and G. Sinclair (2013). 'Status of women police', *International Journal of Law, Crime and Justice*, 41 (2), 115–31

Primoff, E. and A. Sidney (1988). 'A history of job analysis', in S. Gael (ed), *The Job Analysis Handbook*, NY: Wiley, pp. 14–29

Procter, R., F. Vis, and A. Voss (2013). 'Reading the Riots on Twitter', *International Journal of Social Research Methodology*, 16 (3), 197–214

Prokos, A. and I. Padacic (2002). 'There oughtta be a law aganst bitches: masculinity lessons in police training', *Gender, Work and Organization*, 9, 439–59

Public Accounts Committee (2009). *Independent Police Complaints Commission, HC 335*, London: PAC

Public Accounts Committee (2011). *The Youth Justice System*, London: House of Commons

Public Administration Select Committee (2014). *Caught Red Handed: Why We can't Rely on Police Recorded Crime Statistics*, London: SO

Punch, M. (2009). *Police Corruption*, Cullompton: Willan

Punch, M. (2010). *Shoot to Kill*, Bristol: Policy Press

Quinlan, T.L. (2015). *Comparative Post-9/11 Counter-terrorism Policing*, Doctoral thesis, LSE

Quinton, P. (2011). 'Formation of suspicions', *Policing & Society*, 21 (4), 357–68

Quinton, P. and J. Morris (2009). *Neighbourhood Policing*, London: Home Office

Rabe-Hemp, C. and J. Braithwaite (2013). 'Exploration of recidivism and officer shuffle in police sexual violence', *Police Quarterly*, 16 (2), 127–47

Radelet, L. (1986). *The Police and the Community*, NY: Macmillan

Randol, B. and M. Gaffney (2014). 'Are block watch volunteers different than volunteers in community-oriented policing programs', *Police Practice and Research*, 15 (3), 234–48

Ratcliffe, J. et al (2011). 'The Philadelphia foot patrol experiment', *Criminology* 49 (3), 795–831

Redshaw, J. et al (1995). *Core Policing, Ancillary Tasks and Alternative Providers*, Exeter: Devon & Cornwall Police

Reed, E. (2010). 'Early Learning Centres?', *Police*, October, 17–19

Regher, C., V. Leblanc, I. Barath, J. Balch, and A. Birze (2013). 'Predictors of physiological and psychological distress in police', *Police Practice and Research*, 14 (6), 451–63

Reiner, R. (1978). *The Blue-Coated Worker*, London: Macmillan
Reiner, R. (1992). *The Politics of the Police*, Harlow: Harvester Wheatsheaf
Reiner, R. (1998). 'Process or Product? Assessing Individual Police Performance', in J-P. Brodeur (ed.), *How to Recognise Good Policing*, London: Sage, pp. 55–72
Reiner, R. (2010). *The Politics of the Police*, 4th edition, Oxford: Oxford University Press
Reiner, R. (2011). *Policing, Popular Culture and Political Economy*, Aldershot: Dartmouth
Rinkevics, A. and D. Landmane (2013/2014), 'Memory and Suggestibility', *European Police Science and Research Bulletin*, 9, pp. 9–11
Rix, A., F. Joshua, M. Maguire, and S. Morton (2009). *Improving Public Confidence in the Police*, London: Home Office
Robinson, V. (2013). Address to NPIA conference, Bramshill, 27 November
Rogers, C. (1983). *Freedom to Learn*, Columbus OH: Charles E. Merrill
Rogers, C., R. Lewis, T. John, and T. Read (2011). *Police Work*, Abingdon: Routledge
Roh, S. and W. Oliver (2005). 'Effects of community policing upon fear of crime', *Policing: An International Journal*, 28 (4), 670–83
Rosenbaum, D., A. Shuck, S. Costello, D. Hawkins, and M. Ring (2005). 'Attitudes towards the police', *Police Quarterly*, 8 (3), 353–65
Roux, G., S. Roche, and S. Astor (2011). *Minorities and Trust in Criminal Justice*, Grenoble: CNRS Pacte
Rowe, M. (2007). 'Rendering visible the invisible: police discretion, professionalism and decision-making', *Policing & Society*, 17 (3), 279–94
Rowland, R. and T. Coupe (2014). 'Patrol officers and public reassurance: a comparative evaluation', *Policing & Society*, 24 (3), 265–84
Royal Canadian Mounted Police (1992). *The Role of the Strategic Planning and corporate Policy Branch*, Ottawa: RCMP
Rubinstein, J. (1971). *City Police*, NY: Farrar, Straus & Giroux
Sandberg, J. (1994). *Human Competence at Work*, Goteborg: BAS
Schafer, J. (2009). 'Developing effective leadership in policing', *Policing: An International Journal*, 32 (2), 238–60
Scheider, M. et al (2003). 'The impact of citizen perceptions of CP on fear of crime', *Police Quarterly*, 6 (4), 363–86
Schein, E. (2004). *Organizational Culture and Leadership*, San Francisco: Jossey Bass
Schofield, B. (2002). 'Partners in Power', *Sociology*, 36 (3), 663–83
Schon, D. (1972). *Beyond the Stable State*, London: Temple Smith

Scorer, R. (2012). 'Talking tactics', *New Law Journal*, 162 (7503), p. 324

Senjo, S. (2011). 'Dangerous fatigue conditions: a study of police work', *Police Practice and Research* 12 (3), 235–52

Shpayer-Makov, H. (1991). 'Career prospects in the London Metropolitan Police', *Journal of Historical Sociology*, 4 (4), 380–408

Shpayer-Makov, H. (2002). *The making of a policeman*, Aldershot: Ashgate

Semukhina, O. and K. M. Reynolds (2014). 'Russian citizens' perceptions of corruption and trust of the police', *Policing & Society*, 24 (2), 158–88

Sennett, R. (2008). *The Craftsman*, London: Penguin

Sexton, R. and P. Denicolo (1997). 'Formative critical incidents in early professional life', in P. Denicolo and M. Pope (eds.), *Sharing Understanding and Practice*, Farnborough: EPCA, pp. 133–43

Shepherd, E. and A. Griffiths (2013). *Investigative Interviewing*, Oxford: Oxford University Press

Sherman, L. (1992). *Policing Domestic Violence*, NY: Free Press

Sherman, L. and R. Berk (1984). 'The specific deterrent effects of arrest for domestic assault', *American Sociological Review*, 49 (2), 261–72

Sherman, L. and J. Eck (2002). 'Policing for crime prevention', in L. Sherman, D. MacKenzie and D. Farrington (eds.), *Evidence-Based Crime Prevention*, NY: Routledge, pp. 295–329

Sherman, L., D. Farrington, B. Welsh and D. MacKenzie (2002). 'Preventing crime', in L. Sherman et al (eds.), *Evidence-Based Crime Prevention*, London: Routledge, pp. 1–12

Sherman, L. and H. Harris (2015). 'Increased death rates of domestic violence victims from arresting vs. warning suspects', *Journal of Experimental Criminology*, 11 (1), 1–20

Shilston, T. (2011). 'Black box: a qualitative method for improving public confidence in policing', *Policing: A Journal of Policy and Practice*, 5 (2), 125–31

Shiner, M. (2010). 'Post-Lawrence policing', *British Journal of Criminology*, 50 (5), 935–53

Short, T., C. Macdonald, S. Luebbers, J. Ogloff, and S. Thomas (2014). 'Nature of police involvement in mental health transfers', *Police Practice and Research*, 15 (4), 336–48

Shute, S. (2008). *Satellite Tracking of Offenders*, London: Ministry of Justice

Silverman, J. (2013). Address to Academy of Social Sciences Conference, London, 13 October

Simpson, L. (2013). *Does Britain have Plural Cities?*, Manchester: Centre on Dynamics of Ethnicity

Sin, C. Hoong, S. Sheikh, and M. Khanna (2012). 'Police readiness for dealing with tackling hate crime against people with learning disabilities', *Safer Communities*, 11 (3), 145–53

Sindall, K. and P. Sturgis (2013). 'Austerity policing: is visibility more important than actual numbers in determining public confidence?', *European Journal of Criminology*, 10 (2), 137–53

Singer, L. (2001). *Diary of a Police Officer*, London: Home Office

Singer, L. and S. Cooper (2008). *Inform, Persuade and Remind*, London: MoJ

Skills for Justice (2009). *A Guide to the New National Minimum Qualification for Student Police Officers and the Qualification for PCSOs*, London: Skills for Justice

Sklansky, D. (2014). 'The promise and perils of police professionalism', in J. Brown (ed.), *The Future of Policing*, Abingdon: Routledge, pp. 343–54

Sklansky, D. and M. Marks (2008). 'The role of the rank and file in police reform', *Policing & Society*, 18 (1), 1–6

Skogan, W. (2006a). 'Asymmetry in the impact of encounters with the police', *Policing & Society*, 16 (2), 99–126

Skogan, W. (2006b). *Police and Community in Chicago*, NY: Oxford University Press

Skogan, W. (2008). 'Why reforms fail', *Policing & Society*, 18 (1), 23–34

Skogan, W. and K. Frydl (2004). *Fairness and Effectiveness in Policing*, Washington DC: National Academies Press

Skolnick, J. (1966). *Justice Without Trial*, NY: Wiley

Skolnick, J. (2008). 'Enduring issues of police culture and demographics', *Policing & Society*, 18 (1), 35–45

Smith, D. (2010). *Public Confidence in the Criminal Justice System*, London: Ministry of Justice

Smith, G. (2004). 'Rethinking police complaints', *British Journal of Criminology*, 44 (1), 15–33

Smithson, H., R. Ralphs, and P. Williams (2013). 'Used and abused: problematic usage of gang terminology, *British Journal of Criminology*, 53 (1), 113–28

Snow, P. and M. Powell (2011). 'Oral language competence in incarcerated young offenders: links with offending severity', *International Journal of Speech*, 13 (6), 480–89

Sobol, J., Y. Wu, and I. Sun (2013). 'Neighbourhood context and police vigor', *Crime and Delinquency*, 59 (3), 344–68

Sozer, M. and A. Merlo (2013). 'Impact of community policing on crime rates', *Police Practice and Research*, 14 (6), 506–21

Sparrow, M. et al (1997). *Beyond 911*, NY: Basic Books

Stanislas, P. (2014). *International Perspectives on Police Education and Training*. London: Routledge

Steedman, C. (1984). *Policing the Victorian Community*, London: Routledge

Stinson, P. et al (2012). 'Police crime and less-than-lethal coercive force', *International Journal of Police Science and Management*, 14 (1), 1–19

Stone, R. (2013). *Hidden Stories of the Stephen Lawrence Inquiry*, Bristol: Policy Press

Stonewall (2013). *Homophobic Hate Crime*, London: Stonewall

Stout, B. (2011). 'Professional ethics and academic integrity in police education', *Policing*, 5 (4), 300–9

Strang, H., L. Sherman, E. Mayo-Wilson, D. Woods, and B. Ariel (2013). 'Restorative Justice Conferencing', *Campbell Collaboration Library*, 9 (12), 1–59

Strawbridge, P. and D. Strawbridge (1990). *Probationary Training in Major Police Departments of the USA*, London: Metropolitan Police

Suchman, L. (1987). *Plans and Situated Actions*, Cambridge: Cambridge University Press

Suh, B., L. Hong, P. Pirolli, and E. Chi (2010). 'Want to be Retweeted?', Proceedings of IEEE Second International Conference on Social Computing, pp. 177–84, IEEE

Sunshine, J. and T. Tyler (2003). 'The role of procedural justice and legitimacy in shaping public support for policing', *Law and Society Review* 37 (3), 513–47

Survation (2014). *Police Perceptions Poll*. London: Survation

Suva, J. (2012). 'Challenge of competence-based police ethics education', *Internal Security*, 4 (1), 17–24

Swellert, J. (1988). 'Cognitive load during problem-solving', *Cognitive Science*, 12 (2), 257–85

Tal, J-Z. and D. Weisburd (2013). 'Effects of security threats on antecedents of police legitimacy', *Journal of Research in Crime and Delinquency*, 50 (1), 3–32

Tankebe, J. (2008). 'Police effectiveness and police trustworthiness in Ghana', *Criminology and Criminal Justice*, 8 (2), 185–202

Taylor, B., C. Koper, and D. Woods (2011). 'A randomized controlled trial of different policing strategies at hotspots', *Journal of Experimental Criminology*, 7 (2), 149–81

Taylor, F.W. (1911). *Principles of Scientific Management*, NY: Harper

Taylor, G. (2006). *Evaluation of the Victims of Trafficking Pilot Project*, London: Home Office

Tena, O. (2013). 'Strategies to reconcile domestic and paid work duties in Mexican police women', *Acta Colombiana di Psicologica*, 16 (2), 81–91

Terrill, W. and A. Paoline (2012). 'Conducted energy devices and citizen injuries', *Justice Quarterly*, 29 (2), 153–82

Terrill, W. et al (2003). 'Police culture and coercion', *Criminology*, 41 (4), 1003–1034

Tester, K. (2008). 'A more humane material life', *Times Higher Education*, 6 March, 44–45

Thacher, D. (2008). 'Research for the front lines', *Policing & Society*, 18 (1), 46–59

The Guardian (2014). 'Counter-terrorism officer jailed', 6 June, p. 4

Thomas, W.I. (1923). *The Unadjusted Girl*, NY: Little, Brown, & Co.

Tilley, N. (2010). 'Whither Problem-Oriented Policing', *Criminology and Public Policy*, 9 (1), 183–95

Tilley, N. and M. Scott (2012). 'Past, present and future of POP', *Policing: A Journal of Policy and Practice*, 6 (2), 122–32

Toch, H. (2008). 'Police officers as change agents in police reforms', *Policing & Society*, 18 (1), 60–71

Tong, S. (2017). 'Case study of detective training', Research into Practice Conference, University of Surrey, 24 November

Torres, S. and R. Vogel (2001). 'Pre and post-test differences between Vietnamese and Latino residents in a community policing experiment', *Policing: An International Journal*, 24 (1), 40–55

Transparency International (2011). *Corruption in the UK*, London: TI

Transparency International (2012). *Corruption Perceptions Index*, London: TI

Treadwell, J., D. Briggs, S. Winlow, and S. Hall (2013). 'Shopocalypse now', *British Journal of Criminology*, 53 (1), 1–17

Trojanowicz, R. and B. Bucqueroux (1994). *Community Policing: How to Get it Started*, Cincinnati OH: Anderson

Tuffin, R., J. Morris, and A. Poole (2006). *National Reassurance Policing Evaluation*, London: Home Office

Turley, C., H. Ranns, M. Callkanan, A. Blackwell, and T. Newburn (2012). *Delivering Neighbourhood Policing in Partnership*, London: Home Office

Turner, L. (2014). 'PCCs, Neo-Liberal Hegemony and democratic policing', *Safer Communities*, 13 (1), 13–21

Tyler, T. (2006). *Why People Obey the Law*, Princeton: Princeton University Press

Tyler, T., S. Schulhofer, and A. Huq (2010). 'Legitimacy and deterrence effects in counter-terrorism policing', *Law & Society Review*, 44 (2), 365–402

UK Data Archive (2015). *Learning at Work Survey Dataset*, Colchester: UKDS

Ungar, M. and E. Arias (2012). 'Reassessing Community Policing in Latin America', *Policing & Society*, 22 (1), 1–13

UN Office of Drugs and Crime (2006). *The Integrity and Accountability of the Police*, Vienna: UNODC

Van Craen, M. (2013). 'Explaining majority and minority trust in the police', *Justice Quarterly* 30 (6), 1042–67

van de Klomp, M., S. Stronks, and O. Adang (2014). 'Police and Citizens in Conflict', *Policing & Society*, 24 (4), 45–78

van de Velde, B., A. Meijer, and V. Homburg (2015). 'Police message diffusion on Twitter', *Behaviour and Information Technology*, 34 (1), 4–16

Van de Walle, S. and J. Raine (2008). *Explaining Attitudes Towards the Justice System in the UK and Europe*, London: Ministry of Justice

Van Ewijk, A. (2012). 'Diversity within police forces in Europe', *Policing: A Journal of Policy and Practice*, 6 (1), 76–92

Van Maanen, J. (1973). 'Observations on the making of policemen', *Human Organization*, 32 (4), 407–18

Van Maanen, J. (1982). *Varieties of Qualitative Research*, LA: Sage

Van Maanen, J. (1989). 'Observations on the making of policemen', in A. Blumberg (ed.), *The Ambivalent Force*, NY: Holt, Rinehart & Winston

Vasquez, J. (2012). 'Community Policing in Columbia', *Policing & Society*, 22 (1), 43–56

Vuorensyrja, J. (2013). 'Learning in police recruit training', *European Police Science and Research Bulletin*, 8, 4–8

Waddington, D. (2007). *Policing Public Disorder*, Cullompton: Willan

Waddington, D. (2013). 'A "kinder blue"', *Policing & Society*, 23 (1), 46–64

Waddington, D. and K. McSeveny (2012). 'Terrorism and the Risk Society', in S. Bennett (ed.), *Innovative Thinking in risk, Crisis and Disaster Management*, Farnham: Gower, pp. 41–58

Waddington, P. (1999). *Policing Citizens*, London: UCL Press

Waddington, P. (2011a). 'Cop culture', in T. Newburn and J. Peay (eds.), *Policing: Politics, Culture and Control*, Oxford: Hart, pp. 89–110

Waddington, P. (2011b). 'Public evaluations of police behaviour', address to British Society of Criminology Conference, Newcastle, 4 July

Waddington, P., J. Kleinig, and M. Wright (eds.) (2013). *Professional Police Practice*, Oxford: Oxford University Press

Wakefield, A. (2006). *The Value of Foot Patrol*, London: Police Foundation

Walby, S. and J. Allen (2004). *Domestic Violence, Sexual Assault and Stalking*, London: Home Office

Walker, N. (2000). *Policing in a Changing Constitutional Order*, London: Sweet & Maxwell

Walker, S. and V. Bumphus (1992). 'The effectiveness of civilian review', *American Journal of Police*, 11, 1–26

Ward, J., M. Krohn, and C. Gibson (2014). 'Effects of police contact on trajectories of violence', *Journal of Interpersonal Violence*, 29 (3), 440–75

Watson, T. (2002). 'Professions and Professionalism', *International Studies of Management and Organisations*, 32 (2), 93–105

Weatheritt, M. (1986). *Innovations in Policing*, Beckenham: Croom Helm

Webb, S. and J. Burrows (2009). *Organised Immigration Crime*, London: Home Office

Webb, V. and C. Katz (1997). 'Citizen ratings of the importance of Community Policing activities', *Policing: An International Journal*, 20 (1), 7–23

Weick, K. (1976). 'Educational organizations as loosely-coupled systems', *Administrative Science Quarterly*, 21, 1–19

Weinberger, B. (1995). *The Best Police in the World*, Aldershot: Scolar Press

Weinfass, Ian (2016). '"No need for positive discrimination" in police recruitment', *Police Oracle*, 3 August 2016

Weir, H., D. Steward, and R. Morris (2012). 'Problematic alcohol consumption by police officers and other protective service employees', *Journal of Criminal Justice*, 40 (1), 72–82

Weir, R. and M. Bangs (2007). *The use of GIS by crime analysts*, London: Home Office

Weisburd, D. (2012). 'Bringing social context back into the equation', *Criminology and Public Policy*, 11 (2), 317–326

Weisburd, D., S. Bushway, C. Lum, and S-M. Yang (2004). 'Trajectories of crime at places', *Criminology*, 42 (2), 283–322

Weisburd, D., Hinkle, C. Famega, and J. Ready (2011). 'Possible "backfire" effects of hotspots policing', *Journal of Experimental Criminology*, 7 (4), 297–320

Weisburd, D., S. Mastrofski, J. Willis, and R. Greenspan (2006). 'Changing everything so that everything can remain the same', in D Weisburd and A Braga (eds.), *Police Innovation*, Cambridge: Cambridge University Press, pp. 284–304

Weisburd, D., T. Telep, W. Cody, J. Hinkle, and J. Eck (2010). 'Is POP effective in reducing crime and disorder', *Criminology and Public Policy*, 9 (1), 139–72

Westmarland, L. (2001). *Gender and Policing*, Cullompton: Willan Publishing

Westmarland, L. (2011). *Police Integrity Feedback Report*, Buckingham: Open University

Westmarland, L. (2014). 'Ethics and Policing', in J. Brown (ed.), *The Future of Policing*, Abingdon: Routledge, pp. 463–75

Wheller, L. (2013). *Street level drug enforcement*, Ryton: College of Policing

Wheller, L. (2017). 'Building capability and capacity', What Works conference, January 21, British Library

Wheller, L. and J. Morris (2010). *What Works in Training, Behaviour Change and Implementing Guidance?*, London: NPIA

White, D. (2006). 'A conceptual analysis of the hidden curriculum of police training in England and Wales', *Policing & Society*, 16 (4), 386–404

White, D. and R. Heslop (2011). 'What is the attraction of nurse training as a model for professional education?', Fifth Critical Perspectives on Professional Learning conference, University of Leeds, 13 June

White, M., P. Mulvey, and L. Dario (2016). 'Arrestees' perceptions of the police', *Criminal Justice and Behavior*, 43 (3), 343–46

Wickes, R.L. et al (2016). 'From hate to prejudice', *British Journal of Criminology*, 56 (2), 239–55

Wikstrom, P-O. (2014). 'Situational action theory', in G. Bruisma and D. Weisburd (eds.), *Encyclopaedia of Criminology and Criminal Justice*, NY: Springer, 4845–52

Wilensky, H. (1964). 'The professionalization of everyone?', *American Journal of Sociology*, 70 (2), 137–58

Wiley, S., L. Slocum, and F-A. Esbensen (2013). 'Unintended consequences of being stopped or arrested', *Criminology*, 51 (40), 927–66

Williams, M. et al (2013). 'Policing cyber-neighbourhoods', *Policing & Society*, 23 (4), 461–81

Wilson, Jacqueline (2014). 'Ambient Hate', *Howard Journal*, 53 (4), 377–94

Wilson, J.M. (2006). *Community Policing in America*, London: Routledge

Winsor, T. (2011). *Independent Review of Police Officer and Staff Remuneration and Conditions, Part I*, London: HMSO

Winsor, T (2017). *State of Policing*, London: HMIC

Wolf, M. (2017). 'Uses and Abuses of Economics in the Debate on Universities', *Council for Defence of British Universities Conference*, Athenaeum, London, 26 January

Wood, D. and S. Tong (2009). 'The Future of Initial Police Training: a University Perspective', *International Journal of Police Sciences and Management*, 11 (3), 294–305

Wood, J. and C. Shearing (2007). *Imagining Security*, Cullompton: Willan

Wood, J., E. Sorg, E. Groff, J. Ratcliffe, and C. Taylor (2014). 'Cops as treatment providers', *Policing & Society*, 24 (3), 362–79

Woods, N. (2016). *Good Cop, Bad War*, London: Ebury

Wyllie, D. (2016). 'Eight body camera concerns', *Australian Police Journal*, 70 (2), 86–9

Yokum, D., A. Ravishankar, and A. Coppock (2017). 'Evaluating the Effects of Police Body-Worn Cameras', Washington, DC: The Lab @ DC

YouGov (2013). *YouGov/Times Survey Results*, London: YouGov

Young, J. (1994). *Policing the Streets*, London: Middlesex University

Index

The manufacturer's authorised representative in the EU for product safety is Oxford University Press España S.A. of el Parque Empresarial San Fernando de Henares, Avenida de Castilla, 2 – 28830 Madrid (www.oup.es/en or product.safety@oup.com). OUP España S.A. also acts as importer into Spain of products made by the manufacturer.

www.ingramcontent.com/pod-product-compliance
Lightning Source LLC
LaVergne TN
LVHW011512200926
848484LV00001B/15
* 9 7 8 0 1 9 8 8 1 7 4 7 5 *